Conversations
with Neil's Brain

Books by William H. Calvin and George A. Ojemann

Inside the Brain

Books by William H. Calvin

The Throwing Madonna

The River that Flows Uphill

The Cerebral Symphony

The Ascent of Mind

How the Shaman Stole the Moon

Conversations
with Neil's Brain

*The Neural Nature
of Thought and Language*

*William H. Calvin
George A. Ojemann*

A William Patrick Book

Addison-Wesley Publishing Company

Reading, Massachusetts ▪ Menlo Park, California ▪ New York
Don Mills, Ontario ▪ Wokingham, England ▪ Amsterdam ▪ Bonn
Sydney ▪ Singapore ▪ Tokyo ▪ Madrid ▪ San Juan
Paris ▪ Seoul ▪ Milan ▪ Mexico City ▪ Taipei

MIT

2400

Library of Congress Cataloging-in-Publication Data

Calvin, William H., 1939–
   Conversations with Neil's brain: the neural nature of thought and
language / William H. Calvin and George A. Ojemann.
      p.   cm.
   "A William Patrick book."
   Includes bibliographical references and index.
   ISBN 0-201-63217-9
   1. Brain. 2. Consciousness. 3. Brain—Surgery. 4. Epilepsy—
Surgery. I. Ojemann, George A. II. Title.
QP376.C318   1994
153—dc20

                                        93-23661
                                         CIP

Jacket design by Suzanne Heiser
Jacket illustration by Michael Shumate, Image Bank
Text design by Editorial Services of New England, Inc.
Set in 11-point ITC Garamond by Editorial Services of New England, Inc.

1 2 3 4 5 6 7 8 9 10-MA-97969594
First Printing, April 1994

Contents

For our mutual mentor,
ARTHUR A. WARD, JR.

chapter 1

A Window to the Brain

THE TIMED SCRUB is an operating room ritual, and I'm a little out of practice. Keep those elbows down, I remind myself, so that the water drips off them rather than running the other way, from dirty to clean areas. Scrub, scrub. Three more minutes to go on the scrub, then my grand entrance into the O.R.

Though I have to think about it because I do it so infrequently, this scrub is automatic for a surgeon, requiring as little thought as riding a bicycle. A surgeon gets ten quiet minutes to think about the patient, contemplate the novelties of the case, reflect on what the patient said when asked about preferences. In this type of neurosurgery, there may be a lot of on-the-spot tailoring of the surgery to the unique aspects of the patient's brain. And there are often serious value judgments to be made, ones that the patient will have to live with ever after. Conflicts can arise, between getting rid of the patient's epileptic seizures and preserving his language and memory abilities intact. One of the neurosurgical principles in such matters is, "Better some seizures than a loss of language abilities." That's a consideration that could arise later today, when some of Neil's brain is being removed.

There is a window next to the scrub sink, and I look into the O.R. to see how things are going. I see the big blue-green tent, created with sterile sheets, but it mostly hides Neil. I remember seeing him at the pre-op conference: the one patient, and twenty inquisitive doctors. Not the usual patient-to-physician ratio, even hereabouts. The conference

1

brings out many people like me who are interested in how the brain normally works, crowding in with the usual specialists in treating epileptics.

Before the conference, when Neil and I were talking about writers, he said that he was becoming a rather specialized kind of writer himself: writing letters-to-the-editor about wearing seat belts. The skull fracture that caused his epilepsy came from a collision with the steering wheel fifteen years ago, during one of those quick trips to the grocery store.

Like most epileptics who are surgical candidates, Neil is highly motivated. A long day of surgery, he said, was nothing compared to coping with a seizure almost every week. And besides, he added, he had always wondered how his brain worked; maybe he might learn a little.

Unlike many of the mentally ill, epileptics often have quite a bit of insight into their problem. Seizures are only temporary, with little in the way of problems between them. A single seizure usually won't hurt you, unless you are driving a car or flying an airplane. It's all the repetitions that make it a serious problem. About one in four epileptics isn't helped by anticonvulsant drugs. If the epileptic "pacemaker" area can be identified, and is in a place where it is doing more harm than good, it can sometimes be surgically removed. This requires a lot of testing, once the brain's surface is exposed to the light of day, to identify the troublesome region. The patient wakes up after the first two hours and, under only local anesthetic, works quite hard, exercising his brainpower as we watch his brain.

Another minute. Remember the door. Ordinary pedestrians push open a swinging door in a straightforward manner. Surgeons, however, tend to back into swinging doors, shouldering them aside. No outstretched arms. Ever since I had to learn the surgeon's technique for keeping freshly scrubbed hands sterile, I've been keeping my eyes open around the medical school. Surgeons shoulder doors open, even when not scrubbed. If you watch the people entering a lecture hall, you may be able to sort out the surgeons by their shoulder action.

Toss the brush in the trash without touching anything. Shut off the faucet with its knee control. Peer through the window in the swinging door to make sure that someone isn't about to leave the O.R. Lean your back to the door. Pause. Take a deep breath. Let it out. (No, those aren't on the checklist—but everyone seems to do it before going onstage.) Back into the door, push it open, and rotate around its edge into the O.R. Another player enters, stage left.

Nobody seems to notice.

THE SPECIAL SIGN hangs on the O.R. door today: "Quiet, Please. Patient Awake." That's to cut down on all the shoptalk between O.R. staff accustomed to anesthetized patients. It was discovered long ago that awake patients under local anesthesia may not realize that the nurses are talking about last week's patient, or the one in the operating room next door.

But it's hardly a hushed library. The O.R. is awash in sound. The gurgling sounds emanating from the idling suction, the regular muted beeps from the heart monitor, the chorus of monotonous fans hidden inside a dozen pieces of electronics equipment—they go on, not unlike the background sounds of a busy office, but echoing off the tile walls and floors. There's only one telephone, and the number is unlisted. It seldom rings here, but sometimes the circulating nurse has to answer it and relay a quick question.

Indeed, such a call just caused the second-year resident to strip off her gloves and leave the O.R.—a message was relayed from the chief resident, asking for some help down in the emergency room, and the surgeon nodded his agreement. She noticed me on her way out, did something of a double take, and then waved at me as she backed through the swinging doors. Wonder what's going on down in the E.R.?

The anteroom was certainly quiet in comparison to the O.R. This isn't my usual milieu. Although I'm not exactly a tourist, it always seems a bit of Alice-in-Wonderland when I enter, still wet behind the elbows and dripping occasionally. I never had the slightest interest in becoming a physician, much less a surgeon. I started out to be a physicist, but I soon went astray, seduced by a fascination with the brain. How do you command your hand to grasp a cup? What goes wrong in the brain when your mind fools you? How do you make up a grocery list or plan a career?

I generally work at a desk, surrounded by disorderly piles of scholarly magazines, with a computer or two hidden beneath them. My archaeologist friends smile when they see my office: layers reaching all the way down to physics, they ask? I talk often to anthropologists and linguists and computer scientists about our over-lapping interests. And to psychologists and primatologists; I've recently been creating a computer game for a chimpanzee to play, trying to measure precision timing skills.

Most of the time, I make theoretical models of brain functions; lately, I've been investigating an electrical pattern that I call the "hexagonal mosaics of the mind." But I have little to do with sick people other than when my neurosurgeon and psychiatrist friends invite me to come over and see a patient with a particularly interesting problem. I'm a neurophysiologist. Brains—how they work, and how they came to evolve—occupy my working day.

So what on earth am I doing here in the O.R.? I'm about to "assist," lend an extra pair of hands, stand by to solve the minor electronics problems that sometimes arise. And to watch the patient carefully when the neurosurgeon is trying to map out the brain's surface—the cerebral cortex is, after all, largely what separates the humans from the apes. We've got four times more.

You seldom get the chance to see a real human brain—at least, not while its language cortex is holding a conversation with you. And somehow remembering words, piecing them together into a sentence, picking and choosing which sentence to speak aloud and which to leave in the subconscious to gestate a little longer. A unique person emerges from all that—Neil, in this case.

Even more rarely does anyone get a chance to investigate how that sentence comes about. Look for where the names pop out, or where they are strung together into sentences. See what brain areas specialize in reading. Find the spots in the brain where syntax resides, maybe even that "deep structure" that the linguists claim must be built-in.

I wait, hands held high, elbows still threatening to drip one last drop. I finally figured out the change in smell, between the anteroom and the O.R. proper: soap is the primary smell of the anteroom, what with all the scrubbing, but the scent of freshly done laundry dominates the O.R., all of those clean drapes and gowns that have been recently unfolded.

The scrub nurse sees me, but she is busy laying out some sponges for the neurosurgeon. Finally, judging that the neurosurgeon will not run out of sponges for a while, she picks up a sterile towel and walks over to hand it to me. "Let's see, you're seven and a half, if I remember correctly?" That is indeed my glove size. How could she have remembered from so long ago? I'll bet she looked at my hand and guessed.

Neil inside the sterile tent

Once gowned and gloved, I must navigate through all the scattered equipment without touching anything. Hands folded across my chest like a meditating monk or prudent poker player, I work my way around the anesthesiologist's gas machine with its air tanks. I catch a glimpse of Neil under the sterile drapes. Only the anesthesiologist can see Neil's face. But I can see his arms and legs, and he's restless. Small wonder.

I've arrived too late to see the first act, appropriately called "opening." He's lying on his right side so that the left side of his head is up. The left side of Neil's brain is where the problem is. To see the part of the brain that is causing Neil's epileptic seizures, the surgeon must remove a hand-sized piece of bone, opening a window into the brain just above the line between left eye and left ear. The bone must be taken out in one large chunk, because it will be reinstalled in Neil's skull late this afternoon to close that window. Opening is just a matter of drills and saws—although especially nice models, ones that any cabinetmaker would covet, designed to avoid damaging the underlying layers.

Opening is consequently a little noisy. Neil got to sleep through it all. But it's over now, and the intravenous short-acting anesthetic has been stopped, allowing Neil to wake back up. He needs to be alert during the next act. And there is very little to cause any pain at that stage of the operation. Touching the brain's surface doesn't produce any sensations of touch. The brain itself has no sensors for that sort of thing, although it receives messages from sensors elsewhere in the body.

GEORGE OJEMANN'S OFFICE will be even more of an archaeologist's delight than my own, with piles everywhere ("My filing system," he claims. "What year did you loan me that book you need back?"). The patient records are, of course, kept elsewhere, one reason that he can indulge his filing system.

The neurosurgery operating room, the various consulting rooms in the clinic, the patients' hospital rooms, the conference rooms where x-rays are posted and cases are debated—they're all "offices" of a sort for a neurosurgeon, who can wear out a new pair of shoes faster than most of us.

Here in the O.R., the neurosurgeon is like the captain of a ship, navigating difficult waters while directing a cast of thousands (well, a half dozen at the moment). Even the spotlights tend to feature the surgeon—although once you get a view of the sterile field and the patient's brain, you realize that the surgeon is illuminated only incidentally, backlit by the spotlights and with his face lit by the light reflected from the well-lit brain. Reflected glory, indeed.

"We ought to be ready for the handheld stimulator in a few minutes," George says softly to me as I finally inch my way past the last obstacle. My cue to get busy unwrapping the sterile box of electronics. I signal the circulating nurse to come and help me (brief glances and raised eyebrows are an important mode of communication in the O.R.—surgical masks hide most other facial expressions).

"Neil," George continues, raising his voice a bit, "we're doing just fine up here. Move around some more if you want to. How do you feel?"

"I'm okay," the muffled voice replies from beneath the sterile drapes. "What are you guys doing now?"

"Just anchoring the dura, making things tidy for the next act. There shouldn't be any more discomfort," George says. "I put some local anesthetic down on that spot that hurt, but we won't be touching that region of the dura again for a long time, anyway." The dura is a tough "skin" that covers the brain; usually one can cut or stretch it without the patient noticing, but in other patients a little local anesthetic is needed on the dura as well as the usual dose on the skin incision.

The circulating nurse has unwrapped the first layer of sheets surrounding the electronics box without touching the underlying layer. She steps back and, with a flash of the eyebrows, signals, "It's all yours now." I unfold my sterile hands from my chest for the first time and

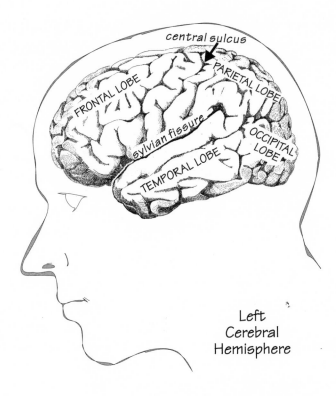

central sulcus

FRONTAL LOBE

PARIETAL LOBE

sylvian fissure

OCCIPITAL LOBE

TEMPORAL LOBE

Left
Cerebral
Hemisphere

proceed to remove the second layer of sheets that protect the box. A spotlight up in the gallery above me is repositioned to shine down on the side table where the box sits, gleaming but transparent, the size of an old-fashioned bread box and filled with the unfamiliar.

Indeed, the only two familiar things in the box seem somewhat out of place in the O.R.: an ordinary clipboard and a sharpened yellow pencil. Sterile, of course. I find the handheld stimulator and unwrap the wires. We use it to pass a little electric current through the surface layers of the brain. Once I tried stimulating my arm with current of the same strength, a few milliamperes, and all I felt was a tingle. Not pain.

I turn around to face the patient, watching George finish "tidying up," flushing with sterile saline solution and then sucking it up. Nothing seems to be bleeding anymore. But Neil's brain looks white and pink and red, simply because there are so many blood vessels spreading out over its surface. It takes a lot of oxygen to run a brain, and so the brain gets about one-fifth of the bright red blood that the heart pumps.

Looks like a normal brain to me, but I'm no expert. And George isn't saying yet. He gently touches the exposed surface here and there, especially in the region closest to Neil's left ear. Does Neil feel anything? No.

"Feels normal, so far," George says. Sometimes scarred tissue feels tough, its resilience like a stale marshmallow. Whatever is stirring up the epileptic seizures that begin in that region, it isn't obvious. Still, it could be a tumor or an old scar. The microscope may tell a different story this afternoon. We're rather expecting some old scar tissue, because of Neil's skull fracture long ago.

"Notice that central sulcus?" George asks me. I peer more closely at Neil's exposed brain surface, searching for the characteristic pattern.

Oops, *what* central sulcus? I missed that—there is a little abnormality after all. The brain's surface is folded into a hills-and-valleys arrangement (better known as gyri and sulci) that increases the surface area—a matter of some importance since the brain's fancier functions

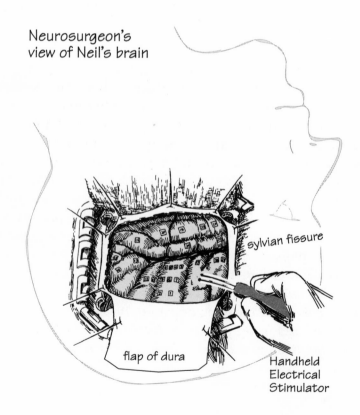

Neurosurgeon's
view of Neil's brain

sylvian fissure

flap of dura

Handheld
Electrical
Stimulator

are performed only in the "cortical" layers near the surface. The more surface area of cerebral cortex, the more "processing power."

You can seldom see down into the "valleys" (some, such as the sylvian fissure, are quite deep), but you can judge how wide the "hilltop" is. And one hilltop is very wide—looks as if the fold we call the central sulcus is simply missing in Neil, at least down near the sylvian fissure where the surgical window gives us a view. Its absence probably means nothing; there is a lot of normal variability.

"You should have stuck around until the end of the pre-op conference," George tells me. "The neuroradiologist waited until the very end of the conference and then said, 'Oh, by the way, you might not see the central sulcus, down where you'll be operating.' No one else had noticed, and she's never going to let us forget it."

Magnetic resonance imaging—those magical machines that seem to slice your brain up into a series of images, and without even using x-rays—is wonderful for revealing details like that, and an MRI is now part of the preoperative workup. It has considerably reduced the number of surprises in the O.R., at least the ones seen at this stage of the operation. Back when George learned how to do this kind of epilepsy surgery from Arthur Ward, about a quarter-century ago, they were lucky to have a good x-ray highlighting the major blood vessels in advance of the surgery, displaced blood vessels serving to warn us if there was a tumor. And back when Arthur learned the epilepsy operation a quarter-century before that, in Montreal, from Wilder Penfield himself, much of the time they were flying blind. Penfield was the pioneer, the neurosurgeon whose maps of motor and sensory strip are frequently seen in textbooks, whose reports of memories evoked by brain stimulation have dominated popular accounts of what memories are stored in the brain.

Now there are a number of ways to image the brain's anatomy. The computerized tomography scanners started the revolution in the early 1970s. The MRI then came along, improving resolution enough that we can see boundaries between gray matter and white matter. We can see the cortical surface folded into hills and valleys. Yet anatomy doesn't always tell you about function. And how well it *works*—that is what's important. Certainly to Neil, who is about to lose some of his brain on the prospect that this will allow the rest of his brain to perform better. Such operations have been done for over fifty years, with many studies of the patients afterward.

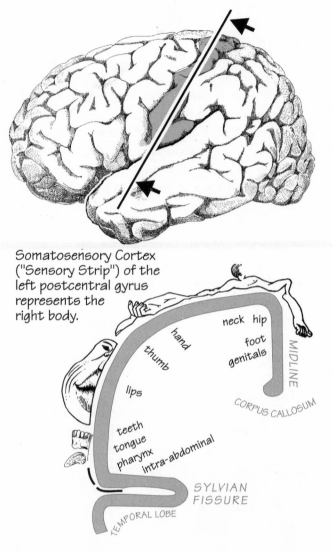

Somatosensory Cortex
("Sensory Strip") of the
left postcentral gyrus
represents the
right body.

neck   hip

hand

thumb

foot

genitals

MIDLINE

lips

CORPUS CALLOSUM

teeth

tongue

pharynx

intra-abdominal

SYLVIAN
FISSURE

TEMPORAL LOBE

Modified from Penfield and Rasmussen, 1950

THE HANDHELD STIMULATOR looks like a little penlight that grew a pair of horns. And, of course, a tail—that wire trailing back to the electronics. The horns are silver wires that end in smooth little balls. George turns and takes the stimulator from me, double-checking the wiring that the nurse and I have created.

"Neil?" he asks, raising his voice. "All settled down for a while?"

"I suppose so," Neil answers from under the drapes. "What's next?"

"Now we're ready to do some of that electrical stimulation that I told you about yesterday," says George. "I want you to tell me if you feel anything."

George lowers the two silver wires until they gently touch the exposed cortical surface, and then lifts them again. "Feel anything?"

"No. Nothing," replies Neil.

By this time, I've maneuvered myself back around the anesthesiologist's gas machine so that I can peer under the sterile drapes and see Neil a little better. He's lying on his right side, with his head propped up on a doughnut-shaped pillow. The tent over him has a flat top, created by the scrub nurse for her big tray of instruments, but one side is open. Neil sees me looking at him, and I silently wiggle my eyebrows at him.

"Hey! Someone touched my hand!" Neil volunteers. Neither the anesthesiologist nor I had come anywhere close to Neil's hand.

"Which hand?" asks George.

"My right one, sort of like someone brushed the back side of it. It's still tingling a little." The right hand reports to the left side of the brain, and George evidently has located the hand area of somatosensory cortex with the stimulator.

"Turn down the stimulator current a little." George glances up at the technician in the gallery, and a voice comes back over the intercom saying that the stimulator is now set at two milliamperes, down from three.

"Felt it again," Neil reports. "Same place as before. But it isn't continuing to tingle." Neil is picking up on our strategy—but then, he's an MIT-trained engineer. And he's been reading a lot about the brain these last few weeks.

"That's on the side of my face," Neil says. "The right side. Cheek, sort of."

"Does it tingle afterward?" George asks.

"No. Didn't feel normal, though. Funny kind of feeling." That's par for the course—stimulated sensations are seldom identifiable with any familiar sensation. No patient has ever reported being tapped with a pencil point, for example.

Everyone is listening to Neil. There is just the busy background noise of the O.R., with no one speaking. There is a pause in Neil's responses, probably because George is stimulating some region that isn't in the primary somatosensory cortex. Most regions of the brain can be briefly stimulated without the patient being aware of it.

George looks up from the sterile field and nods to me. I bend down farther, sterile gloves clutched to sterile chest, and peer intently at Neil's hands and face.

"Somebody moved my hand!" Neil says again. "Felt funny, but I sure didn't move it." George must have stimulated the motor strip. Neil's hand didn't move in any ordinary way. At first, it looked as if he might be reaching for something, but then the hand rotated to be palm upward, with none of the finger positioning associated with grasping. Motor cortex stimulation seldom produces movements that might be useful.

The motor cortex is just in front of the somatosensory cortex. And if I know George, the next thing to move will be Neil's jaw.

Sure enough, I see Neil's jaw tighten and the right corner of his mouth pull back a little.

"Felt like the dentist pulling the corner of my mouth back," Neil reports after the stimulation stops. "But not very gracefully," he adds. There is no sense of volition—patients don't report wanting to move, and then doing it. These are involuntary movements, and rather uncoordinated ones at that.

"Nothing else," I report, meaning that I didn't see the hand move at the same time. I focus on Neil's right thumb, expecting George to try stimulating a point on motor cortex midway between his two previous positions.

And sure enough, Neil's right thumb flexes inward. Neil notes that someone is moving his hand again. Although the jaw and the thumb

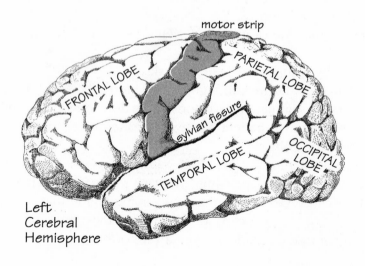

motor strip

FRONTAL LOBE

PARIETAL LOBE

sylvian fissure

TEMPORAL LOBE

OCCIPITAL LOBE

Left
Cerebral
Hemisphere

may not be adjacent to one another within the body, the jaw's motor cortex patch is adjacent to the one for the thumb.

"Didn't see any jaw movement," I report afterward. Near the boundary, the electrical stimulation may spread enough to evoke both movements.

I didn't see Neil's left arm or face move either, although that goes without saying. It would really be newsworthy if I had seen the left side move while the left brain was being stimulated. That the left brain has something to do with the right side of the body was discovered

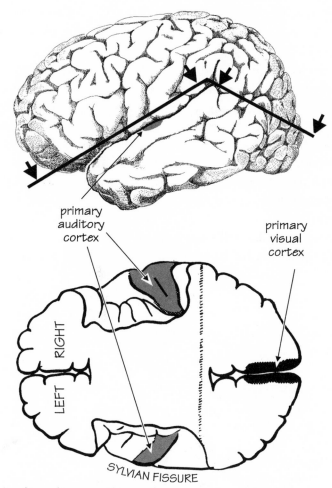

primary
auditory
cortex

primary
visual
cortex

RIGHT

LEFT

SYLVIAN FISSURE

Looking down on the
top of both temporal lobes
at the primary auditory cortex
and, in the rear, visual cortex.

by the ancient Greeks. Hippocrates noticed that injuries to one side of the head often caused the other side of the body to become paralyzed or suffer seizures.

The notion of "maps" on the brain surface has been around for about two centuries. By the early nineteenth century, the phrenologists, such as Franz Joseph Gall in Vienna, proposed that the brain had rather detailed functional maps, even suggesting that there was a separate area for grammar. Phrenology then went down the wrong track with the notion that these maps could be located by feeling the bumps on the skull, and that there were different areas for "Democrats" and for "Republicans." These maps, still popular among artists, are largely wrong—but they serve to remind us of how the science got started, with a good idea.

The orderly map on the brain's surface representing movement commands has been known for a little more than a century. A British neurologist, John Hughlings Jackson, observed the way an epileptic seizure progressed. The patient's tongue might first protrude. Then his face would begin to twitch. Next the fingers, then the arm, and so on to the rest of the body. The slow progression of the seizure served to map the motor strip, much as we do more cleanly with the handheld stimulation in the O.R. The electric current is a crude but effective stimulus to motor strip, so long as you are careful to keep the current strength well below the levels that would start a local seizure.

ON MY RETURN TRIP around the sterile field, I see that big piece of Neil's skull, being kept moist in a protected spot amid the scrub nurse's array of instruments and supplies. Once I get back to stand next to George, I notice that he has placed some little numbered pieces of sterile paper atop Neil's brain, resting lightly on its surface. Number 1 marks the first site that George stimulated, and so on. The scrub nurse undoubtedly has kept track of how many have been used, just to make sure that, along with the sponges, they are all removed later. For now, they serve as landmarks to remind us of the stimulation results.

Alongside the motor strip, but just to its rear, is the sensory strip. In the usual textbook pictures of an average brain, a deep infolded groove, the central sulcus, separates the two maps. But, as our neuroradiologist predicted, Neil doesn't have that anatomical dividing line, at least not down in the region we can see through today's window in the skull. The numbered tags for sensory responses lie right next to the motor response tags, atop the same wide gyrus. No infolded region separates them.

The texts show typical maps of the sensory strip and the motor strip, but patients exhibit a lot of variability. That's the reason it has to be mapped carefully in each patient undergoing epilepsy surgery. Brain maps are just as variable as faces. No one knows whether such details of cortical organization are important—but they might reflect the differences between the clumsy and the well coordinated, the articulate and the tongue-tied.

There are several more motor maps; they are hard to detect in the operating room with the stimulating technique, but are known from laboratory studies of monkey brains. The motor strip, for example, is not the exclusive commander of the muscles. It certainly isn't the exclusive commander of the neurons in the spinal cord that actually run the muscles; the premotor regions just in front of the motor strip have just as many connections down to the spinal cord as does the motor strip itself. But the loss of motor strip tends to produce muscle weakness and, if the damage is extensive enough, paralysis.

Indeed, this is the origin of that dubious factoid: "You use only 20 percent of your brain anyway." This is true, but only in a very limited sense. Before the hand starts acting weak or paralyzed, a slowly growing tumor has to kill about 80 percent of the cells in the hand region of the motor strip. Yet that is a very crude test of function. A pianist or mechanic would probably notice problems long before then. And a stroke that suddenly killed perhaps 30 percent of the neurons in the motor strip would also cause paralysis.

There is more than one map of sensations from the skin, too, and an orderly map of the visual world at the back of the brain—losing that piece of the brain causes blindness. But it isn't the only one. No one knows how many visual maps there are in humans, but there are several dozen in monkeys, and more are discovered every year. However important some maps may be (you could be paralyzed or blind without them), we can't think of them as "the center of things" anymore.

Both the sensory and the motor maps extend to include the rest of the body, but those regions are still hidden under Neil's skull. The legs and feet are represented up over the top of the cerebral hemisphere, where it turns to dive vertically down the midline.

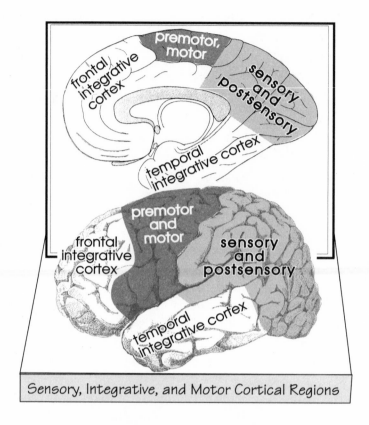

Sensory, Integrative, and Motor Cortical Regions

The representation of the larynx is also inaccessible today, as is most of the auditory cortex, because they're buried in the depths of that big infolding called the sylvian fissure. The maps of visual space are in the back of the head, quite inaccessible except when a tumor must be removed from there. The only parts of Neil's brain that are visible today, because of the surgery he requires, are the left temporal lobe and some parts of the frontal and parietal lobes. But that's a very interesting area—it includes most of the language cortex.

I notice George lightly touching the temporal lobe, exploring for scar tissue once more. And since Neil is busy talking to the anesthesiologist and won't hear me, I risk a little computer joke in a soft voice. "Still trying to find the reset button?"

"No," quips George, just as quietly. "I'm looking for the seat of consciousness."

Definitely an in-group joke, neurological variety. There is no seat of consciousness. Or at least not of the most interesting aspect of consciousness.

CONSCIOUSNESS certainly seems to be the Big Question. Where's Neil? Is he down in his brain stem, since that's what keeps him awake? Poking around down there is fraught with hazards—the patient might stop breathing, or his blood pressure might soar.

Or is he in his thalamus, since it helps determine what he pays attention to?

Or here in the language areas of his brain, so visible now, that allow him to express himself in ways that chimpanzees can't? It will take at least three chapters in this book to describe how a voice arises from brain mechanisms.

Or is he up in his frontal lobes, which he uses for speculating and worrying and planning? It's what he used to decide whether or not to undergo this surgery today.

Is there a "command neuron" among the billions of nerve cells in his brain that triggers a particular action, or a cell whose specialty is representing his grandmother?

Is Neil "conscious" when he answers accurately but cannot form a memory of the event? Indeed, how does Neil memorize something? And perceive his world, select what to recall from memory, then decide how to act?

How does he create something new, a novel sentence that he's never spoken before, or a plan for a career? Or (the flip side of frontal lobe functions, which we will consider in a later chapter), how would he get sidetracked into obsession, or suffer hallucinations?

And, finally, how does Neil manage to put all of this together, to see himself in terms of the stories that he has constructed about his past? How does he see himself poised at the intersection between his various stories about the past and his various imagined futures? And choose from among them? That, surely, is conscious.

A "voice" emerges somehow, somewhere in that brain before us. It mostly talks to itself (and what does *that* mean?). It narrates his life story. It is the voice of Neil. He didn't have it when he was born, but he was telling himself stories by the age of four and his inner voice was full blown before he reached his fifth birthday. How did he create it? In the course of this attempt to cure Neil's seizures, we will explore Neil's brain and learn something about how it creates his unique voice.

chapter 2

Losing Consciousness

The music from these spheres from the galaxy within our head is our consciousness. Consciousness is the continuous, subjective awareness of the activity of billions of cells firing at many times a second, communicating instantaneously with the tens of thousands of their neighbors. And the organization of this symphony of activity is such that it is sometimes externally oriented (during waking), sometimes remarkably oblivious to the outside world (during sleep), and sometimes so remarkably aware of itself (during dreams) that it recreates the external world in its own image.

J. ALLAN HOBSON, *The Dreaming Brain*, 1988

NEIL LOSES CONSCIOUSNESS only occasionally during his seizures, and then only for a few minutes. But back when he was first injured fifteen years ago, he was unconscious for a long time. His head injury had damaged his brain stem. In a family letter written while he was still recovering, his wife, Judy, described what happened:

Neil's accident was several months ago, and his recovery has been slow but steady. At first we didn't think he was going to make it, or maybe not ever wake up. Those first few days were just terrible. He wouldn't respond to a voice. His heart and lungs were okay, but when the doctor pinched him anywhere, he'd just straighten out his arms and legs. He became all stiff, with his back slightly arched. The doctor called this "decerebrate rigidity" and said it was a bad sign.

After a few days, Neil would bend his arms when pinched, though his legs were still rigid. The doctor said this was a good sign, "decorticate rigidity"—though it didn't look any better to us, and Neil still didn't respond to his name. In a few more days, Neil tried to push the doctor's hand away when he was pinched, another good sign, according to the doctor.

But the day I remember is when Neil finally opened his eyes when I called his name. It was such a relief. And thereafter, you could always awaken him—he was only asleep and no longer in coma, though the doctor called it "stupor" for a few more days until Neil was more alert to what was going on in his room. Pretty soon, he recognized us and was sitting up and talking, even walking down the hall for exercise. He could do most things. He looked wide awake, almost normal except for his memory, which he complained about a lot. It was then that he was transferred from the neurological floor to the rehabilitation hospital across town.

Neil doesn't remember anything about the accident. Or much about his stay on the neurological floor before that transfer. Even now his memory isn't very good. He remembers a lot from before the accident, his name and mine and his childhood and how to do his job. While he now remembers most things that have happened in the last few weeks, his memory for what happened before the transfer to the rehabilitation hospital is still spotty. For example, Neil doesn't even recall his birthday party during that last week on the neurological floor, when he seemed almost normal to us, serving people from the punchbowl we set up in the lounge, and talking about college days. He doesn't remember seeing his new niece, even though he held the baby for the longest time and talked about her that evening after they all left. That's very distressing to Neil, discovering that he isn't able to retain those experiences in his consciousness. But then he forgets his distress, until he's reminded again of something that he's lost.

Neil's new memories just didn't stick around for very long. As artificial intelligence expert Marvin Minsky points out, "When somebody says they are conscious, what they are saying is I remember a little bit about the state of my mind a few moments ago." Minsky is, of course, mocking the loose use of the word, saying consciousness is "one of those words we have for things we don't understand."

But is memory an important aspect of consciousness? Neil certainly seemed conscious after that terrible first week, despite his inability to recall his previous state of mind. We usually separate memory problems from consciousness—and wish we could separate a few more things, since the word is rather overburdened. There are many connotations of the word in *Webster's*:

○ Perceiving, apprehending, or noticing with a degree of controlled thought or observation. In other words, fully aware.

○ Personally felt, as in "conscious guilt."

○ Capable of or marked by thought, will, design, or perception.

○ Having mental faculties undulled by sleep, faintness, or stupor: "She became conscious after the anesthesia wore off." In other words, fully awake.

○ Done or acting with critical awareness: "He made a conscious effort to avoid the same mistakes." Here, *deliberate* may substitute for *conscious.*

○ Likely to notice, consider, or appraise: "He was a bargain-conscious shopper."

○ Being concerned or interested: "She was a budget-conscious manager."

○ Marked by strong feelings or notions: "They are a race-conscious society." For these last three uses, *sensitive* may substitute.

Sharing the same word in English—*consciousness*—does not mean that these connotations share the same neural mechanism. Other languages, after all, group these connotations under different words. Yet many people discussing consciousness regularly confuse these connotations with one another, acting as if they believe there is a common underlying entity such as "The Little Person Inside the Head." To avoid this presumption, we can use different English words for different aspects, such as when we use *aware* and avoid *conscious.*

But even *aware* has its problems. In the early days after his head injury, Neil was probably unaware of his surroundings—but we don't really know that. He might have been aware of the voice and the pinch, but unable to respond; because he also had memory problems, maybe he couldn't report that later. Occasionally, one encounters a patient who can recall conversations she overheard at a time when everyone thought she was still in coma. She was aware but effectively paralyzed.

And so, rather than consciousness or awareness, neurologists prefer to talk about something they can objectively measure: levels of arousibility. A sleeping person can usually be aroused to full alertness, just by a loud voice. But sometimes the arousal achieves only a level of stupor, even when a pinch is used. And sometimes no purposeful movements result, in which case we talk of deep coma.

Arousal is not the same as attention, another aspect of consciousness. Arousal is general, not specific like attention. The errors that people make during overarousal tend to be errors of commission or overcorrection—they jump to conclusions. In underarousal, one tends to get errors of omission instead—things aren't noticed as they should be. Vigilance tasks, such as the sentry or the radar operator trying to stay alert for the rare event, lead to loss of arousal within times as short as a half-hour. But that's quite different from fatigue, which is commonly due to overarousal. Stress is, in some sense, overarousal.

Levels of arousal may not be included in those consciousness connotations in *Webster's,* but that's what neurologists usually mean when they use the word. When physicians are forced to use the

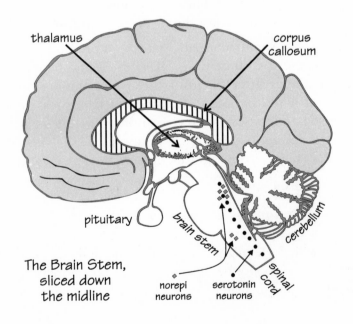

The Brain Stem, sliced down the midline

"C-word," that's the connotation that they will usually retreat to, the only firm ground in the whole morass.

But equating *conscious* with *arousable* creates appalling problems. It tends to be interpreted as ascribing consciousness to any organism that has irritability. And irritability is a basic property of all living tissue, plant as well as animal, the first-trimester fetus as well as the severely demented Alzheimer's patient—even the bacterium in your gut is conscious by that definition. A recent president of the United States used that definition in explaining his stance against abortion, although no reporter thought to ask him what he therefore thought of the consciousness of, say, a sperm.

With so many major synonyms (*aware, awake, deliberate, sensitive, arousable,* and more), you can see why everyone gets a little confused talking about consciousness, the subtle thinkers as well as the literal-minded. Modern discussions of consciousness in the scientific community usually include such aspects of mental life as focusing your attention, things that you didn't know you knew, mental rehearsal, imagery, thinking, decision making, awareness, altered states of consciousness, voluntary actions, subliminal priming, the development of the concept of self in children, and the narratives we tell ourselves when awake or dreaming.

NEIL'S STAGES OF RECOVERY correspond to more and more of his brain stem recovering from the bruising it took during the sudden stop. The first good sign was when his arms flexed, even though purposelessly; the second good sign was when he tried to push away the hand that pinched him. Then he achieved stupor, and finally he was awake and observing his surroundings. And now, fifteen years later, he is an experienced engineer asking lots of questions about his brain. In the weeks before his surgery, I gave him much to read, and we met in the hospital cafeteria to discuss it.

Neil found me in the atrium one afternoon, in my favorite corner behind the espresso machine, just as a psychiatrist friend was leaving. So we had the round table to ourselves, amid the smell of fresh coffee and the sound of rain on the glass roof. It was where we'd met the previous week, when Neil had brought me the copy of the letter his wife had written fifteen years before, and it proved to be the table at which most of our pre-op conversations were held.

After we had discussed his cab driver's tales about other passengers she'd brought to this medical center, he asked about coma and consciousness.

"So that's just the 'wake-up-call center' down in my brain stem?" he asked. "Is coma merely deep sleep, where the brain's alarm clock doesn't work in the morning?"

"Yes and no," I answered. (Actually, I wasn't that succinct, but I'm going to condense my answers a little). We know, from animal studies back in the 1940s, that there are certain parts of the brain stem that control awakening. They're crucial. Animals with damage there appear to be continuously asleep and don't awaken spontaneously. Many neurons—that's what we call nerve cells—down there deliver norepinephrine all over the brain and spinal cord. And so diffusely that we think of it almost as a lawn-sprinkler system. A lot gets delivered to the sensory strip. About half of these "norepi" neurons are in a brain stem cluster known as the locus coeruleus. They are rather inactive during sleep, and most active when you startle at something unexpected.

"I figured out that adrenaline is another name for epinephrine," Neil commented. "I suppose that noradrenaline is just a synonym for norepinephrine?"

Right, epinephrine does things outside the brain somewhat similarly to what norepi does inside. Adrenaline is released from the adrenal glands, which sit atop the kidneys, and is carried in the bloodstream as a hormone. When you get a rush from almost getting hit by a car, that's adrenaline, raising your heart rate and setting up your muscles for fight or flight. It adds to the startle effect that norepi produces within the brain.

There is another diffusely broadcasting group of neurons scattered along the centerline near the surface of the brain stem. These deliver serotonin to wide areas of the brain and spinal cord. The activity of these serotonin neurons may determine levels of arousal, but they don't increase their activity with sensory input. The norepi neurons do, and are thought to be more important for the emphasis of attention. Now it looks as though the serotonin neurons have another big role, that of regulating pain perception. Drugs that enhance the effectiveness of norepinephrine and serotonin are commonly used as antidepressants. Ones that enhance the serotonin effects are often helpful in chronic pain disorders.

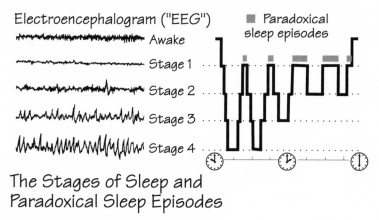

The Stages of Sleep and
Paradoxical Sleep Episodes

After Andreasen, 1984

During coma, neither the serotonin nor norepi systems are working well, which is probably why the patient can't be aroused.

BUT SLEEP IS FAR MORE COMPLICATED than coma, I continued. About two hours every night is spent in light sleep. People awakened from that stage of sleep report mulling things over but never getting very far along a line of thought. They'll call this thinking, not dreaming. In the deeper parts of this "orthodox" sleep is when bed-wetting occurs, as well as night-walking episodes. Both norepi and serotonin neurons are ticking along at only about half of their waking rates.

About every 100 minutes or so during sleep, both the norepi and serotonin systems virtually shut down. Then the sleeper experiences an episode of "paradoxical" sleep. This is when most of the muscles are unusually relaxed—except (and here's the paradox) for the eyes, which dart back and forth under the closed eyelids, and except (in males) for the penis, which becomes erect. If you wake up people in this stage of sleep, they'll often report dreaming, not thinking. There are well-formed sensory impressions, though sometimes quite bizarre. A series of actions seems to occur, often with an improbable juxtaposition of people, places, and times. Strong emotions may be experienced.

And the dreamer seems to accept, uncritically, what's happening in the dream—memory recall doesn't work very well in sleep. Making new memories is even more impaired. If you wait as much as five minutes after the end of the rapid eye movement sleep to awaken sleepers, they won't remember much of the dream. Dreaming is mostly visual, with some auditory and tactile sensations as well as a sense of movement—but seldom does anyone report pain, or smells or tastes.

"So they're not really like daydreams, are they?" Neil asked, munching on a scone he'd bought at the espresso stand.

People indulge in fantasies while awake, I told him, but these are seldom as vivid and bizarre as in nighttime dreams. Furthermore, real dreams are like delusions; you have very little insight, and while the dreams are occurring, you tend to think it's all real. Emotions aren't normal in dreams. Anxiety, fear, and surprise are likely to be exaggerated. Yet shame and guilt play little role in dreams, even when seemingly engaging in shabby behavior that would stir your conscience if you were awake.

You don't gain access to established memories very well during sleep, and you usually can't establish new memories either. Actually, it's a bit of a puzzle why you ever form permanent memories of dreams, given how poor the recall usually is. But there's a way around that, at least if you awaken before the five minutes are up. If you recall a dream before it fades, when your circuits for memorizing new things are working once again, then you can memorize the *recall* rather than the original happening. If you make a habit of reviewing your fading dreams upon awakening, you can memorize quite a collection of nonsense. Keeping a dream diary can thus clutter up your head with a lot of things that didn't really happen—and we have enough trouble as it is, just keeping straight those things that really happened from all those things that we merely imagined or planned.

"So why do therapists like to talk about dreams so much?" Neil asked.

Psychotherapists may find it useful to ask about dreams as a way of getting patients to talk about something other than their current problems, if they are dwelling on them. Talking about dreams can be a psychotherapist's version of talking about the weather, simply a way of getting a conversation started so that it can move on to something that the patient would not think to mention spontaneously. A lot can be learned simply from the way a patient chooses to interpret a dream. But seeking significance in dreams—which is what patients may mistakenly think the therapist's questions are all about—is not much better than seeking it in tea leaves. Randomness predominates in both, yet we usually try to make it fit into some sort of story line.

"So, that's the kind of sleep you can't do without," Neil went on. "You go a little crazy if you don't get enough dreaming sleep, don't you?"

You normally dream about two hours every night, I told him, in addition to your two hours of mulling things over in light sleep. If you were awakened each time you started to go into dreaming sleep, you'd play catch-up the next night, dreaming more than normal. If this happened night after night, you'd become rather irritable—and not just because of awakening. You can be awakened just as often in orthodox sleep without becoming so cranky.

"I read somewhere that, in dreams, we all have the experience of being psychotic or demented or delusional. It almost sounds like we have a quota for being psychotic, and if we don't fulfill it at night, we become psychotic during the day!"

That's like what René Descartes said back in 1641: "I am accustomed to sleep and in my dreams to imagine the same things that lunatics imagine when awake." Psychiatrists consider psychosis a little more complicated than that—but yes, dreams do show you normal physiological processes that, when nothing better is happening, could correspond to the symptoms of mental illness.

There are people called narcoleptics, I went on, who suddenly fall asleep during the day. The problem was identified centuries ago, but we now know that narcoleptics go immediately into dreaming sleep— real daydreams, complete with the psychotic features of nighttime dreams. Usually dreaming sleep doesn't occur until after at least 20 minutes of orthodox sleep, but in narcolepsy the transition can be very rapid. Indeed, the onset of the muscle relaxation accompanying dreaming sleep is so sudden in most narcoleptics that they may collapse while standing up.

"I saw that happen to my roommate in the rehab hospital. Another survivor of seat belt neglect. I told him that he was taking 'falling asleep' too literally."

About three-quarters of narcoleptics sometimes do that, I said. Others get enough warning to lie down, or at least to rest their heads somewhere. Narcolepsy can be from a bruise to the brain stem, but most cases are probably inherited; there's a "gene for narcolepsy" in 98 percent of narcoleptics.

THE VARSITY CREW ROWED past us as we walked along the waterway behind the medical center during a brief, sunny period. That's when Neil brought up one of his vocabulary questions.

"I suspect you use the word *stroke* differently from the way the coxswain does," he said.

In medicine, I told him, the meaning of *stroke* was originally closer to "Felled by an unseen blow." It meant any sudden collapse and loss of awareness. At least, that was the label for those cases in which the loss of consciousness wasn't temporary, as in fainting or a seizure. It could, of course, have been a heart attack, but we now have a separate label for those cases of sudden collapse, since we understand them so well. So these days, *stroke* refers to what's left over—sudden damage to the brain caused by blood-supply problems.

Sometimes paralysis occurs, but it all depends on what brain region was damaged. Often no loss of consciousness occurs and the stroke manifestations are subtle.

"What causes the stroke? The usual plumbing problems?"

Leaks and stoppages, yes. And the occasional burst pipe can cause major structural damage rather quickly.

Just as in a bruise under the skin, a blood vessel in the brain can leak. Blood is very toxic to neurons, which stop working and often die when the blood comes in direct contact with them. When there's not an obvious external event like a hit on the head, bleeds are usually caused by the ballooning of an arterial wall, rather like an old tire that develops a blister on its sidewall. The balloon—called an aneurysm—may never cause any trouble, but occasionally it ruptures, pumping blood into the surrounding tissues. If a blood vessel in your leg were to rupture, the leg would just swell up. But the brain is surrounded by the skull, and all that escaped blood takes up space, squeezing the brain. That compression of the brain is what kills a lot of stroke victims.

Or the stroke may be caused by a plugged-up blood vessel. Usually a clot forms, or an atherosclerotic plaque accumulating on an arterial wall comes loose—whichever, this embolus is swept along in the blood stream until it reaches an artery that is too small for it to pass through. Sometimes that unfortunate artery is in the lung, sometimes in the brain. It's all pretty random, what artery becomes plugged. And so some region of the brain might lose its oxygen supply. If the obstruction is flushed through or dissolves in a short time, the neurological symptoms may be brief; one side of the face might sag, for example, but then begin to recover several minutes later.

Such temporary strokes are known as transient ischemic attacks. But if the artery stays plugged up for something like 15 minutes or more, permanent damage occurs. Once the dead cells are cleaned out, there's a hole in the brain.

"But I don't have any holes in my brain, right?" Neil sounded a little anxious.

Just the usual cavities that everyone has—those big reservoirs of cerebrospinal fluid we call the ventricles. There was a lot of excitement about the ventricles during the Renaissance. The first phrenologists were actually religious scholars who lived 500 years ago. They thought that the subdivisions of the soul were housed in the various cavities of the brain: memory in one; fantasy, common sense, and imagination in another; thought and judgment in a third.

"I'll have a hole after the operation. What's going to fill in the hole?"

Cerebrospinal fluid fills all the space inside the skull that isn't brain or blood. You'll get an enlarged ventricle, so to speak.

"I'll have more soul, eh?" Neil chuckled as we walked back inside the cafeteria. "What about those people—I've seen them mentioned in magazine articles—who are discovered to have big holes in their heads—even though they have normal intelligence? They only seem to have a thin layer of brain."

Actually, most of their brain is normal, but they have a big, fluid-filled cyst, with only a thin layer of cerebral cortex in many places. People confuse the cerebral cortex with the brain in general, perhaps because the cortex is what seems to house the fancier functions such as language, planning ahead, and worrying about tomorrow. Back when the first computerized tomography scanners were being tested on medical students, one was discovered to have a big cyst like that, with only a thin layer of cortex. But that cortex worked pretty well. Of course, a thin layer of cortex is all that any of us has. It's just a thin shell, weaving in and out of the folds in the brain's surface.

"In the pictures I've seen, it seems to vary in thickness from one place to another."

To explain that, I told him, would require that we get a piece of cake.

With dessert in hand, I explained that most of that apparent variation in cortical thickness is just the cortex being sliced on an angle, rather than along the local vertical, just as if you took a layer cake and cut it on a slant. You can make it look two or three times thicker that way, by cutting on a really oblique angle. But in reality, the cortex is never any thicker than a stack of maybe two coins. It's the icing on the cake.

"Fooled me. So that thin little surface layer does all the interesting stuff? All the language? All the planning?" He thought for a minute.

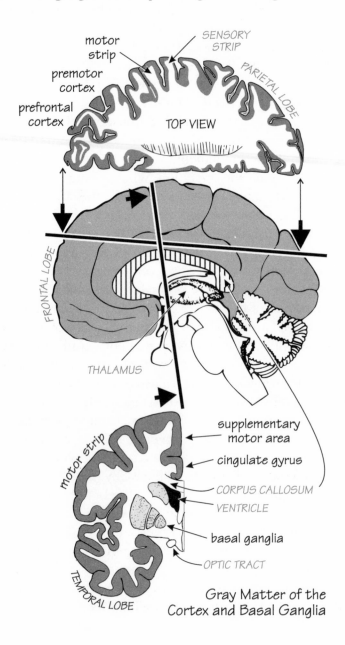

Gray Matter of the
Cortex and Basal Ganglia

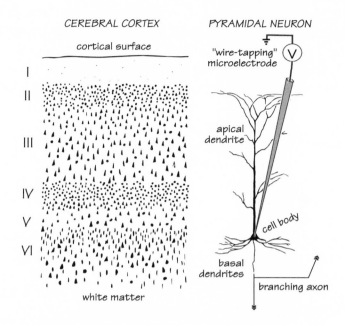

"So what's the rest of the space between my ears, if there's only a couple of thin layers of cortex doing all the work?"

Wires. Lots and lots of wires. Except we call them axons or sometimes nerve fibers. If you've ever toured a telephone company's central office, you'll remember seeing huge bundles of wires rising out of the floor, continuing through the ceiling, and often ascending through several more floors of the building. But when you finally see the computer that switches all the calls from one circuit to another, you discover that it isn't very large. It's small enough to fit inside a closet.

The brain does things much fancier than mere switching, but the wires still take up most of the room. That's what the white matter is. The part of cerebral cortex doing all the fancy stuff is just that thin surface sheet, wrinkled into hills and valleys.

THE CEREBRAL CORTEX is an important proportion of the gray matter. But there is a lot more in the depths of the brain, concerned with things like sleep, directing your attention, and regulating your memory. Some gray matter, such as the thalamus, has an intimate back-and-forth relationship with the cerebral cortex.

Of course, the gray matter isn't really gray. It's closer to brownish red.

"Gray matter isn't gray anymore?" Neil said, laying down his fork in mock disgust. "My disillusionment is complete."

It's only gray in a very dead brain. But then, that's the only condition under which most people ever see a brain, assuming they ever see one at all. It's only in the operating room that we get to see that the natural, workaday color of the gray matter is really a nice rich reddish brown—rather like color pictures of the Grand Canyon.

"I hesitate to ask, but is the white matter really white?"

Fear not, the white matter is indeed a pale porcelain white, not unlike skim milk diluted with a little water. The color is contributed by the fatty insulation, known as myelin, wrapped about the wires. There is some myelin insulation within the gray matter as well, but other things contribute some color too—all those other parts of the neuron, such as the cell body and dendrites, and lots of little blood vessels. In the white matter, you find only the long, thin, tubular part of the neuron—its axon—sometimes with myelin insulation wrapped around it, sometimes not.

"Those wires carry the electrical signals, right? That's where brain waves come from?"

Yes and no. Yes, the axons carry electrical signals, called impulses, which are about a tenth of a volt in size and absolutely essential for moving information over long distances in cerebral cortex. But no—brain waves don't come from axons in the white matter, but from another part of the cell—the dendrite—that is closer to the cortical surface. The electroencephalogram—EEG for short—is a pretty crude measurement. There's nothing in the computer world that is as crude as the EEG. Still, it allows us to see little seizures happening that we otherwise wouldn't know about, because they didn't cause any muscles to contract.

"But isn't the EEG voltage proportional to the message traffic in some way—to the mail trucks arriving and leaving?"

It's not even as precise as those little tubes the traffic engineers lay across the street to measure traffic flow. But you don't have to count every car and truck to get an idea of the traffic patterns. Just imagine using a tape recorder and hanging the microphone on a light pole. Set the tape speed very slow and let it run for a day, then watch the sound level indicator as you replay the tape.

Do you know how you can wake up in a hotel room in a foreign city and guess whether it's morning or not, without ever opening your eyes? If the traffic noise outside is just the occasional truck, it's probably still four in the morning. Traffic starts to build about six, and so does the traffic noise. If you go back to sleep at six, you'll probably wake up next during the height of the rush-hour noises.

The EEG shows some rhythms that led to the term "brain waves." They are very much like the traffic rhythms you would notice. There are big, sustained peaks twice a day—during the morning and evening rush hours. There are more rapid rhythms too. If you plotted out the loudness of the traffic noise, you'd get a rhythm of about thirty little peaks every hour.

"The traffic signals down the block probably cause the traffic to bunch up."

Right, I said. The rush-hour rhythm isn't as pronounced on the weekends, and so there are cycles within cycles. The stop-and-go cycle becomes more pronounced during rush hours. So, too, the various EEG rhythms wax and wane in amplitude, depending on whether you

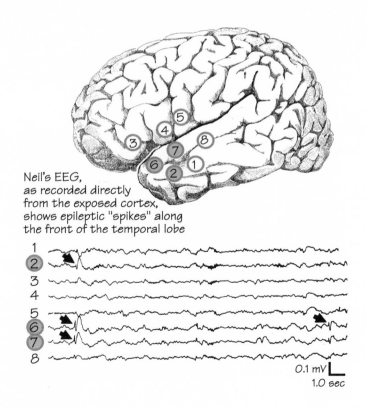

Neil's EEG,
as recorded directly
from the exposed cortex,
shows epileptic "spikes" along
the front of the temporal lobe

0.1 mV
1.0 sec

are resting or alert, busy or waiting. The rhythms are very useful, even though quite imprecise. Sometimes we try to synchronize a lot of activity, just to see how the EEG responds.

"That's the test I had, with the clicks once a second, the one called the average evoked response?"

Exactly. Just think of a loud noise—say, a dish breaking on the floor—that stops all the conversation in a room. Everything becomes unusually quiet. Then everyone begins talking at once. We can learn a lot about how some parts of the brain are working by using little disruptions like that. We can't always figure out an appropriate stimulus to stop and restart the conversations. But for the visual cortex, light flashes work pretty well.

NEIL WAS CURIOUS about his EEG abnormalities. He's been through dozens of EEGs over the years but never understood exactly what the neurologists were looking for. We were sketching some EEG patterns on the napkin he'd fetched from the espresso stand.

"So what's your analogy for the spike they find in my EEG? They said it's the hallmark of a resting epileptic process, in between seizures."

The spike is more like a backfire—not normal, but not serious by itself. Usually an occasional backfire is just the sign of an engine that needs a tuneup, and I suspect that's what most EEG spikes signify, too. It's when you get a whole series of backfires, or a whole series of spikes in the EEG, that there's a chance of a breakdown any minute. Sometimes you can see a series of spikes in the EEG that remind you of an old truck, surging ahead but bucking with another backfire, then surging again, threatening to shake itself to pieces with the repeated backfires, and finally all but collapsing in the street. That's a lot like how we imagine a seizure starts.

"How many neurons are involved in one of those EEG spikes?" Neil asked me.

Probably millions, I replied. An EEG electrode glued to the scalp records signals from a region of brain at least the size of a dime. I once calculated that there are 133 million neurons in a dime-sized sheet of cerebral cortex. The troublemakers are probably only a small minority of that but, much of the time, their signal gets diluted by all the rest. A lot of seizures don't produce muscular movements, yet they keep that part of the brain from getting any useful work done for a while.

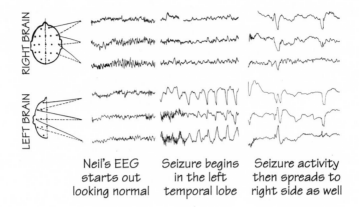

Neil's EEG   Seizure begins   Seizure activity
starts out   in the left   then spreads to
looking normal   temporal lobe   right side as well

From the scalp, we can see only the larger mobs in action. When they reach the level of overt movements, they're involving many millions of neurons.

"Lots and lots of busy little neurons," Neil said. "How many all told?"

The count is now up to about 200 billion, I told him. That's for the whole brain. For just the cerebral cortex, the subtotal is about 30 billion. People confuse the cerebral cortex with the entire brain, but the cortex has only a fraction of the total number of neurons. The cerebellum, atop the brain stem, has many more, thanks to so many little granule cell neurons. And, of course, the number of synapses is even larger—they're the points of contact between neurons, and each neuron has many thousands of them.

But even if the totals were constant across individuals, the subtotals would still vary between different parts of the cerebral cortex. If you were to look at the primary visual cortex in a number of normal individuals, you'd notice that it wasn't always the same size. Some individuals have three times more than others.

"So do those people see better?"

IS BIGGER REALLY BETTER? In the case of the visual cortex, no one knows yet. Language cortex probably varies a lot, too. Among various animal species, the depth of the cortical layers varies somewhat, but the number of neurons beneath a square millimeter of cortical surface stays quite constant, not far from 148,000.

"That's interesting. Sounds like some sort of packing principle is involved, that's universal."

Perhaps. The major growth of cerebral cortex, as our ancestors became fancier and fancier primates, was sideways. In chimpanzees and gorillas, the total is less than a standard sheet of typing paper. Humans have the equivalent of four sheets of paper. Rats have less than a square inch of cortex, less than humans by a factor of 500. Increased surface area is presumably what led to so many wrinkles in the cortical surface, all those narrow valleys that increase the amount of surface area that can be packed into a given volume.

"Does a smart person have more cerebral cortex than an idiot? Is cortical size what makes us smarter than a chimpanzee?"

Cortical area has something to do with being smart, I conceded, although it's hardly the whole story. If you measure the amount of gray matter using an MRI scan, individuals with high IQs have significantly more than those of average IQ. But the cortical area accounts for only a fraction of the variability in IQ. Something else must affect intelligence. The internal efficiency of the circuitry probably matters more than the total amount of cortex.

"I'm going to lose some cortex when they do the surgery. What'll happen to my IQ? My wife is concerned about that too. And I know my business partners are!"

IQ measurements usually go *up* after operations like these, and rather significantly. But that's because the patients are so impaired before the operation, either by the lingering effects of recent seizures or by high drug dosages and their side effects. And so individuals test lower than their biological endowment.

Neil thought about this for a minute as we carried our trays over to the cafeteria's conveyor belt. "So I'm likely to come out of this operation somewhat smarter than I am now—but not as smart as I was fifteen years ago, before I banged up my head. But I was so smart back then that I didn't wear my seat belt!"

Just goes to show that good habits can be more important than IQ. Intelligence, or at least what IQ tests measure, has a lot to do with "being quick" mentally—able to get through a lot of questions in a fixed amount of time. And IQ also has a lot to do with being able to juggle many things at the same time, as in those analogy questions that ask "A is to B as C is to ___ ?" And then you get three choices—D, E, and F—so that, to solve the problem, you have to keep six items in mind simultaneously.

Things like judgment and creativity and a good storehouse of knowledge may be far more important in real life than whatever IQ measures. You don't want to be so quick that you jump to the wrong conclusions, or so indecisive that you never make up your mind. It's a matter of the right balancing act, what controls when you move on to the next problem. Having a "good brain" often isn't a matter of how much brain there is. Quality can usually make up for quantity.

chapter 3

Seeing the Brain Speak

"TIME FOR THE PICTURE SHOW, I see," Neil says from under the drapes. I glance up briefly from studying Neil's brain to see that the neuropsychologist is indeed maneuvering the slide projector box around the anesthesiologist, positioning it so that Neil can clearly see its back-projection screen.

Neil's conversational commentary on what he sees comes from the brain before me, so brightly illuminated and colorful. Nothing gray about it. The sounds may emerge from Neil's mouth, but the words were chosen and sent on their way by something soft that lies just beneath Neil's exposed brain surface—that very cerebral cortex I'm looking at. Somehow, it creates a "conductor" for the orchestra of nerve cells—a "voice" that talks to itself much of the time and only occasionally speaks out loud.

A society of bees may create a beehive, but a society of nerve cells can create a person, one capable of pondering ethics, writing poetry, and performing neurosurgery. One that may be capable, someday, of understanding itself. Each time I gaze through this surgical window into a talking brain, I reflect that the view back to Earth would be anticlimactic, should anyone ever offer me a ride on a moon rocket. A person *lives* in that brain I am now seeing. Somehow the real Neil, an authentic voice, emerges from all those nerve cells. And narrates its life's story. Somehow.

I may marvel at it all, but George is probably busy thinking about exactly which parts of the brain are essential for language abilities. Not for patients in general, but for Neil—his version of all the possible variations on the basic plan. Neurosurgeons must avoid crippling language abilities. When epileptic areas are close to language areas—and often they are—it becomes very important to map language abilities before removing anything.

We finish recording the electrical activity from the surface of the brain, obtaining more details than we'd seen in the pre-op EEGs. The characteristic signature of the idling epileptic process—those backfire-like spikes—are seen in Neil's temporal lobe, and in regions that are often involved with language processes. George cannot simply remove those areas, because he would cause more trouble than he would cure. So the next question is, Exactly where does Neil's language come from?

JUST LOOKING AT THE SURFACE of the brain, you can't see any anatomy that is peculiarly language cortex. Indeed, it is very hard to see the four "lobes" of each half of the brain (frontal, parietal, occipital, and temporal).

As Neil said when we discussed this earlier, "It's hardly a four-leaf clover." Just as there aren't any agreed-upon boundaries in the United States between "the East" and "the Midwest," so it is hard to say exactly where the parietal lobe stops and the temporal lobe begins.

"At least," Neil replied, "the right half is just the mirror image of the left."

But no—the two cerebral hemispheres are actually quite asymmetric in various ways. A hemisphere isn't usually half, as the right side is often a bit wider than the left side. The right side protrudes in the front, slightly beyond the tip of the left frontal lobe; conversely, in the rear, the left occipital lobe protrudes beyond the right.

"So the average brain is skewed?"

Yes, and that's not all. The sylvian fissure, the great infolded cleft that separates the temporal lobe from the rest of the cerebral hemisphere, is usually long and straight on the left side. On the right side, it is shorter and curls upward more noticeably. This reflects a right-left difference in the size of several brain areas. One of these is the "planum temporale," the part of the temporal lobe buried in the sylvian fissure, extending from the auditory area to the back end of the fissure.

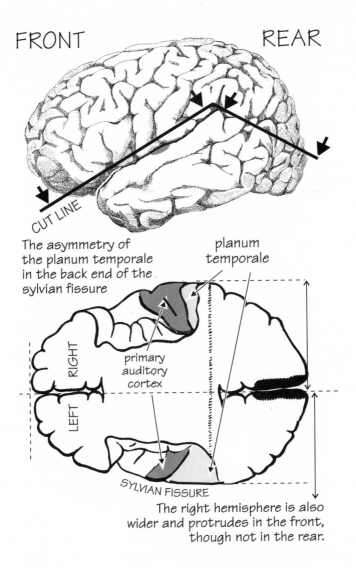

FRONT   REAR

CUT LINE

The asymmetry of
the planum temporale
in the back end of the
sylvian fissure

planum
temporale

RIGHT

primary
auditory
cortex

LEFT

SYLVIAN FISSURE

The right hemisphere is also
wider and protrudes in the front,
though not in the rear.

Functionally, the two halves of the human brain aren't symmetric
either. Some brain functions are "lateralized," especially language,
which usually resides in the left side of the brain. Several decades ago,
the neurologist Norman Geschwind observed that the planum temporale was larger on the right side in some people—and in about the
same percentage of the population as had right-brain dominance for
language. He inferred from this that the relative size of this area was
an "anatomic marker" for lateralization of language, although the
actual function of this area is not known.

"Do the apes have that asymmetry?" Neil asked.

It is present in orangutans and chimpanzees, suggesting that at least one anatomic substrate for language appears earlier in evolution. But it is not present in gorillas—which evolved midway between orangs and chimps—and gorillas can be taught a simple gestural language. So it isn't simple.

"Well, then, when does the fetus first start getting asymmetric?"

The planum temporale asymmetry can be identified in fetuses of 26 weeks gestational age, the beginning of the third trimester. So babies are born with an anatomical specialization that is probably related to language.

But the anatomy provides only this thin layer of clues about where language is located. Altered function provides many clues.

When something goes wrong under the hood of a car, we may at last discover what some peculiar-looking part had been doing all along. The brakes stop working, and once we get around to looking under the hood rather than at the wheels, we discover fluid leaking from a part that a diagram in the owner's manual mysteriously labels the "master cylinder."

Thanks to what stops working (the brakes), we can finally identify the function of that particular part of the clutter in the engine compartment. Greek philosopher-physicians of 2,500 years ago used similar reasoning when they recognized that the left half of the brain seems to control the right side of the body while the right half of the brain controls the left side.

"If the car's engine compartment were organized along crossover lines," Neil observed, "the left wheels' power would come from the right side of the engine. And the left wheels' brakes would come from a master cylinder on the right side. And vice versa."

Instead, modern cars get power to all wheels from the same engine that occupies both sides of the engine compartment.

"And on most American cars, the brakes on both the right and left sides are controlled from a master cylinder on the left side of the engine compartment. Steering is similarly left-sided."

That arrangement is, you know, rather like language in the human brain. In 1861, the French surgeon Paul Broca said that, in his experience, it was usually damage to the left side of the brain that affected language, not right-sided damage. Such aphasia—as damage-induced disturbances in language abilities are collectively known—is distinguished from mere difficulties in speech itself. The "power" for speech obviously involves both sides of the chest and tongue and lips, but the mechanism that selects the words is on the left side of the brain, just as the steering and braking originate from the left side of the car. Broca called the left brain "dominant" for language.

"Does that have anything to do with the right hand being, well, right-handed?"

That kind of cerebral dominance was subsequently confused with that other specialty of left-brain function: running the right hand. It used to be thought that left-handed persons were the ones with right-brain language, that their brains were just mirror images in a few aspects, similar to the ways that cars in the United Kingdom or Japan differ from cars in Europe and the Americas.

"But they're not? They're just all mixed up?"

It now appears that most left-handers have language in the left brain, just like right-handers. About 5 percent of all people have language in the right brain and another 5 to 6 percent have significant language function in both halves. Although left-handers are found more often in the reversed-dominance and mixed-dominance groups, no pattern of hand use reliably predicts the side of the brain where the major language area resides.

Broca also had an example of where language might live within the left brain. He had been caring for a stroke patient who seemed to understand much of what was said to him. Leborgne could follow directions and help care for some of the other patients in the hospital—but couldn't get out any word except "tan." His condition wasn't explained by a paralysis of the relevant muscles, as Leborgne could eat and drink and say "tan-tan."

When Leborgne died, Broca examined his brain to see what had been damaged. The stroke turned out to have affected a region of the brain just above the left ear, including the lower rear portion of the frontal lobe, the lower front portion of the parietal lobe, and the upper part of the temporal lobe. Despite this varied damage involving three of the four lobes, Broca was most impressed with the frontal lobe damage because it extended deeper than elsewhere.

Broca proposed that the damaged lower rear portion of the frontal lobe was responsible for this patient's language problems. He suggested that this region controlled language output. Neurologists soon came to speak of "Broca's aphasia" or "expressive aphasia" when

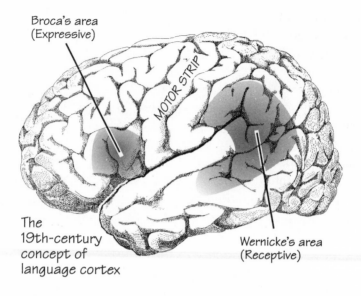

Broca's area
(Expressive)

MOTOR STRIP

Wernicke's area
(Receptive)

The
19th-century
concept of
language cortex

encountering that characteristic language problem, and "Broca's area" to describe the lower rear portion of the frontal lobe on the left side that is in front of the motor strip.

Actually, Broca made a little mistake here. It turns out that "Broca's aphasia" does not reliably result from damage to only "Broca's area." There needs to be damage to many of those other areas that Leborgne's brain showed were damaged, but that Broca deemphasized.

"Is that what Wernicke discovered?" Neil asked.

No, it took more than a century to correct that erroneous guess. What the 26-year-old German neurologist Carl Wernicke described in 1874 were patients with a different set of language problems. These people talked fluently, even excessively. But they sometimes used words that made no sense. Usually they did not understand what was said to them, in contrast to Broca's patient: although their hearing seemed unimpaired, they couldn't make sense out of the strings of words they heard.

Soon neurologists were talking about "Wernicke's aphasia" and later "receptive aphasia." They inferred that language involves the transfer of what is heard or read, first to Wernicke's area for decoding, and then on to Broca's area for spoken output.

It wasn't just the symptoms that distinguished such groups of patients: the Wernicke-type patients seemed to have stroke damage located further toward the rear of the brain ("posterior"), usually in the rear of the temporal lobe and up into the parietal lobe at the back end of the large sylvian fissure. Broca's area is about the size of a quarter, while Wernicke's area is closer to the size of a silver dollar.

"So is listening to speech really done in a different part of the brain than talking?"

Dichotomies ("It's either *this* or *that*") are very popular, and here were two of them in parallel, seemingly different versions of the same thing: Broca-Wernicke (talking-listening, expressive-receptive) and front-rear (anterior-posterior). And so they all became tied together in textbooks (and, of course, if language was left brain, something else was going on in right brain—another tricky dichotomy we will tackle in the next chapter). Dichotomies make researchers happy, they ease the burden of overworked students, they sell books and shortcut study guides—but in reality, things are usually more complicated, and therefore harder to remember.

Imagine a desert nomad trying to figure out the controls on his new car: he pushes a switch and discovers that it causes some hidden lever arms to pop up and sweep back and forth before his eyes. It may entertain the children but, unless it happens to be raining at the same time, the function of the wipers—to clear away raindrops—isn't obvious.

"Many of us have similar trouble, figuring out the controls on videotape recorders."

Neurophysiologists have similar problems in figuring out the functions of the various portions of the brain ("localization of function"). Electrical stimulation of the motor strip may cause some crude movements, but stimulation of Broca's area or Wernicke's area does not, alas, cause speech. Just as the wipers require rain for their function to become clear, so does stimulation require a string of words that it can modify. If the patient is already speaking, the electricity merely causes errors. If not, nothing seems to happen. The anatomy doesn't come with labels and, unless the brain happens to be speaking at the same time, the functions of the cortical language areas aren't obvious.

THE SLIDE SHOW is finally underway, with Neil naming the objects that pop up on the back-projection screen every few seconds. He's well rehearsed at this task, and we know that he can correctly name all of the slides.

Neil's slide show, as naming sites are mapped

"I know what that is," Neil says. "It's a, ah, a. . . ." George removes the handheld stimulator from Neil's cortex. "An elephant," Neil says at last, with some exasperation.

Another slide pops up on the screen. "This is an apple," Neil says routinely. George was nonetheless stimulating the cortex, but at another spot, a short distance away from the previous site. This new site seems unrelated to naming. The electric current has been set to confuse a small brain area, about the size of a pencil eraser. Stimulation causes Neil to make mistakes and is thought to work by inactivating or confusing that small part of the brain (or regions to which it strongly connects).

When some sites are stimulated, Neil can't name common objects that he ordinarily has no trouble naming immediately. George is searching for those sites. The slide projector keeps Neil busy for some time while George explores; we're listening for any difficulties that Neil might have. Neil has been instructed to say the phrase "This is a. . ." before the name of the object. There are a few places, particularly in and around Broca's area, where Neil cannot even utter the preamble: he cannot talk at all.

But arrest of all speech can occur for many reasons and doesn't truly define the language cortex. Anomia, Neil's inability to utter the name after successfully speaking the preamble, is closer to being a specific problem with language. Because all of us suffer from anomia on occasion ("Whatever is her name? It's right on the tip of my tongue!"), naming difficulties are thought to be a mild momentary inefficiency in language processing in our brains—which is what makes it a good survey test for use in the operating room.

The site where stimulation blocked "elephant" is not specific to elephants; stimulation later while showing other objects reveals problems in naming them as well. This seems to be a "naming site," not an elephant site. Unlike computer memories that store things in pigeonholes, a memory such as "elephant" is stored in a distributed way throughout whole areas of the brain, overlapping with other memories in ways we do not yet understand.

EVEN IF THERE AREN'T ELEPHANT SITES, I suppose that there might be places for particular classes of words, such as nouns or verbs. Or, as Neil asked the other day, is there a place for animals, another for vegetables, and another for minerals?

Are there places where word phrases are constructed, and other places that decode what you hear for its meaning? Do bilingual persons

have a different place for each language? Is language cortex organized differently in men and women, in the articulate and the tongue-tied, in the deaf using sign language? There are many possibilities, but only limited ways to get any answers.

For brain functions other than language, most of what we know comes from studies of the brains of other animals. Mimicking speech sounds is not, of course, language, any more than a tape recorder is capable of generating language. Parrots can acquire a vocabulary, but interest has centered on the protolinguistic abilities of our closest ancestors among the apes.

Apes, unfortunately, are not usually very good at mimicking human speech sounds. But if their teachers point at the appropriate symbol on a chart when speaking a word, the ape can "speak" the word later by merely pointing at its symbol. The same symbol-board technique is widely used with autistic children, so they can eventually manage to convey the meaning they associate with the symbol, just by pointing. Relatively few apes have been taught any type of language, and then with vocabularies (a few hundred words) that are small by human standards (typically 10,000 to 100,000 words).

The good students among the bonobos (pygmy chimps) can understand novel sentences as complicated as "Go to the office and bring back the red ball," where the test situation is novel (balls are not usually found in the office) and has many opportunities for error (numerous balls, some red, are in plain sight in the same room). They do this about as well as a two-year-old child, although they (and such a child) may not construct such sentences on their own. The sentences they do construct are usually within the realm of protolanguage, rather like that of the tongue-tied tourist with a similarly small vocabulary, or the Broca's aphasic.

While many such sentences are "Give me" requests, a bonobo will occasionally construct a request such as "Sue chase Rose" (watching a chase scene is preferred entertainment for young bonobos, almost as good as being chased themselves), which does not involve the bonobo itself as either subject or object of the verb.

But while some animals respond impressively to commands, they (and young children) are not known for being able to answer free-form questions (not even "Name three kinds of fruit") or to converse about the weather. This may change as more infant apes are reared to use symbolic languages from an early age, learning from skilled preschool language teachers. The abilities of the bonobos, in particular, seem quite promising. Yet almost nothing is known about the brain organization underlying language in such apes. Most observations on language still must be made in humans.

"And only after strokes, I suppose?" Neil had asked.

Until recently, most of our understanding of the human brain organization for language depended on the accidents of nature rather than on carefully designed scientific experiments. Both are useful. It is like the difference between a natural history museum and a science museum: one shows you the varied experiments of nature that have survived, while the other shows you what makes them tick. Understanding the mechanisms may someday provide workarounds for the disabled, speed everyone's learning, even increase the versatility of our language-based reasoning about the complexities of the everyday world. For a long time, the natural history museum of aphasia and dyslexia was all we had.

All types of language disorders involve some difficulty in naming objects. That is why object naming is used to screen brain areas for their role in language during Neil's operation. Occasionally, anomic aphasia—finding the right name—is the only problem after a stroke. But usually the patient's problems are more specific than simple, everyday anomia; sometimes the difficult words are a particular class of words, giving us some insight into how language is organized in the brain.

In the years since Broca, researchers have noticed that patients with stroke damage to Broca's area utter mostly nouns. When they do utter word phrases, they tend to omit the verb endings, most pronouns, and the conjunctions. Talking about a movie, such a patient said, "Ah, policeman . . . Ah . . . I know! Cashier! . . . Money! . . . Ah! Cigarettes . . . I know . . . this . . . beer . . . mustache. . . ."

They also have difficulty mimicking sequences of movements that are modeled for them involving simple movements of the tongue and mouth. Sometimes they can sing words that they cannot speak. They are very aware of their problems. And, violating the expressive-receptive, front-back dichotomy, they also have some problems understanding what others say. They especially have trouble with the words that reveal sentence structure, such as conjunctions and prepositions. But their understanding of other types of words is often intact.

Patients with damage to Wernicke's area usually have reasonable sentence construction but often misuse words. They may substitute a word that, by either sound or meaning, is related to the correct one. They seem unaware of their problem. And they often talk at some length: an aphasic patient named Blanche, when asked her name, replied, "Yes, it's not Mount Everest, Mont Blanc, blancmange, or almonds put in water. . . . You know. You be clever and tell me!"

There are many other kinds of aphasia. Given the Broca-Wernicke dichotomy that established the framework, it is perhaps natural that these variants were ascribed to some combination or interconnection, such as damage to the pathways between the frontal and parietal language areas. Some aphasics can repeat back a sentence containing words they find hard to use when constructing a sentence themselves. Such transcortical aphasia also has a converse, called conduction aphasia, in which the words can be used spontaneously but the patient has difficulty when asked to repeat back a sentence.

Surprisingly, the language problems produced by other forms of damage do not necessarily follow these principles derived from stroke patients. Wernicke's aphasia is rare with head injuries or tumors, even when Wernicke's area is damaged. This has led to the suggestion that Wernicke's aphasia is a feature of a special population of patients, elderly individuals prone to strokes who may have, in addition to the local injury from the stroke, more widespread brain damage from age or chronic disease of the brain's blood vessels. The symptoms depend on the baseline from which you start.

"Well," Neil once said, "at least brain damage isn't the only way to find out if a region of the cerebral cortex has something to do with language. Now you've got all the fancy techniques to try out on me."

For example, injecting a short-acting anesthetic into the left carotid artery that supplies the left side of the brain, and then later into the right carotid that supplies the right side of the brain, can demonstrate whether language is housed in the left or the right brain. A failure of naming ability during the several minutes when one side is asleep suggests that it is the side where language lives. Neil was given this test as part of his evaluation prior to surgery, establishing his left-brain dominance for language.

Sometimes catheters can be threaded into the smaller arteries of the brain, and the drug squirted out to temporarily block smaller cortical areas. The most localized blocking method, the electrical stimulation

When performing a finger
movement sequence,
two regions of increased
blood flow are seen.

If only mentally rehearsing
the repeated movements,
only the supplementary
motor area is active.

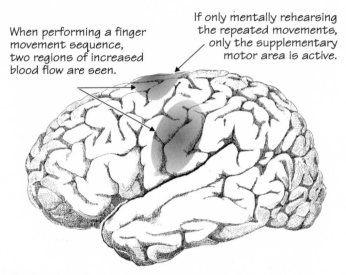

Data from Roland et al., 1980

mapping that is part of Neil's operation, requires some neurosurgery first but can localize functions to areas about the size of a pencil eraser.

The applied electric current does not damage the brain. If I touch the handheld stimulator to the back of my hand, I feel a slight tingle. The current just confuses things, reversibly blocking functions such as language. And this allows a wide range of traditional experimental designs developed from studying nonlanguage functions in animal brains to be imported to the study of language in humans. But, for ethical reasons, such high-resolution methods that temporarily manipulate brain regions can be used only on those persons already undergoing neurosurgery for their own benefit and volunteering their time.

There are also survey methods for producing images that show how hard the brain is working. Since they can operate through the intact skull, they are often suitable for use in normal volunteers for hours at a time. One new technique measures magnetic fields and has recently revealed a wave of activity that regularly sweeps the brain from front to back. Other important methods measure regional changes in blood flow within the brain. When nerve cells become very active, they increase the blood flow to their local region of brain, and such activity measurements can be combined with clever selection of tasks to yield images of what's where.

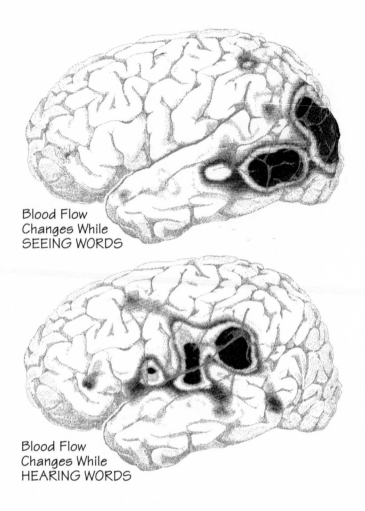

Blood Flow
Changes While
SEEING WORDS

Blood Flow
Changes While
HEARING WORDS

PET images modified from Raichle, 1992. ("Moats" are actually intermediate intensities, not gaps; see the original color versions.)

Using positron emission tomography (PET) imaging, the localities are identified by a radioactive tracer. There is an even newer technique with better spatial resolution, in which groups of cells about one millimeter apart can be distinguished. In functional magnetic resonance imaging (sometimes called "fast MRI" or FMRI), the change in the amount of oxygen in the blood can be determined by changes in tissue resonance in a magnetic field, and a map made of where such changes occur. When subjects speak the same word repeatedly, different regions of the brain "light up" than when they mentally rehearse the same word without speaking aloud.

The fundamental technique is one of looking at differences in blood flow between one state of the brain and another. For each subject, there is a measurement of resting blood flow when the subject is doing nothing more than looking at a small cross in the middle of a video display. Then a word is shown (but the subject makes no verbal response), and a map is made of the blood flow during that condition. Then the first image is subtracted from the second to show the regions of additional activity during reading. In a third condition, the subject might read the word aloud; the image from silent reading is then subtracted to show what vocalization adds in the way of neural activity. In a fourth condition, the subject might be asked not to read the word

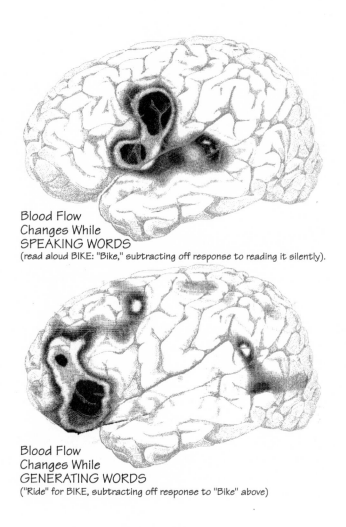

Blood Flow
Changes While
SPEAKING WORDS
(read aloud BIKE: "Bike," subtracting off response to reading it silently).

Blood Flow
Changes While
GENERATING WORDS
("Ride" for BIKE, subtracting off response to "Bike" above)

aloud but to instead speak a verb that matches the noun on the screen, such as saying "ride" when the word *bike* is presented. The third condition is then subtracted, to emphasize what verb-finding adds to the blood flow changes associated with speaking a noun aloud.

When nerve cells are active, they also alter the reflectance of light from the brain surface. "Before" and "after" pictures can be digitally subtracted from one another, yielding an image of which cortical sites are working harder. This "intrinsic signal" technique presently requires exposure of the brain surface and can be used only at operations like Neil's; it is beginning to provide information on language activity localization that complements that obtained from susceptibility to disruption by electrical stimulation.

The imaging techniques show where neurons are active; stimulation mapping shows where they are essential for naming. All of these kinds of information—strokes, tumors, stimulation, and activity—provide a different perspective on brain language organization. In most cases, they suggest that language extends well beyond the naming sites defined by electrical stimulation. Avoiding damage to those naming sites seems adequate to head off language deficits after neurosurgery, so there are both "essential" and "optional" language areas. An adequate understanding of how the brain generates language will need to account for the results from all techniques.

NEIL'S NAMING SITES are not exactly what would have been pre-dicted from the nineteenth-century Broca-Wernicke model, even as modified by later findings from many other stroke patients. Naming in Neil is blocked in only three areas, each smaller than a dime. One of these areas is in the lower part of the frontal lobe, just in front of the face motor area where Broca's area is said to be. The other two are in the back part of the temporal lobe where Wernicke's area is said to be. They are separated by an extensive area where stimulation at the same strength fails to block naming.

Each of these naming areas is much smaller than the textbook Broca's or Wernicke's area. Each area seems to have rather sharp boundaries, for movement of the handheld stimulator by less than half a pencil eraser changes the effect from blocking to unblocking. The pattern found in Neil is the most common one seen in a series of patients undergoing such operations on the language side of the brain.

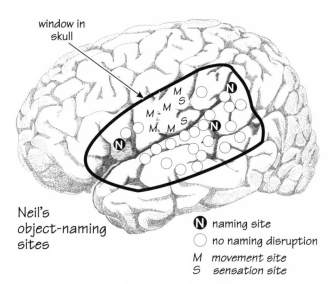

window in
skull

Neil's
object-naming
sites

Ⓝ naming site
◯ no naming disruption
M movement site
S sensation site

This pattern of brain organization, with multiple discrete areas separated by gaps, is also commonly seen in studies of sensory and motor maps in many primates.

Many different patterns of naming areas are encountered in patients with left-brain dominance for language. In a few such patients, only frontal naming areas could be identified: apparently these patients have no posterior language area, although their language seems normal. In a few other patients, only temporal naming areas are present: stimulating Broca's area simply does not disrupt naming.

It is particularly difficult to be sure of the location of Wernicke's area using the naming test. There does not seem to be any one consistent temporal-lobe site for naming in most of these patients. Some patients have temporal naming areas in the rear, others midway along the sylvian fissure.

Broca's area is a little more consistent: nearly 80 percent of patients had a naming area somewhere near Broca's area—that is, in the part of the frontal lobe just in front of the face motor cortex. In some patients, naming sites cover less than the traditional Broca's area, while in others the anomia extended further forward or upward.

This degree of variability in the location of language was unexpected. It might be a result of language areas appearing quite recently in evolution, so that they may not have yet settled into a consistent pattern across all humans. But language is not alone in this variability; sensory and motor maps in cats and monkeys have also shown considerable variability in exact cortical location.

Does the variability make any difference in performance? (That was one of Neil's questions before the operation.) Part of the variability in human language areas seems to be associated with sex and IQ. ("Ah, it's about time that we're getting to the sexy part," he said.) Most of the patients having no identifiable Wernicke's area were female. In the

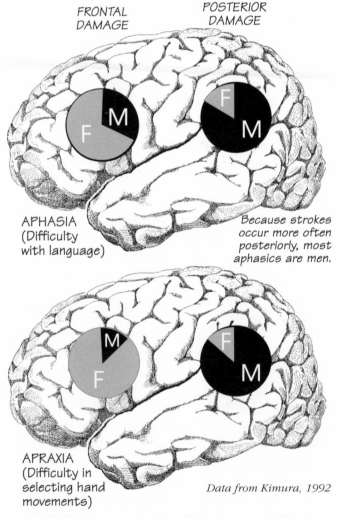

FRONTAL DAMAGE

POSTERIOR DAMAGE

APHASIA (Difficulty with language)

Because strokes occur more often posteriorly, most aphasics are men.

APRAXIA (Difficulty in selecting hand movements)

Data from Kimura, 1992

Judging from strokes, women's brains are organized differently than men's for language and hand movements.

lower-IQ half of the patient population, females were less likely than males to have naming sites in the parietal lobe. Similar differences in language organization between males and females have also been noted from the effects of strokes. Wernicke-area strokes in some women had less effect on language than similar strokes in men. Together these findings suggest that although most men and women have similar language organization, there is a group of women who have fewer naming sites in the rear. What this "means" is still an open question.

If all this language is in the left side of the brain, what are corresponding areas of the right brain doing? The nineteenth-century English neurologist John Hughlings Jackson was the first to suggest that, just as language was located on the left, we might find visual and spatial functions in the right brain. This idea was ignored for a long time, but now it is widely accepted, even to the point of great exaggeration in the popular mind.

While flipping through the reading material that I handed him for our next meeting, Neil said, "There must be a whole shelf of books claiming to tell you how to tap the right brain. And become more creative, escaping the domination of your overly logical left brain. Somehow, I don't see any of those books on your right-brain reading list!"

chapter 4

If Language Is Left, What's Right?

THE *"HALF-A-BRAIN" TEST*. That's the name Neil had invented by the time we next met in the atrium. In the intervening week, he'd experienced one of the major diagnostic tests used on all epilepsy surgery candidates.

"So I passed," he smiled, as I sat down and took the first sip of my cappuccino. "I qualified for the epilepsy operation. What's the test's proper name, anyway? *Wada* something?"

George says that the test is properly known as the intracarotid amobarbital perfusion test. But I've never heard it called anything other than by the name of the man who devised it, a Japanese-Canadian neurologist with a conveniently short name, Juhn Wada. The test not only shows which side of the brain contains the major language functions, but it is also used to determine whether each side of the brain is capable of managing recent memory functions on its own, when the other side is inactivated.

Just as in the arterial dye studies, a radiologist threads a long catheter into a leg artery. The tip of this hollow tube is guided up into the internal carotid. If you then inject a short-acting anesthetic like amobarbital into the left carotid, the right brain stays awake and working. But the front two-thirds of the left brain stops working, at least for a few minutes.

"They had me hold my arms out, and my right arm drifted down even when I tried to keep it up," Neil said.

Arm drift is just the way that neurologists tell that the anesthetic has arrived. They were also very interested in whether you could keep talking—to make sure that you are not one of those people with language in the right brain rather than the left. But your language failed, as it should when language is on the left side.

"They also said that I'd failed to identify some music."

That was during the right-sided anesthesia. Identifying simple musical rhythms—not selections of music, per se—seems to be one of the things that the right brain does.

"But how come nothing very dramatic happens when the right half of the brain isn't working?"

Depends on what you mean by *dramatic*. Woodrow Wilson apparently suffered a right-brain stroke during the Versailles peace conference just after World War I. It didn't paralyze him, but his fellow statesmen noticed that his personality seemed to change overnight; he became harsh and vindictive, whereas earlier he had been farsighted and conciliatory. But he also became more socially outgoing rather than showing his usual reticence. Then a few weeks later, he had another stroke that paralyzed his left side.

Despite this perfectly obvious paralysis, he claimed that nothing was wrong with him—and that's what really distressed the people working around him. He even fired his secretary of state for trying to discuss this puzzling situation with the cabinet. Dramatic enough for you?

"I guess so! You mean, as in setting the stage for World War II?"

Exactly. Wilson couldn't argue effectively for League of Nations membership before Congress and, of course, he'd fired his secretary of state for "usurping power" as part of his denial of illness. So the United States' withdrawal effectively crippled the League.

World War II, several decades later, had many additional "causes," but you can certainly imagine a different outcome if Woodrow Wilson had not become so strangely disabled by his right-brain stroke.

Actually, Wilson had suffered a series of strokes, starting at age thirty-nine when he was a history professor at Princeton. After the stroke that left him paralyzed on his left side, President Wilson's wife and doctors kept quiet about how disabled he had become after Versailles and they essentially ran White House affairs for the next year. They kept Wilson's illness—and his denial of it—so quiet that Wilson's lack of insight into his disability never made it into the history books until a half century later, when a neurologist with a historical bent wrote a book about it.

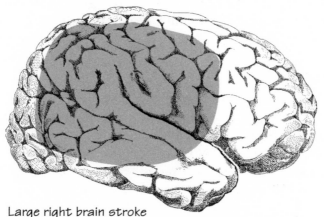

Large right brain stroke
of the type suffered by Woodrow Wilson in 1919
producing "denial of illness" and defective body image.

By far the strangest aspect of right parietal lobe damage is what neurologists now call "denial of illness." Despite the obvious evidence of paralysis, the patient claims that nothing is wrong. Or that he merely has a head cold. To be fair, the characteristic problems you get with right-brain strokes were only beginning to be recognized by neurologists in 1919, when Wilson's major strokes occurred.

Usually when a leader fails, subordinates can take up the reins. But there was nothing that the vice president and secretary of state could do: because Wilson's language was not impaired, he could order them around. He could hold on to office even though so severely disabled as to be unable to lead. Although the 25th Amendment to the U.S. Constitution has since provided procedures for some kinds of presidential disability, Wilson's type of disability—a lack of insight regarding his illness—could still confound the intent of the amendment and leave the United States with yet another leadership vacuum.

Or it could leave the United States with a president having an altered personality. In 1974, while still on the Supreme Court, Justice William O. Douglas suffered a right-brain stroke. He, too, denied his illness, even issuing a press release that suggested his left arm had been injured in a fall.

Wilson developed an uncharacteristic obsession with being overheard and with protecting the secrecy of his papers. Douglas also developed some mild paranoia that, in a president, might have had far more serious consequences. Unlike Wilson's subordinates, Douglas's fellow justices were eventually able to persuade him to retire; for about a year, however, they had to cope with a Justice Douglas who was not his former self.

WILSON'S STROKES had many of the other features we now associate with right-brain damage, such as defective body image. A person may be lying in bed, with the left side of his body paralyzed, and still deny that anything is wrong. If you pick up his left hand, place it on his right chest, and then ask him about it, he may deny that it's *his* hand. He may become obsessed with what another person is doing in bed with him.

In less dramatic cases, you can see what neurologists call "neglect." While the right eye sees both to the left and to the right side of the nose, everything to the left of the midline is sent to the right brain. The right brain winds up with what is seen by both eyes of the left side of the visual world. And vice versa. Some patients with right-brain strokes tend to ignore anything on the left side of their visual world.

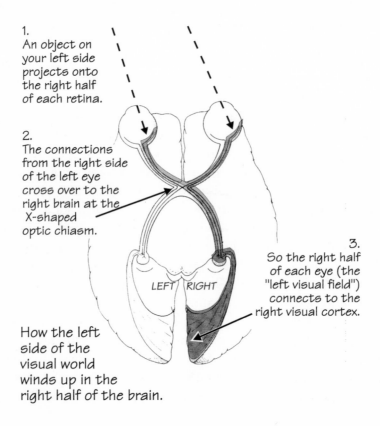

1.
An object on your left side projects onto the right half of each retina.

2.
The connections from the right side of the left eye cross over to the right brain at the X-shaped optic chiasm.

LEFT RIGHT

3.
So the right half of each eye (the "left visual field") connects to the right visual cortex.

How the left side of the visual world winds up in the right half of the brain.

Others pay attention to objects on their left side—but only if there is nothing else on their right side to compete for their attention. When driving a car and approaching an intersection, such a person may be able to see cars approaching from the left just as readily as cars approaching from the right, but only so long as they don't approach from both directions at once. If they do, the patient may ignore the car on the left and pay attention exclusively to the car on the right.

For some patients, such as my father after he had a small left parietal lobe stroke, the neglect is temporary; his lasted only a few days. But for others, it persists and becomes a big problem. Such patients must stop driving, but it is difficult to persuade them to do so; as far as they can tell, nothing is wrong with them.

"That's hard to believe. They really have no insight into their condition?"

The very first neurology patient I ever saw, at a Saturday morning conference at Harvard Med, had this kind of problem. He seemed normal in every other way, and he was quite articulate. It was very impressive to see the neurologist stand behind this patient and bring his hands slowly forward around the patient's head while the patient was looking straight ahead. The patient reported seeing the hand off to his left when it had reached halfway around his head. When the neurologist repeated the test on the right side, the patient saw that hand normally as well. But when the neurologist brought both hands around at the same time, the patient reported only the one on his right—even though the neurologist was waving his fingers on the left, trying to attract the patient's attention. The patient had stopped driving, at the insistence of doctors and family, but maintained that everything seemed normal from his point of view.

A self-portrait painted by the German artist Anton Räderscheidt after he suffered a right-brain stroke illustrates what neurologists mean by "neglect" and "defective body image." The portrait fills only the right half of the canvas, and in that right side, only one side of the face is accurately depicted.

"If you don't have an internal image of the left half of your body, to say that nothing is wrong with it does have a certain logic," Neil said.

Agreed. But the problems caused by this kind of right-brain stroke are anything but trivial. Imagine a president who claims to be normal and still speaks in an authoritative tone of voice. He has no interest in participating in rehabilitation and does not know his own limitations. These are among the most difficult of all the brain-damaged patients to rehabilitate because they have so little insight into their problem.

"Which raises the question, Where *do* we get insight?"

Well, the psychotic patient often lacks insight into the illness. And we suspect that animals lack the mental capacity for such insight.

"Maybe insight is part of consciousness," Neil said. "Whatever that is. Something else to add to the consciousness list."

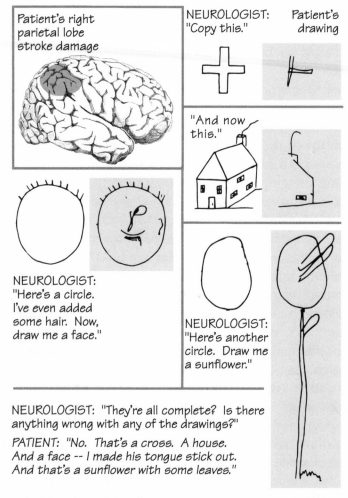

Patient's right parietal lobe stroke damage

NEUROLOGIST: "Copy this."　Patient's drawing

"And now this."

NEUROLOGIST: "Here's a circle. I've even added some hair. Now, draw me a face."

NEUROLOGIST: "Here's another circle. Draw me a sunflower."

NEUROLOGIST: "They're all complete? Is there anything wrong with any of the drawings?"

PATIENT: "No. That's a cross. A house. And a face -- I made his tongue stick out. And that's a sunflower with some leaves."

"Neglect" of left side of visual space

UNUSUALLY GOOD FUNCTION OF THE RIGHT BRAIN is said to characterize those who excel in the visual arts: painters, sculptors, architects, moviemakers. Neurologists suspecting a right-brain stroke often try to test for elementary versions of these abilities.

Neurologists like to draw a circle and ask the patient to fill in a clock face. The right-brain stroke patient knows that there should be numbers from one to twelve, but he is likely to crowd all of these into his "good side," the right half of the circle between twelve and six o'clock.

"The patient just ignores the left half of the clock face?"

Right. Ask such a patient to draw a cross, and it is likely to be drawn missing the left arm. You can get a house that has only details on its right side, a face with only one eye, a flower with only half of its petals—all drawings that the patient will claim are complete and normal sketches. The auto mechanic with such a stroke may be able to identify all the parts of an engine, but nonetheless be unable to assemble them. Subtle forms of this "constructional apraxia" are tested in the mental rotation of objects, seen in the multiple-choice questions on standard intelligence tests. These are all examples of "visual-spatial" functions.

The other deficit often present with a large right-hemisphere stroke is "dressing apraxia": the patient can't get his arms into the sleeves, even though not paralyzed. The patient can name sleeves or pant legs and describe their use, but still can't perform, apparently because his image of his own body is defective. Even if Woodrow Wilson hadn't been partially paralyzed, it is likely that Mrs. Wilson would have needed to help him get dressed every morning.

"So does sign language operate out of the right brain?" Neil asked.

In a word, no. Deaf patients using sign language are just as impaired with left-brain strokes as the rest of us, and their sign language is just as unimpaired by right-brain strokes as ours is.

People have also wondered if the pictographs of some Asian languages involve the right brain. But a language, no matter how it is implemented, seems to be a language—even for pictographs or hand gestures. And it depends primarily on the left brain, although some emotional aspects of prosody—the way your voice rises at the beginning of a question or falls at the end of a sentence—are affected by right-brain strokes. People with right-brain strokes sometimes talk in more of a monotone than they did before.

Clearly, right-brain strokes and left-brain strokes have different symptoms. You can see where the popular notions of left brain for language, versus right brain for spatial skills, have gotten their impetus. But the reality of biology is much more complicated. As George likes to say, the popular view is slightly more than half right. For every patient who has bilateral or right-brain language, there are 13 with left-brain language. Yet lateralization of spatial skills to the right brain is not the reverse. Nothing there is as strongly lateralized as even six to one.

"Lateralized?" Neil asked, raising his eyebrows.

That's when functions with no left-right intrinsic aspect are not equally represented in both hemispheres. Functions like judging the distance of an object are not lateralized: both sides of the brain can do it, seemingly equally well. You usually measure lateralization by reviewing numerous patient records to see if right- and left-brain damage is equally likely to disrupt a particular function, such as knowing how to put on a shirt. Maybe five patients have dressing apraxias after right-brain strokes, for every one patient with a dressing apraxia after a left-brain stroke. Only two patients show constructional apraxia after right damage, for every one with that symptom after a left-brain stroke. So constructional abilities are "less lateralized" than dressing abilities, but they are both lateralized, compared to depth perception.

"Estimating distances sounds like one of those survival mechanisms, handy for hunting with spears and such."

The ability evolved much earlier than that. Lateralizations were originally thought to be uniquely human, but now they're thought to go back to the monkeys, probably to a specialization for hanging on to the tree branch with the left hand while using the right hand to move food to the mouth. Monkeys have a minor version of our tendency to use the left brain for listening carefully to rapid sound sequences. So it's a matter of the extent of lateralization, as well as the emergence of additional specialties such as language. And the corpus callosum can be a real bottleneck, simply because impulses travel rather slowly on that pathway. Coordination has its price.

Many patients with strongly lateralized language do not necessarily have strongly lateralized visual-spatial functions. Visual-spatial functions are more strongly lateralized in males than in females, probably because they depend on adequate levels of testosterone, the male sex hormone, during brain development, back when you were a fetus in your mother's womb. The difference between individuals in the degree of lateralization of different functions is just another example of how variable individuals are.

"So does your degree of lateralization make any difference in your abilities—say, as a painter?"

That's still an open question. Certainly some evidence suggests that more lateralization is associated with better function. When both sides of the brain have some language ability, certain types of language disability seem to be more likely. Stuttering, in particular. It's as if the two language areas can't coordinate their act properly, with all of those messages being sent back and forth through the corpus callosum.

"I know. I worked for a company where the higher-ups were split, half on the East Coast, half on the West Coast. They could never make up their collective mind. People said that when we introduced a new product, we stuttered. Now I run a start-up with two other guys. We don't have that problem."

COMPARED TO THE LANGUAGE SUBDIVISIONS in the left brain, we know much less about how these visual-spatial abilities are housed in the right brain. For the right brain, we're not even up to the nineteenth-century Broca-Wernicke level of theoretical summary.

We find it difficult even to place neglect, denial of illness, and defective body image on a right-brain map—or to be sure that their definitions don't overlap. The strokes that produce these visual-spatial problems tend to be large, with smaller strokes producing symptoms that are difficult to recognize by present methods. Defects of body image may be more likely with a stroke centered in the lower portions of the parietal lobe. Neglect is more likely with strokes higher in that lobe.

And that's consistent with the generalization that's made about monkeys, about what happens in analyzing the visual world after the information leaves the primary visual cortex. Damage to the underside of the temporal lobe tends to interfere with object recognition, but damage to the parietal lobe tends to impair awareness that objects are even there—and, of course, making movements toward them.

"So the temporal lobe takes care of *what* something is and the parietal lobe handles the *where?*"

Pretty much, though there is always overlap. For example, we know a lot about the parietal lobe's Area 7 from the study of single neurons—at least in monkeys, which probably aren't very lateralized. With a little wiretapping, you can figure out what the neurons in Area 7 are interested in. They respond best to objects moving in the space just beyond your skin. Those neurons are truly egocentric.

"Just outside—you mean, like when I hold a fork?"

No, mostly for things you're not touching—yet. The next time you're on an airline flight, watch the flight attendants as they serve trays of food in very close quarters. You can watch the elbow of a flight attendant, poised inches away from the head of a person in the row ahead, and marvel at how well she seems to know where that person's head is, even though no longer looking in that direction. Out of sight, perhaps, but not out of mind.

I once asked a flight attendant about this. She claimed that she had eyes in the back of her head. Those "eyes" were probably neurons in her parietal lobes, contributing to a mental model of her extrapersonal space. The parietal lobes are probably what keep our visual experiences from looking like an amateur videotape, jerking from here to there. Our eyes do indeed jerk from here to there, even faster than a camera, but we don't perceive it that way. The seeming stability of our perceived world is probably because it is, in large part, actually a mental model of our visual world—that we update from all those jerky images we get.

THE RIGHT TEMPORAL LOBE functions are a little better known, compared to those of the right parietal lobe. The right temporal lobe is interested in faces, among other things.

"The man who mistook his wife for a hat?"

Not exactly. But the ability to recognize faces can be disrupted by temporal lobe strokes damaging either side of the brain, particularly if they involve the undersurface of the back part of temporal lobes. The famous patients who cannot recognize familiar faces, such as that of a spouse, may have a more general problem. Someone tested such patients on a series of pictures of cars, perhaps just as a control to testing them on portraits of people. The patients who couldn't pick out the faces of relatives from among the portraits also could not pick out a picture of their own car from among other somewhat similar cars. They

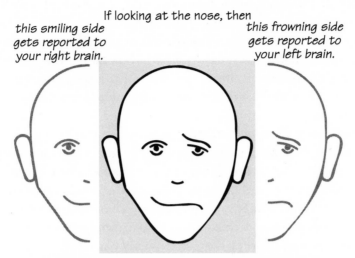

If looking at the nose, then
this smiling side
gets reported to
your right brain.

this frowning side
gets reported to
your left brain.

And, since your right brain is probably more sensitive to
emotional expressions, you will likely think he's smiling.

can get the general category—cars and faces—but not unique examples. Their problem is with proper nouns, not ordinary nouns.

The right temporal lobe is particularly interested in the emotional content of the facial expression. This was discovered by using the fact that the image from the left half of your retinal images goes to the right brain. If half of a face is smiling, and the other half frowning, the side to the observer's left is likely to be picked.

Better yet, you get yourself a set of pictures of faces, those of actors trying to portray an emotion—using both sides of the face—such as happiness, sadness, disgust, anger, and so on. George has tried stimulating the right temporal lobe while showing patients such actors' faces depicting a standard emotion like disgust. Normally, the patients are quite reliable at naming the emotion being acted out. But they make mistakes when stimulated at some sites in the temporal lobe.

"Do they see happy or angry? I mean, is the right brain a pessimist or an optimist?"

Sorry, but they make errors in both directions. They just pick the wrong name, from among the possibilities. In the real world, that could lead to some serious misunderstandings.

"So when another animal approaches you, and you misread its facial expression as one of friendliness rather than hunger, you aren't likely to leave many offspring behind."

Yes and no. Basically, that turns out to be the wrong evolutionary argument. Primates usually don't eat others of their own species. And you don't need to check out the expression on his face to know that an approaching tiger presents a threat. But facial expressions are extraordinarily important among the apes, for judging the intentions of other members of the group. That's how an animal solicits help in a dispute, judges what the dominant animal will permit without retaliation, or just finds a grooming partner.

Reading the emotional state of another member of your species is probably more important for sexual selection than for staying alive. Males that misread the body and facial postures of a potential mate get bitten or kicked. That's the real law of the jungle. Those that are particularly good at judging readiness to mate may wind up with a lot more offspring. Staying alive is the name of the game when you're a juvenile, which,

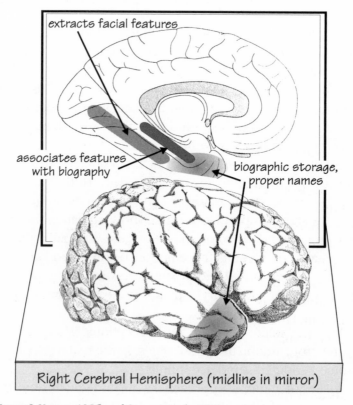

Right Cerebral Hemisphere (midline in mirror)

After Bruce & Young, 1986 and Sergent et al., 1992

because of all that juvenile mortality, is when most natural selection occurs. But sexual selection may be more important in adulthood.

In the temporal lobes of monkeys, neurons can be found that are interested in faces—but only faces of the appropriate species, and then only the eyes or the mouth. Nearly two-thirds of the neurons recorded from the human temporal lobe seemed to be interested in faces. In monkeys, there are a number of face-specialist neurons in the first fold below the sylvian fissure. And the monkeys are also lateralized for emotional face features, reacting more appropriately when the emotional clues are in the left half of their field of view.

We think there is a series of steps in recognizing a face as a familiar person. One of the higher-order visual areas, running along the underside of the temporal lobe, is particularly good at extracting facial features such as eyebrows. The front of the temporal lobe is thought to be involved with storing biographical information and proper names. A third area, in between them, is thought to be an association area that relates facial features to the biographical information. The right brain is far more involved with this job than the left brain.

"So what about my storehouse of people's names? Do I lose it with this operation that's going to shave off the front of my left temporal lobe?"

No, but patients occasionally complain afterward that they have more trouble with proper names than with memories in general. We like to talk about areas of the brain having specialties, but the information is usually stored redundantly over a wide area. And removing the front end of one temporal lobe still leaves the other temporal tip.

"So how about adding two and two together? Where do I do that—in the right brain?"

Either right- or left-brain damage can disturb arithmetic, particularly when it involves the parietal lobe. When you see disturbances in calculation abilities after a left-brain stroke, it's usually complicated by some links with language abilities. There's a constellation of symptoms known as Gerstmann's syndrome in which calculating fails—but also the labeling of body parts, especially fingers. And those patients get confused about labeling things as being right or left.

"Sounds as if they were counting on their fingers! But what about fancier counting abilities, balancing the checkbook, and so on?"

There are some stimulation mapping studies on calculating abilities done in the O.R. George has occasionally asked patients undergoing right-brain operations to do some simple problems of addition, subtraction, division, and multiplication while he stimulates sites in the right parietal lobe. He identified a number of sites where only one of these four functions was altered, and few sites where more than one was altered.

But no checkbook-balancing studies. The existing studies do suggest, however, that there are somewhat different neural systems for each type of calculation. With the evidence of difference between sexes in the degree of lateralization of visual-spatial functions—it's greater in males—and now this evidence of specific right-brain mechanisms in mathematics, you can see how eventually we might answer some of the questions about why males are so overrepresented in the "tail of the distribution" for math abilities. We're talking here not about the average engineering student sweating his or her way through advanced calculus, but about those extremely gifted in mathematics, regardless of schooling or environmental emphasis, most of whom are male. And more are left-handed, allergic, and dyslexic than you'd normally expect.

MUSIC IS SIMILAR TO LANGUAGE in its neurology, but some differences have been seen. For example, George tells about a patient who was a country and western musician, a quite gifted amateur. After he had the worst headache of his life, his doctors diagnosed a bleed, a hemorrhage from an aneurysm in the left superior temporal gyrus, immediately below the sylvian fissure. For a few days, the patient had some difficulty saying exactly what he wanted to. And some of his words were nonsense, but this all cleared up. When his speech was normal, he tried to sing one of his favorite songs—and discovered that he couldn't do it. When the neurologists explored this a little further, they found that he couldn't hum the melody or sing the lyrics to any of his old favorites. But he could *speak* the words. And it works the other way as well. Patients with Broca's aphasia can often sing words that they can't speak.

Such findings suggest that music depends on both sides of the brain. After the front of the right temporal lobe is removed, there is some reduced musical ability—memory for a set of tones or for rhythms. But that's only for amateurs. Disturbance of musical abilities in professional musicians usually takes left-brain damage. It's been suggested that as you gain proficiency in music, it is increasingly organized like a language, dependent on your left brain. But not on exactly the same areas as spoken language.

George has also wiretapped some neurons in the temporal lobe while having the patient listen to music. Short recordings of classical music caused their activity to decrease, sometimes to levels half of that before the music started. Classical music may be soothing, literally.

"I'm going to have to get you to explain the wiretapping business one of these days. But go ahead."

In music with a pronounced rhythm, activity of some neurons was entrained by the beat, just as if the neurons were clapping in unison. When rock music with a heavy beat was played, the activity of the neurons usually increased, and their firing patterns became even more emphatic. Some observers have commented, half seriously, that these neurons are firing in the "bursting" pattern reminiscent of that seen in recordings from epileptic areas.

As George likes to say in an ominous tone of voice, perhaps everything your grandmother told you about rock 'n' roll is true.

LANGUAGE IS NOT SOLELY A FUNCTION of the left hemisphere, but the changes after right-brain strokes are more subtle than the dramatic language changes seen after left-brain strokes. When you hear a sentence, you have to make a mental model for what that string of sounds represents. A full understanding of an utterance may well involve many right-brain functions.

Right-brain stroke patients may not understand all of the connotations of a common word. They may become more "literal-minded," having trouble appreciating figures of speech. Ask them to paraphrase a short story, and they may repeat it verbatim without making changes. They have trouble with antonyms. The spontaneous speech of such patients is often rambling.

As you might expect from the flat tone of voice used by many right-brain stroke patients, they may also have trouble interpreting the speaker's tone of voice. Testing them on narratives is particularly revealing. Unlike aging patients who are quick to admit when they are uncertain about a memory, right-brain stroke patients seldom indicate a lack of confidence when making mistakes in recalling test stories.

They are particularly bad about retelling a story in the right order, tripling the normal number of errors. This is almost as bad as the patients with left-brain strokes causing aphasia.

"So if they can't keep the story straight, jokes must be wasted on them. They won't be surprised at the punch line."

Yes, subtleties go right past them. Their own attempts at humor are often crude, off-color, or inappropriate. So while the left brain may be more involved with the building blocks of language, the right brain is quite helpful in interpreting it all.

> Whereas the left hemisphere might appreciate some of Groucho's puns, and the right hemisphere might be entertained by the antics of Harpo, only the two hemispheres unified can appreciate an entire Marx Brothers routine.
>
> HOWARD GARDNER, HIRAM H. BROWNELL,
> WENDY WAPNER, DIANE MICHELOW, 1983

chapter 5

The Problems with Paying Attention

WE WERE SITTING ON THE PARK BENCH behind the medical center, our attention riveted on a particularly handsome sailboat that was idling impatiently in midchannel, waiting for the drawbridge to go up. Attention is the gateway for memory—which is why I still remember that sailboat with its sails unfilled. If you don't pay attention to something at the time it happens, you are unlikely to be able to recall it tomorrow.

That isn't to say that you can't "play back" a strange noise that awakens you in the middle of the night. Or recall a conversation that you accidentally overheard while talking to someone else—provided that you start mulling it over within the next few minutes. But memory works best for what you had your attention focused on at the time, and gradually recall becomes impossible for anything else.

"So what kinds of memories do you suppose I'll recall when George stimulates my temporal lobe?" Neil asked. He was, I noticed, jumping the gun a little, as I knew that George wanted more tests before going ahead with a decision to operate.

Probably nothing will flash into your mind, I said. Wilder Penfield's "experiential responses," which everyone seems to have heard about, are actually infrequent. Experiences evoked by electrical stimulation happen to less than one patient in a dozen in the published studies, and George sees even fewer. They're nearly always from the temporal lobe. Sometimes they're impressively detailed, but usually they're just voices heard offstage. George once had a patient who heard Led Zeppelin music each time a particular temporal lobe site was stimulated. Sometimes it was the same song, sometimes a different one from the same album.

"So that's the impact of decades of Top 40 Radio. They no longer have to be broadcast—by now it's all *imprinted!*"

Penfield got many reports of lullabies and classical music, too. Sometimes the recall was a particular piece of music, sometimes a specific scene from the patient's past—such as Penfield's patient who recalled her mother talking to her aunt on the telephone about a visit. Usually it wasn't a complex "multimedia" hallucination but just some unidentifiable experience.

Penfield, especially after he retired as director of the Montreal Neurological Institute in 1963, emphasized his belief that memory is like a tape recorder, capturing and storing all the detail. That's easily the most widespread popular belief these days as well. Back in 1980, a survey showed that even most psychologists believed in a videotape analogy.

"Videotape is probably the only technological analogy available to most people."

But modern memory research tends to dispute the videotape metaphor, emphasizing that attention is needed at the time, and that what does get stored is surprisingly malleable, easily distorted by later events. In particular, things tend to get "out of order," mistakes being made about what event followed another, in a manner that videotape doesn't do. And modern neurosurgeons tend to think that those stimulation-evoked "experiences" are actually little seizures that evoke hallucinations—that they are more like the fragments of our nighttime dreams than like a fully formed sensory experience being replayed.

"So what happened? Did these people have a seizure at the same time as this experience, that burned in the details?"

That's possible. Patients who have experiential responses from temporal lobe stimulation are also particularly likely to have them as part of their seizures as well. But this could be just an accidental association. Certainly it's not just a matter of the stimulated site. George likes to go on—using his mock-ominous tone of voice again—about his patient who heard Led Zeppelin music, saying the patient's "Led Zeppelin area" was naturally removed since George dislikes such music.

Some years later, George then reveals, he was talking to the patient about that experience. George asked the patient if he remembered the moment in the operating room when he heard that music. Yes, indeed. Then George asked if his musical interests had changed after the operation. "Oh yes," came the patient's reply. "I'm into deep rock now!"

Removing that whole section of temporal lobe (the Led Zeppelin area was, of course, part of the epileptic focus and scheduled for removal anyway) didn't eliminate the patient's abilities to recall the music or the experience afterward. So it was hardly the sole site of memory storage.

One of the reasons people now believe that these "recalls" are just seizure-associated hallucinations is that all of the more complex ones are associated with minor seizure activity—what we call afterdischarges—both locally and in the deeper structures of the temporal lobe. And the more you turn up the strength of the stimulating current, the more likely you are to evoke these reports—and to see afterdischarges spreading more widely.

"Does it cause a full-blown seizure?" Neil asked.

If the current is strong enough and lasts long enough, even normal cortex can be pushed into a seizure. That's one way psychiatrists produce seizures during electroconvulsive shock therapy for severe depression. In the O.R., we always keep the strength below the threshold at which afterdischarges start to occur locally, and well below the threshold for its spreading outside the local area.

SEIZURES COME IN ALL SIZES. There are little seizures and medium-sized seizures. And then there are big seizures.

"I hate the big ones," Neil said. "I'm unconscious, just like in the little ones. So it's not that. But everybody says I put on a show with the big ones, stiffening up and then jerking all over. It's embarrassing as hell. Sometimes I lose my urine and bite my tongue. Then I always feel groggy and sore all day."

Every part of the cerebral cortex is capable of going into a seizure if provoked hard enough. What provokes it is usually a seizure in a neighboring area, so the seizure may spread like a burning fuse, involving one area after another.

"But my big seizures come all at once. Both arms and legs, and on both sides of my body, all at the same time."

That's what's called generalization of the seizure, I told him. An EEG then will show epileptic activity on both sides appearing all at once, at the same time as the patient suddenly stiffens. It's as though some mechanism had spread a small seizure throughout the whole brain instantly, the way an aerial bomb blast can start many widespread fires at the same time. The major effect of the anticonvulsant drugs is to prevent that kind of spread.

Sometimes the generalized seizure seems to be the only kind of seizure a patient has, which deprives the neurologist of the best clues. Such a seizure could have started almost anywhere in the brain. It's only the beginnings of a seizure, before generalization, that can tell you where the trouble is. If the patient has little seizures in between the medium and big ones, the neurologist has much more information for locating things.

"Mine start when I go blank. I'm sort of 'out of it' despite still sitting there at the dinner table. Sometimes I may start tapping a spoon on my plate. Or chewing and swallowing, even though dinner hasn't been served yet."

Now, to a neurologist, that immediately waves a red flag. Automatisms can originate from almost anywhere in the temporal lobe, but seldom from any other part of the brain. What else happens to you, especially before those automatic movements?

"Well, mostly I don't remember very well. But often there's an awful smell. I don't really know how to describe it—it's not like anything real. Maybe a bit like burning rubber. And that's the last thing I remember."

Those kinds of hallucinations are known as the "aura" of a seizure. They're actually little seizures and, at least when we can find their source, we tend to call them focal seizures. That particular kind, associated with a brief unpleasant smell, often can't be seen on the EEG recordings from the scalp. With smells like that, there is usually a small seizure occurring in the uncus, the inner part of the temporal lobe that bulges out, almost touching the brain stem.

"That's what my doctor said."

When they involve automatic actions like fumbling with a spoon and chewing without food, with no memory for these actions, we're more likely to call them complex partial seizures. Patients are likely to take about half an hour to fully recover from one of these, although they are unresponsive for only a few minutes. That kind of seizure is more likely to show up on a scalp EEG, in which case they're often localized to the temporal lobe.

Patients report a variety of feelings and experiences with temporal lobe seizures. Some experience déjà vu, that feeling of unusual familiarity, as though they had been here before. Or illusions—for example, distortions of size or shape in which individuals appear as giants or little people. Some suffer hallucinations, auditory or visual— even smells.

"My neurologist told me about a patient of hers who saw a bucolic farm scene before each seizure. The patient even drew the scene for her. It sounds like 'visions' from the Bible or some such thing."

Paul's vision on the road to Damascus, sure. Maybe he had temporal lobe epilepsy. The voices that told Joan of Arc to save France may well have been auditory hallucinations with temporal lobe seizures. They say that when Joan was burned at the stake, her heart wouldn't burn. One thing that could cause that is calcification of the covering of the heart—calcific pericarditis—which is a consequence of tuber- culosis. Brain tuberculomas—little tumors of tubercular tissue—are common in widespread tuberculosis, and seizures are a common symptom of those tumors. So it wouldn't be surprising if she suffered from little seizures in the temporal lobe.

"Temporal lobe epileptics are such interesting company— Dostoyevsky, van Gogh. I've heard it said that Jonathan Swift and Lewis Carroll probably had it too, because of all the little people they wrote about in *Gulliver's Travels* and *Alice in Wonderland.*"

Yes, seeing giants and little people can be symptoms of temporal lobe seizures. If they never progress to bigger seizures, they may never get diagnosed as epilepsy.

"So what's the difference between the little seizures and the big ones?"

The big seizures—*grand mal* or just generalized seizures—start out the same way as the littlest. But they recruit more followers and so progress further through the brain.

"I can never tell if one of mine is going to be big or little."

The big ones don't stop with fumbling movements. All of the sudden, a patient will stiffen all over. When I was out shopping last year, I saw a guy stop in the middle of the sidewalk. He looked confused and swallowed repeatedly. After maybe ten seconds, he looked like a frozen statue, his right forefinger pointing toward heaven.

His head was drawn back, so it looked as if he were gazing toward heaven as well.

"Sounds like a lot of religious paintings I've seen from the Middle Ages. The saints, frozen just like that."

Hippocrates, in the fifth century B.C., called epilepsy "the sacred disease." But this man on the sidewalk: after a few seconds of this frozen posture, both of his arms began to jerk, as if he were gesturing to the gods, jabbing with that forefinger. And his legs jerked too. He would have toppled over if two companions hadn't grabbed him. They laid him down on his side and folded a coat under his head, which is exactly the right thing to do. They looked so competent that I just sat in my car and watched as they reassured the pedestrians. The jerking stopped in a few minutes, but it was fifteen minutes before he was sitting up. He looked hungover but five minutes after that, he was able to walk away looking fairly normal.

"After I have one of those, I just get my secretary to cancel my appointments and drive me home. Complete loss of the day."

There are other kinds of generalized seizures that are basically inhibitory, like briefly turning off a switch. Those patients tend to look awake but briefly out of contact. This seizure type is more common in kids. These seizures are sometimes called *absence,* pronounced as in French—the name probably derives from the phrase, *absence d'esprit,* or "absence of mind." In the old terminology, the French and everyone else called them *petit mal*—the "little sickness."

"So what spreads the focal seizures around, to make a big one?"

They co-opt the selective attention circuitry. Some neurons seem to have connections to everywhere, such as those neural circuits that help keep you awake and alert. Remember when we were discussing coma, particularly those serotonin and norepi connections from the brain stem that spread diffusely through the cortex? The ones I likened to underground lawn sprinklers, spreading liquid fertilizer to grow thoughts?

"So the seizure spreads into that system and then gets broadcast everywhere?"

Well, that was Penfield's notion, although it may require some neural connections that aren't very obvious. Since then, another possibility has appeared, that there is wrong-way impulse traffic in that attention system. Just imagine that plumbing system working backward, as if someone were forcing water from a hose down one of the sprinkler heads, and it came back up through all the others. Neurons are normally one-way streets, but occasionally they can be forced into working backward.

SELECTIVE ATTENTION seems like a spotlight, highlighting some aspects of the sensory environment while keeping others in the background.

We appear to use the same system to focus inward, the way you'd try to remember the name of someone you saw years ago, while trying to ignore the distractions of the sights and sounds of the cafeteria. This is the circuit that selects which sensations we will emphasize, out of the many we are exposed to. What we store in memory, what we retain as our conscious experience. Which we will try to recall from memory. So selective attention is perhaps the closest we will come to finding one system in the brain that determines the current content of our conscious experience.

"Now we're getting somewhere. So that's the real me? Selective attention is like a television producer in the control room, deciding which camera's view should go out over the air?"

Sometimes the spotlight can't be moved very well, as in those right-brain patients who neglected things to their left. That's an example of a posterior parietal lobe area that is involved in focusing selective attention, and the plumbing of that norepi system seems to favor such areas. Drugs that reduce the effectiveness of norepi interfere with the ability to focus your attention, as in paying attention to what the teacher is writing on the board.

Some blood flow studies of the brain have been done during vigilance tasks, such as watching for the traffic light to finally change to green. These are very much right-brain tasks, involving both that posterior parietal area and a region of frontal lobe. And you see exactly the same two areas light up even if it isn't a visual task, such as waiting for a tap on the big toe.

Various parts of the frontal lobe and brain stem are used in orienting toward a stimulus, as when a cat hears a noise, then turns her eyes, points her ears, and finally rotates her whole head around toward the source of the sound. But that seems to be different from staying alert for a particular type of stimulus—what we'd use to listen for a baby crying upstairs in the midst of traffic noises from outside. The frontal

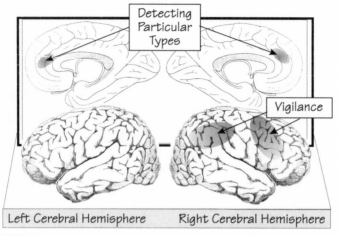

Selective Attention Specialties

Data summary from Posner, 1992

lobe is particularly involved in representing things during their absence, and you seem to use some regions of the midline regions of the frontal lobe, the cingulate gyrus just in front of the corpus callosum, to stay alert for a class of words—such as when you are looking for Italian surnames while scanning a telephone book.

Both anterior and posterior attention systems have many subcortical partners in doing their job, especially in the thalamus. The brain stem mechanisms for arousal from sleep are a fairly general system, but the high-end version of the system in the thalamus is somewhat more specific.

WHILE THE THALAMUS isn't really the center of things—the thalamus and frontal cortex are a closely linked system—some of the best examples of how selective attention works come from operations on the thalamus, which are done for the treatment of Parkinson's disease.

A little microtremor is normal. But a year or two after a patient thinks he just has the coffee jitters, he starts having more than the usual problems with writing checks. Or swinging an arm. Or cutting steak with a knife. The stiffness finally shows up in overall posture or in a shuffling gait. The voice often fades.

So it's the stiffness and the tremor that finally prompt a visit to a neurologist. And the neurologist will try to explain that some neurons that make dopamine—one of those neurotransmitters with a broad distribution like serotonin and norepi—aren't doing a very good job of it anymore, because many of them died decades earlier. There is a drug, l-dopa, that helps the remaining neurons of the substantia nigra to manufacture more dopamine, and that often helps.

But some of the patients will still have a tremor, even though their stiffness is satisfactorily controlled by the drug. It's those patients who may benefit from an operation on the thalamus.

"I thought that the trouble was in the substantia nigra," Neil said.

That's the pigmented region of the brain below the thalamus, from which many neurons are missing. The thalamus is probably normal. However, most brain systems are really two systems, one pushing while the other pulls. What's so important is the balance between them. Killing a small portion of thalamus seems to roughly compensate for the loss of those neurons in substantia nigra, reestablishing a balance in the system that regulates tremor.

"So how do you get to the thalamus if it's so deep inside the brain?"

Through a little hole in the skull, positioned over an area without major blood vessels. It's all done with local anesthesia. The neurosurgeon just sinks a needlelike probe down about three inches into the thalamus and coagulates a little of the thalamus around the tip of the

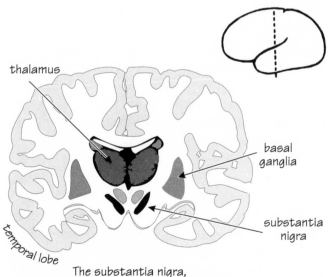

The substantia nigra,
whose cell loss causes Parkinson's disease.
And the thalamus,
where lesions can abolish the tremor.

probe. The patient's tremor usually stops immediately. The trick is in knowing how to aim the needle and how to be sure where the tip is.

"No kidding. 'These are professional surgeons, kids—don't try this at home.' So how do they know where the tip is located—using X-rays?"

Right, but since brains vary in function as well as anatomy, neurosurgeons tend to stimulate from the tip of the probe while asking the patient to perform some relevant task. One of the tasks George uses when he does a thalamotomy for parkinsonism is to have the patient watch a projection screen while slides are shown. First, there is a slide showing some common animal or object, such as an elephant. So the patient says, "This is an elephant."

Then it gets more interesting. A second slide pops up, and all it shows is a number. The patient, being well-rehearsed beforehand, starts counting backward from this number. Then about six seconds later, a third slide pops up that says simply, "Recall." The patient is supposed to recall the name of the object on the first slide: "Elephant." But you can make this task harder, so that the patient will make errors half of the time. Just have the patient count backward by threes. Then the patient has a harder time hanging on to the elephant name over the distracting task.

If George adjusts the difficulty of the task so that the patient normally makes errors in recall about half the time, he sees a very interesting effect of stimulating the thalamus while the elephant or whatever is on the screen: not only is naming more accurate, but there aren't as many recall errors later. Stimulation makes memory better!

"What happens if George stimulates during the other two slides?"

The patient will be able to count backward during thalamic stimulation, but during the third slide—with the current turned off—he'll remember only about half the names. Same as without stimulation. Stimulation during the third slide results in many more errors.

So it looks as if the thalamic stimulation made the patient pay attention to what he was seeing at the time. Thus, stimulation during the first slide improved his recall during the third. And stimulation during the third slide forced his attention toward the screen rather than allowing him to focus inward, to retrieve the prior name. The selective-attention circuit was acting like a gate, allowing information into or out of recent memory, but not both at the same time: you either

PRESENTATION

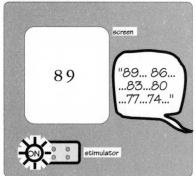

DISTRACTION

Testing Neil's memory recall after a 6-second distraction accompanied by brain stimulation

CUED RECALL

daydream or you pay attention to me, but not both. Paying attention conflicts with recalling things from short-term memory.

"Short-term memory? There's another kind?" Neil asked with a smile. "I've begun to wonder why names keep slipping away."

Immediate "working" memory, short-term post-distractional memory, and long-term consolidated memory seem to involve different brain mechanisms. But I can't explain them—and certainly not the "memory problems" that people complain about—until we discuss those synapses and electrical signals inside neurons.

All of this, so far, is for patients having an operation on their left thalamus. But the right thalamus sometimes gets operated on too, and the results in those patients are quite different. Object form and shape, rather than words, are selectively attended to and remembered. George often uses slides showing complex shapes. After the distracting task of counting backward, the patient is asked to pick which of three shapes was the one he saw earlier.

"So what happens?"

Same thing as with left thalamic stimulation: recall is improved. But what's really interesting is if there is a conflict between right and left thalamus, between names and lines. Stimulate the right thalamus when the patient is naming objects, and there is no special effect. Stimulate the left thalamus during object naming, and you get improvement in recall later. But if you show complex shapes while the left thalamus is being stimulated, there will be many more errors—as if the shapes were being ignored while the left thalamus was stimulated.

The left selective-attention system directed at retaining verbal information dominated the choice of what was to be selectively retained from the environment. As George says, it shows true dominance of the left brain over the right brain—not in general, but for this particular aspect of selective attention.

OUR PERCEPTION OF THE WORLD depends first on what our sensors detect—for example, we can't see the infra-red of heat, or the ultraviolet that gives us sunburn. But second, it depends on what our selective-attention circuits select from all the sensations. What gets through that set of filters is what we might retain in memory.

That makes selective-attention circuits very important for learning. They allow you to acquire new information more reliably. When selective attention is not directing you toward the external world, you can browse through your memories, either in search of someone's name or that more free-form retrieval we call fantasy or daydreaming.

Defective function of these circuits seems to be the basis for attention deficit syndrome and minimal learning disorders, situations in which a child has difficulty sustaining attention. These might well involve those selective-attention circuits passing through the left thalamus that focus attention on verbal information such as object names.

More severe malfunctions in these circuits are probably a part of autism, in which there is an overall limitation in attending to the external environment, especially in attending to the presence of other people and perhaps to verbal information. This limitation is coupled with severe distractibility and an intense focusing of attention on a limited selection of environmental features.

The brain circuits that are defective in autistic children are not well established. While many of their problems with imagination and social inappropriateness are reminiscent of frontal lobe patients, subtle disorganization of neural circuitry has been found in both the thalamus and the language cortex. Their behavioral pattern suggests that very poor function of thalamic selective-attention circuits is likely to be present, as though the autistic child is largely oriented only to what has been previously acquired, and limited in the ability to acquire new material from the environment. They're stuck.

Although many autistic children are also mentally retarded, not all are. But even the brighter ones have trouble with make-believe, such as pretending to feed a doll with an empty spoon, and may not understand that other persons may have different viewpoints and beliefs. And even the more able autistic individuals may have a hard time making a mental model of another person's state of mind. They cannot understand deception. Being so literal, they don't appreciate humor or irony, can't read between the lines. They lack a "theory of mind" with which to understand others.

Sometimes autism is the result of brain damage in early life. Sometimes there seems to be a genetic component. If one of identical twins is autistic, the probability is very high that the other one will be; for fraternal twins, who do not have identical genes, that probability is very low.

"I wish I'd had one of those thalamic electrodes in place when I had to learn Spanish. I could have turned it on each time I had to learn a new word and retained it better for the exam."

Yes, but if you'd accidentally turned on the stimulator during the exam, you'd have remained focused on the questions and unable to retrieve the answers from memory. We joke a lot about medical students wanting a thalamic stimulator while learning gross anatomy. But someday we might be able to use one with certain kinds of autistic kids to help them out of their withdrawal.

"What gets to me," Neil said as we prepared to leave, "is that this isn't science fiction. Everything you come up with in real science seems to open up a whole new set of possibilities."

And mostly in applications that we'd never have guessed.

chapter 6

The Personality of the Lowly Neuron

Immense numbers of individual units, the neurons, completely independent, simply in contact with each other, make up the nervous system.

The neuroanatomist SANTIAGO RAMÓN Y CAJAL, 1909

THE "GRAY" MATTER OF THE CEREBRAL CORTEX is just a thin sheet atop the white matter. But within that reddish brown icing on the white cake, you can see the neurons arranged into a half-dozen layers. In this case, it's the icing that has the layers, not the cake itself.

Just as do the floors of a telephone central office, wires rise up from the depths and ascend through these cortical layers. And other wires head back down into white matter. Or just sideways. The dendrites of each neuron also rise up through a few layers, connecting with many different input sources.

Each neuron is a node where thousands of wires converge, where incoming mail is digested and sometimes turned into outgoing mail. Each neuron is a little computer summing up thousands of influences on its dendrites (those tree-like branches) and occasionally sending out mass mailings to thousands of recipients using electric signals via its long, thin branch, the axon.

There is a certain "tailbone-is-connected-to-the-hip-bone" logic to some connections. The fourth layer gets most of its inputs from the thalamus, down in the very center of the brain, which tends to relay messages from the sense organs—eyes, ears, skin, muscles. The fourth-layer cortical neurons receiving that thalamic input send most of their outputs up to the second and third layers of cortex.

Some neurons in the second and third layers send messages down to the fifth and sixth layers. The sixth layer sends messages back down to the thalamus via the white matter. And the fifth layer sends signals to other deep and distant neural structures, sometimes even the spinal cord. A simple path would come into layer four, then up to three, down to five or six, and then back out of the cortex to some "subcortical" structure.

"That's a simple flowchart," Neil said, looking up from the sketch on his napkin. He'd just come from his latest clinic appointment, after taking what he hoped was the last of the neuropsychological tests. "So, have you got the circuit diagram all worked out by now?"

Not very much of it.

"Sounds like the fourth layer gets the job of sorting the incoming mail."

Right. And the deep layers specialize in the outgoing mail, though without envelope lickers and postage meters. The upper layers generate a lot of interoffice stuff, often sending messages sideways in the cortex—a horizontal, rather than a vertical, aspect of the organization chart. We call them corticocorticals—sometimes a message goes just

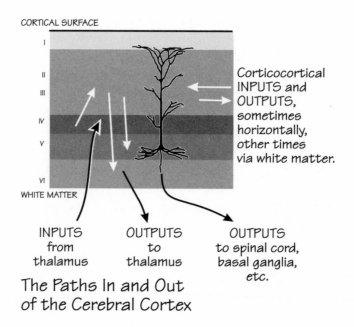

CORTICAL SURFACE

Corticocortical INPUTS and OUTPUTS, sometimes horizontally, other times via white matter.

WHITE MATTER

INPUTS from thalamus

OUTPUTS to thalamus

OUTPUTS to spinal cord, basal ganglia, etc.

The Paths In and Out of the Cerebral Cortex

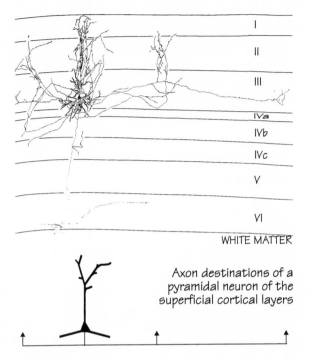

I

II

III

IVa
IVb

IVc

V

VI

WHITE MATTER

Axon destinations of a
pyramidal neuron of the
superficial cortical layers

Adapted from McGuire et al., 1991

a millimeter or so sideways, but sometimes from the front of the brain to the back of the brain. Or from the left brain to the right brain, passing through that biggest of all the wire bundles, the corpus callosum.

Often these internal-to-the-cortex messages are mass mailings with a certain inscrutable logic, rather like the post office delivering it to the first house on each block and skipping the others.

"Now that's what I call a selective mass mailing."

And that's if the mailing originated from the first house on a block. The third house on the block would send to the third house on the next block, and maybe a few more distant houses—but always the third house on a block.

"How long is the block?"

About a half millimeter, but it isn't defined by "cross streets," only by that gap between deliveries. The message may also go "across town," with a connection that dips into the white matter and then resurfaces in some distant gray matter. The mass mailings from an average cortical neuron contact fewer than 1 percent of the neurons within a millimeter radius.

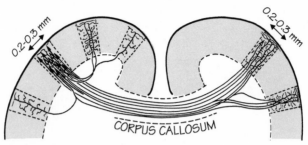

Corticocortical connections
are organized in columns.

Modified from Szentagothal, 1978

All together, there are 148,000 neurons beneath a square millimeter of cortical surface, roughly a hundred million per square inch. They are often organized into little minicolumns of about 100 neurons apiece. Those in turn are sometimes organized into macrocolumns of perhaps 300 minicolumns with 30,000 neurons.

"Sounds like a modular architecture to me," Neil said, his engineering background resurfacing. "Almost like a housing development. So what do the elementary modules do?"

You'd think we could figure out a modular wiring diagram from all this information, but it's surprisingly difficult. In the sensory strip, you'll see a macrocolumn specializing in skin sensations, but the adjacent one might specialize in reports from the muscles and joints. In the visual cortex, a minicolumn will specialize in lines of a certain orientation, while adjacent minicolumns specialize in other angles. And the macrocolumns there are organized by eye—first you might see a set of minicolumns favoring the inputs from the left eye, then encounter another macrocolumn next door that favors what's coming in from the right eye. But for most cortical areas, we don't know much about the columnar organization.

"Don't different cortical areas look different under the microscope?"

The half-dozen layers vary in their thicknesses. But the total cortical thickness stays about the same, all over the brain. Just imagine a city with a height limit of six stories for its buildings. But the ceiling height isn't equal for all the floors—you might see a ceiling on a ground floor that is higher than the ceilings on the other floors. In one part of town, suppose buildings were constructed with the third floor extra tall for

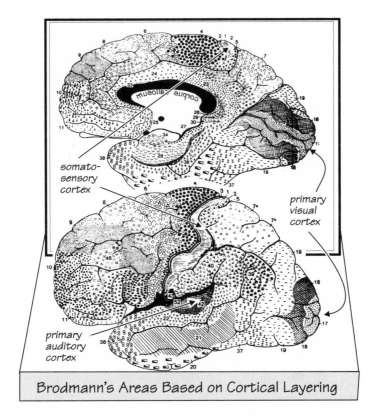

somato-
sensory
cortex

primary
visual
cortex

primary
auditory
cortex

Brodmann's Areas Based on Cortical Layering

some reason, but with the fourth floor having a ceiling so low that you hit your head. Early twentieth-century neuroanatomists defined 52 cortical areas in that way, using neuron size and the relative proportion of layer thickness, and gave them identifying numbers. Area 17, for example, is otherwise known as the primary visual area.

In the motor cortex, also known as Area 4, there isn't much of a fourth layer because it doesn't receive much information coming up from the thalamus. Yet back in the primary visual cortex, the fourth layer is the most impressive of all. That's because it has so many inputs from the eye (via a relay in the thalamus) that a lot of extra neurons are found in the fourth layer, bringing the total up to 357,000 neurons under a square millimeter. Because the extra neurons are densely packed, and the axons from the thalamus are so segregated, you can see a horizontal stripe in the fourth layer, even without a microscope. At the edge of Area 17, where it abuts Area 18, the stripe abruptly stops—that's why the primary visual cortex was originally known as the "striate cortex." Unfortunately, the language cortex isn't as obvious in structure.

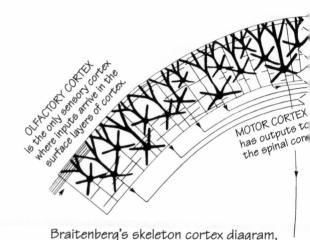

OLFACTORY CORTEX is the only sensory cortex where inputs arrive in the surface layers of cortex.

MOTOR CORTEX has outputs to the spinal cord

Braitenberg's skeleton cortex diagram,

BACK WHEN SIGMUND FREUD was peering through a microscope, the gray matter looked like a great spider web of crossing axons. Everything seemed fused together. At some of the intersections, instead of a trapped fly, there was a black bulge, the cell. No "arrows" anywhere, suggesting how information flowed. Freud probably found this rather frustrating, and by the time visualization techniques were improved, he had moved on to view the brain from a very different perspective—psychoanalysis.

With Camillo Golgi's method of staining a few neurons at a time with silver, Fridtjof Nansen and Santiago Ramón y Cajal independently deduced that the axon actually came to a dead end just outside another cell—that there was really a gap, rather like the no man's land between the two independently maintained border fences of neighboring countries such as Israel and Syria.

That was back in 1888. About 1900, the neurophysiologist Charles Sherrington gave this point of near-contact a name—the synapse. But the synapse wasn't seen in more detail until 1953, following the advent of the electron microscope that showed those parallel border fences. The synapse is the border-crossing point, where the output of one neuron's axon becomes the input to another neuron's dendrite or cell body.

What crosses this border is information, in the form of chemicals. It's analogous to opening a bottle of perfume at one border fence and letting the molecules waft across the no man's land (the synaptic cleft) to the other border fence (the cell membrane). When reaching the

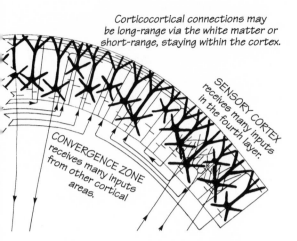

Corticocortical connections may
be long-range via the white matter or
short-range, staying within the cortex.

SENSORY CORTEX
receives many inputs
in the fourth layer.

CONVERGENCE ZONE
receives many inputs
from other cortical
areas.

...ripped of all cells except pyramidal neurons.

other side, the perfume is "sniffed" by special receptor molecules embedded in the cell membrane.

These "perfume molecules" are the neurotransmitters. There are dozens of different types, such as norepi and dopamine. A common one in the cerebral cortex is glutamate.

Some neurotransmitter types are released at a considerable distance from the target neurons and diffuse around a neighborhood, rather like cooking aromas. They change the excitability of target neurons in a general way. This is called "volume transmission."

"Sounds like hormones."

Hormones are the long-distance version of this principle. The hormone is released at a distant site, such as the kidney, and carried by the bloodstream to its target cells, such as a muscle. The other extreme of the principle is the traditional synapse seen in the electron microscope, where the neurotransmitter is released so close to the target cell that it can't miss—it has little chance to diffuse away and affect any other neurons. But there's this intermediate version, where the molecules reach a whole neighborhood of target neurons.

"A tonic of sorts? They get in those neighborhood neurons and turn up their volume control?"

They can certainly change neuron properties, so that bursts of impulses are produced more easily. Of course, the neurotransmitter usually doesn't enter the "downstream" neuron. It only tickles its surface receptors.

"It's not absorbed? So what happens to the neurotransmitter?"

It gets recycled, much of it back into the presynaptic side of the border fence. Many drugs interfere with this recycling of transmitters back into the cells that release them. We call the interference "blocking," but it is closer to slowing down, less like a strike of the garbage collectors than a work-to-rule slowdown. For example, cocaine blocks recycling at synapses using dopamine as their neurotransmitter, among other actions. Common antidepressant drugs often block recycling at synapses using serotonin. It has long been known that many insecticides block recycling at acetylcholine synapses.

"What's the purpose of slowing down recycling?"

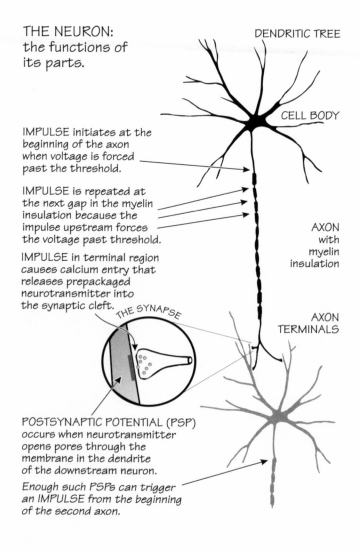

THE NEURON: the functions of its parts.

DENDRITIC TREE

CELL BODY

IMPULSE initiates at the beginning of the axon when voltage is forced past the threshold.

IMPULSE is repeated at the next gap in the myelin insulation because the impulse upstream forces the voltage past threshold.

AXON with myelin insulation

IMPULSE in terminal region causes calcium entry that releases prepackaged neurotransmitter into the synaptic cleft.

THE SYNAPSE

AXON TERMINALS

POSTSYNAPTIC POTENTIAL (PSP) occurs when neurotransmitter opens pores through the membrane in the dendrite of the downstream neuron.

Enough such PSPs can trigger an IMPULSE from the beginning of the second axon.

So the neurotransmitter can hang around longer. This fools the downstream cell. Blocking recycling usually makes the postsynaptic cell think extra neurotransmitter was released upstream—something that usually happens only when a more imperative message is being sent from the presynaptic terminal. Overdoing it, of course (as in the case of insecticides), can make the synapse fail to communicate the arrival of subsequent signals because, like a sticky doorbell button, the postsynaptic receptors never reset.

The flow of information is one way, most of the time. It goes from the upstream "presynaptic" neuron to the downstream "postsynaptic" one: only one side has the perfume to release, and only the other side has the receptor molecules. And that defines one end of the axon as

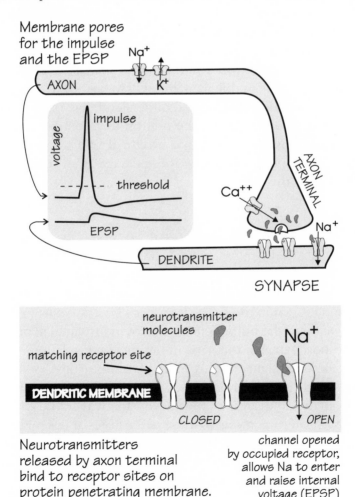

Neurotransmitters released by axon terminal bind to receptor sites on protein penetrating membrane.

channel opened by occupied receptor, allows Na to enter and raise internal voltage (EPSP)

the output, the other end as the place where the inputs last have a chance to interact. While neurons don't come with arrows attached, they are effectively one-way streets for this fast flow of messages. Back in Freud's day, no one knew this—the neural network just seemed like one big web with no input-output organization, no uphill or downhill.

"So let me see if I've got this straight. Something releases a packet of neurotransmitter molecules into that no man's land between cells. Some are recycled, and a few tickle the receptors on the postsynaptic side—and then they're recycled too." Neil thought for a moment. "Sounds as if neurons compute on some sweet-or-sour principle using cooperative or conflicting perfume?"

Only very indirectly. Some of the minutes-to-days reactions of neurons are indeed chemical, but on the timescale of reaction times and speaking sentences, computation is largely electrical. Sweet is a positive electrical change, and sour is a negative one. The perfumelike process at the synapse is just a middleman.

But it's an adjustable middleman, thought to be the basis for learning and memory. The only way you can understand that adjustability is to look at the electrical aspects of the neuron that control computation and synaptic strength—how much electrical effect a synapse produces. And the aspects that move the message from one end of the neuron's axon to the other.

ELECTRICITY CARRIES THE MESSAGE, except at the synapse itself. The event that usually releases the neurotransmitter, like a puff from a perfume atomizer, is the arrival of a puff of electrical charge. Though only a tenth of a volt from bottom to top, the "impulse" is the biggest voltage change seen in the brain. It moves like a wave from the input end of the axon to the output end—except in insulated axons, where it seems to hop between the gaps in the myelin insulation.

"So this electrical signal doesn't move almost instantly, as in wires?"

No, this is more like burning fuses. The speeds vary among axons, ranging from the equivalent of the slowest freeway traffic jams for the smallest uninsulated axons, up to those of the fastest trains for the largest insulated axons. The impulse lasts only for about 1/1000 of a second at any one spot (a millisecond is also about as long as a fast camera shutter remains open), but that's long enough to trigger the release of some prepackaged neurotransmitter, emptying it out into the synaptic cleft.

And what happens on the other side of the synapse is also electrical in many cases. The neurotransmitter sticks to the receptor molecule, and together they are able to open a pore in the cell membrane. An electrical current then flows into (or out of) the postsynaptic neuron for a short time, producing an event known as a postsynaptic potential. All this can repeat, many times each second, depending on the impulse initiation rate.

"Whoa! What started the impulse?"

Postsynaptic potentials in the dendrites spread to push the voltage past threshold at the beginning of the axon, near the cell body. It's like a trigger on a gun, an unstable equilibrium.

"I've never understood where the electricity comes from."

One use of the food you eat is to charge up your batteries. Each cell in your body has such batteries, created when their cell membrane throws certain kinds of salts out of the cell and captures other kinds to hoard inside the cell. All this takes energy. Typically, sodium ions are excluded and potassium ions are hoarded. That's the battery part. All of the interesting events, like impulses, involve making currents flow, using those batteries.

When the flow of sodium into the neuron is smaller than the outward potassium flows, the voltage simply heads back to the resting potential. Just imagine a mixing faucet with a mind of its own: whenever something turns up the hot water, it turns up the cold water even more, until the water stream returns to some standard lukewarm temperature.

But suppose your faucet is also designed such that, when the temperature rises beyond some trigger value, the hot water comes on much harder than the cold, and you get a blast of hot water before any compensation occurs to cool things off. The threshold is an unstable equilibrium: slight increases in the voltage above the threshold, and it's off to the races.

"I know some hotels with showers like that."

Their faucets aren't that diabolical, only sticky. That blast of sodium ions entering the neuron is the impulse starting. Should the inward sodium flow exceed the potassium reactions, then voltage rises—and even more sodium comes in, and the voltage rises even further. It's a vicious cycle. Eventually it stops at the peak of the impulse, where the potassium flow has finally increased enough so that the two flows cancel each other out.

"But what stops the impulse? Why doesn't the voltage hang up there?"

That's because the sodium pores tend to slowly shut themselves off at the higher voltages. The potassium pores don't do this, so they eventually win.

So these pores (we usually call them channels) open or close, depending on the local voltage. They're quite different from the neurotransmitter-sensitive pores that produce the synaptic potentials and the *initial* rise of the impulse. The voltage-sensitive pores then take over to produce the rest of the impulse.

"What makes the impulse travel down the axon so slowly?"

This is something like the Pony Express passing on the message to a new horse and rider; the impulse has to be recreated next door, and next door to that.

"Ah! The domino theory is alive and well—in neurophysiology!"

Very much so. The fatty insulation wrapped around the axon has gaps, called nodes of Ranvier, about a millimeter apart—and the impulse seems to jump from one gap to the next. That takes time, more in some axons than in others—just as it takes time for each domino to fall.

And the long axons may have thousands of such dominos. The impulse is repeated all the way down to where the axon branches. Then impulses travel down both branches, and so on, until shifting the presynaptic voltage at a thousand different synapses. That's why the mass-mailing analogy is appropriate: the same message—say, a pair of impulses—is sent to all the recipients.

"But what's to prevent an impulse from traveling backward along the axon? Just as there's nothing to keep me from driving the wrong way up a one-way street?"

Not much. Of course, an impulse has to get started somehow—and normally the only place they start is at the beginning of the axon, near the input synapses for that neuron. But impulses can start anywhere, given enough impetus. You can start them from the middle of the axons that wrap around the back of the elbow, for instance. Sometimes this even happens with little provocation, as in the people with slipped disks that traumatize the nerves to their leg.

"About your lawn-sprinkler metaphor—do those impulses starting at the end of the axon have something to do with the spread of the medium-sized seizures to cause a big seizure?"

That's one idea, and it's also a possible cause of muscle cramps. Since the anatomy is simpler for the motor neuron and the muscle, it's better to start there. Each time a motor neuron back in the spinal cord fires an impulse, the muscle fibers also repeat the impulse and thereby twitch (the synapse between axon and muscle is so strong that it always creates an impulse in the muscle cell). For some of the hip-and-leg muscles, the motor neuron's axon branches enough to connect with several hundred muscle cells. Thus, the impulse in the motor neuron's axon sets off the twitches in many muscle cells. A series of twitches builds up muscle tension into a sustained contraction.

Now suppose something set off an impulse in one of the many axon terminals—which ordinarily would never happen. Just changing the environment around the terminal branch of the axon could do it; maybe it gets a little starved for oxygen because blood flow is insufficient. So off the impulse goes, the wrong way up that one-way street, heading back up to the spinal cord.

"That must confuse the poor spinal cord."

Probably not very much. The problem is that this wrong-way impulse sets off a muscle contraction in each of those several hundred muscle fibers. Each time the impulse travels past a branch, going off to another muscle fiber, an impulse starts down that branch. And sets off a twitch. So some fraction of the whole muscle gets a little twitch.

A single twitch occasionally may be irritating, but it's not a serious problem. But should that abnormal site of impulse generation set off repeated impulses, then it will be just as if the motor neuron back in the spinal cord sent a whole series of impulses down the axon in the usual way. A sizeable contraction now develops.

"And so I get a cramp that just won't stop," Neil said. "It's totally out of control. At least, out of *my* control."

Right. Except for massaging the muscle or stretching it out by contracting other muscles, there's nothing you can do about it. The brain just doesn't have any pathways to where the trouble is located that can possibly affect this erroneous barrage. Willpower doesn't work anymore, because the impulses aren't starting inside the brain or spinal cord.

"This is what happens when one of my medium-sized seizures suddenly generalizes into a full-blown *grand mal?*"

That's the idea. The neurons in the brain have axons with a lot of branches going different places. And so a wrong-way impulse generated by massive environmental changes in one place—and seizures dump a lot of potassium out of neurons—can travel backward and set off impulses going forward down each branch that it passes on its backward journey. If there's a real barrage of wrong-way impulses similar to those preceding the muscle cramp, then you can get big effects that are widespread in the brain—both sides, arms and legs. And virtually simultaneously.

"That happens only for the axons of the selective attention system?"

No, it probably happens for many of the axons entering and leaving an area where there is a medium-sized seizure. An average cortical neuron has an axon with perhaps 10,000 side branches. But a neuron in the selective attention system or the brain-stem arousal system has a lot more side branches than average—maybe a million—and so it amplifies the mischief more effectively.

"You said that the anticonvulsant drugs helped to stop this spread?"

Either that, or the drugs make the distant sites more resistant to starting their own seizure when the backward barrage arrives—say, by increasing the stockpiles of inhibitory neurotransmitters so that they can't be exhausted quite as easily when such a barrage invades. It takes a lot of wrong-way impulses to start a seizure in normal cortex. Just as with starting seizures with electrical stimulation, a lot of synchronized input—that keeps repeating for a while—is capable of driving any cortical area into a seizure.

INTERFERING WITH NEURAL TRANSMISSION is the more classic way to influence the flow of information within the brain. Local anesthetics may block impulse replication in mid-axon. Muscle paralyzing agents tend to interfere with the synapse between nerve and muscle. Some agents like curare plug up the receptors that guard the postsynaptic pores, so that acetylcholine can't bind. Other agents prevent recovery after an impulse arises, and so interfere with replicating the succeeding impulses.

Furthermore, the ions that enter the postsynaptic neuron through the opened pore may do more than just change the internal voltage. The calcium that enters through some synapses, for example, may change a variety of regulatory processes inside the neuron.

"It has a dual role in life?"

It sends a second message, in addition to the voltage change it produces across the cell membrane. Some synaptic actions don't involve membrane pores or voltage changes at all. Instead, the neurotransmitter binds to a receptor molecule on the outside of the cell membrane. This G-protein then manages to cleave a high-energy chemical bond inside the neuron, something of a trip wire that sets in motion various chemical reactions—some even send messages to the cell nucleus, affecting the manufacture of proteins. This is a much slower process, sometimes producing voltage changes but sometimes merely modulating others, in the manner of pressing the pedals on a piano to modulate the sound produced by the keys.

The calcium-blocker cardiovascular drugs attempt to alter these internal effects. While some of the actions are prompt, it make take weeks for the antipsychotic and antidepressant drugs to do their job.

"And, I presume, some anticonvulsants take a long time to act."

Yes. But second messengers aren't the only slowpokes on the scene. Many synaptic enhancements don't involve the postsynaptic neuron, but rather act to increase the neurotransmitter available to stimulate it.

"Such as those things that block recycling?"

Exactly. Many antidepressants just slow down the reuptake of the neurotransmitter into the presynaptic terminal.

EXCITATION AND INHIBITION have a range of connotations, even Freudian ones, but to neurophysiologists they mean something close to addition and subtraction, or deposits and withdrawals. The neuron doesn't subtract a molecule of inhibitory neurotransmitter from two molecules of excitatory neurotransmitter, however. The neuron avoids the "adding apples and oranges" problem by adding the positive and negative electrical currents that the neurotransmitters produce.

"Ah! Electricity is the currency of computation in the neuron?"

Instead of dollars, this currency is measured in nanoamperes of synaptic current. In the mixing faucet analogy, this would be the temperature of the water mixture emerging: the excitatory synapses "turn up the hot water," and the inhibitory synapses turn up the cold. In general, all of the thousands of outputs from a neuron tend to have the same postsynaptic action, and so we can often speak of inhibitory neurons and excitatory neurons.

"Do they look different?"

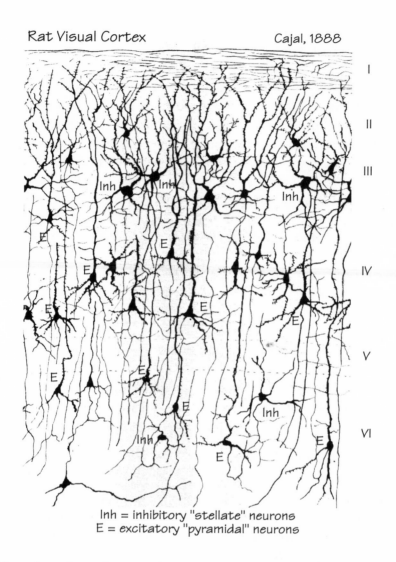

Rat Visual Cortex   Cajal, 1888

Inh = inhibitory "stellate" neurons
E = excitatory "pyramidal" neurons

Often they do, at least in the cerebral cortex. There you can easily spot most of the excitatory neurons because they have a big "taproot" growing toward the surface called the apical dendrite. It arises vertically from the cell body (which is sometimes triangular, leading to the name "pyramidal neuron" for the whole class of taproot neurons). And, strangely, the apical dendrites of a dozen neurons may bundle together. The bottom of the cell body has some basal dendrites surrounding it like a ruff.

The axon emerges from the cell body and dives into the white matter, en route to delivering a message far away. But the axon also has a series of side branches that end nearby. They are the most prolific source of cortical synapses in most areas of the cortex. Pyramidal neuron axon terminals are likely to release the excitatory neurotransmitters such as glutamate or aspartate.

And the neurons downstream from them have receptors that can open up pores to sodium ions and so produce a voltage change known as the excitatory postsynaptic potential. But you can also raise the temperature by turning down the cold water in the existing mixture, and that's how serotonin synapses from brain-stem axons work in the cortex, by reducing the resting potassium current.

"So they're also excitatory. What about the inhibitory neurons?"

If you see a cortical neuron that doesn't have the taproot design, it's usually an inhibitory cell—and it usually releases gamma aminobutyric acid (GABA) from its axon terminals as a neurotransmitter. But what makes it inhibitory is the *post*synaptic action of its neurotransmitter.

"The cold water treatment, I presume."

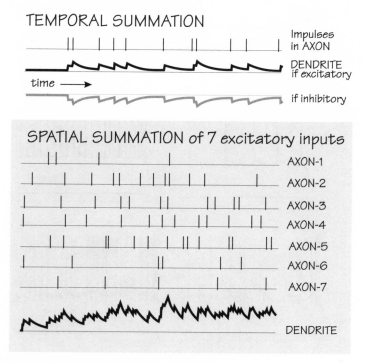

Modified from Calvin, 1980

What inhibitory synapses do is to oppose excitatory synapses elsewhere in the dendritic tree and cell body. The way this usually works, there's a pore that doesn't let sodium ions through, just mostly potassium or chloride ions. And so it produces an inhibitory postsynaptic potential that subtracts from the excitatory ones. About 40 percent of a neuron's potential inputs, on average, are inhibitory.

So it's all a big balancing act. Excitatory synapses tend to raise the voltage above the impulse threshold and "fire" an impulse down the axon. But, individually, they are seldom strong enough to do this; it's likely to be only a small percentage of the voltage change needed to kick off an impulse.

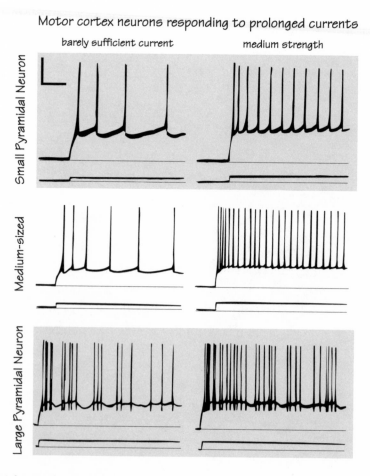

Data of Calvin and Sypert, 1976

"Except at the muscle synapse. Sounds like the brain is more subtle. And varied?"

It's almost as if different neurons had different personalities. Some are specialists in rapid change—they ignore maintained conditions. Others do the opposite. This turns out to be of major importance in dyslexia. You often hear it as an easy-to-remember dichotomy—"fast" versus "slow" cells, jittery versus steady, movement-sensitive versus static, magnocellulars versus parvocellulars. But there are lots of in-between types too, simply because there are more than a dozen types of pores into neurons, and the mix of these types (which is under genetic control and well as being affected by drugs and experiences) determines the neuron's personality, just as different blends of whiskey determine its taste.

Cortical neurons are often silent—George often sees human temporal lobe neurons that respond at rates slower than once per second. When neurons become active, they need more oxygen and glucose. They have ways of asking for more blood supply and, since we have nice ways of measuring that increased blood flow with PET scans and functional MRI techniques, we can produce colorful images of the brain at work.

THE AMOUNT OF NEUROTRANSMITTER RELEASED may vary among the thousands of output synapses. Another way in which the synaptic "strength" is varied is to change the number of postsynaptic receptors to the neurotransmitter. Or you can change the recycle times for the neurotransmitter.

For these and other reasons, the synaptic potentials produced in the many postsynaptic neurons are not all of the same strength. While the synapse is only an inefficient chemical middleman in what are otherwise efficient electrical processes, it is a malleable middleman. Without this adjustability, the neural circuitry would be as rigid as that in our consumer electronics. The ability to adjust these "synaptic strengths" is what learning and memory are all about.

In the short run, synapses change strength with use. Sometimes synaptic potentials decline in size and we speak of synaptic depression.

"That's depression?"

Not the psychiatric use of the term, but an unrelated use of the same word by physiologists. And when one impulse follows closely upon another, there may be *more* neurotransmitter released by the second impulse than by the first—that's called synaptic facilitation. Following a burst of impulses, any impulse in the next minute or so may release more-than-standard amounts of neurotransmitter. That's known as post-tetanic potentiation, or when even longer times are involved, long-term potentiation—enough of a mouthful that it's usually abbreviated LTP.

"So synapses are what's changeable. Now we can talk about how learning and memory works?"

Such impatience. Well, just as a preview—temporary changes in synaptic strength such as synaptic depression and facilitation probably underlie our fading short-term memories. And it is the short-term memories that may provide the basis for the construction of permanent memories. If you lose something from short-term memory, it never gets kept in a more permanent form.

"Why's that?"

Probably because some short-term changes provide the scaffolding for making permanent changes, casting things in concrete. LTP is an interesting candidate—it's seen in only certain malleable parts of the nervous system. Among them are the upper layers of cerebral cortex that manage all that interoffice stuff. And LTP is one thing that makes synapses grow bigger and stronger, changing the brain structure in the long run. It's how your thoughts rewire your brain, so it's a different brain tomorrow than it is today.

chapter 7

The What and Where of Memory

THE ATRIUM WAS SUNNY when I found Neil waiting for me the next week, memory on his mind. The decision on operating still hadn't been made, and Neil was impatient. He'd taken the summer off from work to get his seizure problem fixed and, at the same time, read up on brains. But it was halfway through the summer, and still no date had been set for an operation. Indeed, I knew, George had some reservations about whether to operate at all.

"George sure worries a lot about memory with these temporal lobe operations," Neil said. "I guess finding out about my memory was really the main reason for the Wada test, that making sure my language was on the left side wasn't the crucial issue."

That's my understanding, too.

"But even though I 'passed' the Wada test, George still seems to have memory concerns. What was the significance of passing the Wada test, anyway?"

It's now thought that recent memory requires one functioning temporal lobe.

"But I have two."

That's the point. The Wada test is supposed to temporarily mimic the effect of removing one temporal lobe—in your case, the left one—by briefly anesthetizing that side of the brain. If you have two *working* temporal lobes, then there shouldn't be a major memory problem after removing one of them. But what if, unknown to anyone, your right temporal lobe was so badly damaged that it couldn't support memory? Then both your seizures and memory would depend on the same temporal lobe—the left one—and taking it out would leave you with a severe memory deficit. Better not to operate at all.

If your memory is okay during the brief period when the left side of the brain is inactivated by the anesthetic—and it was—then it probably will be after the operation. And especially so if your memory is poor when your right side is similarly inactivated. That would indicate that the right side is responsible for most of your memory.

"How did they figure that out?"

Measuring memory with the Wada test came about in the 1950s because of a couple of instructive cases studied at the Montreal Neurological Institute, particularly by Brenda Milner and Wilder Penfield. Before that time, no one had paid much attention to a memory role for the temporal lobe, although it had been suggested as early as 1900. One of Milner's cases has become quite famous under the patient's initials, H.M.

H.M. had portions of the inner side of both temporal lobes removed in 1953 for seizures and psychiatric symptoms. And he immediately developed a severe memory problem that has persisted to this day. Yet H.M.'s general intelligence is quite intact—his IQ measured a bit higher after the operation than before. Nearly all his problems are a matter of remembering things. The neurosurgeon who had done the operation sent H.M. to see Milner, and she documented the nature of the memory loss. They reported the case quite widely, so that no one else would surgically remove both temporal lobes.

The other pivotal case was more like the problem that the Wada test addresses. That was a patient of Penfield's who seemed to have damage to only the left temporal lobe, but after its removal for his seizures, suffered a considerable memory loss. He, too, seemed to be otherwise intact after that operation, returning to his job, but having to write everything down because he couldn't remember things. Penfield and Milner guessed that there was damage to his other temporal lobe that wasn't evident with the tests available in those days. And sure enough, when that patient died of a heart attack years later, the examination of his brain after death showed old damage in the remaining hippocampus, one of the structures on the inner part of the temporal lobe, and the structure many people now believe is a crucial one for memory.

"But did H.M. lose all his memory for everything? There seem to be a whole lot of different types of memory. And every writer seems to subdivide memory differently and use his own terms to label the different types. I found it really confusing!"

Welcome to the club. Essentially, a new label is added each time someone devises a different way of presenting new material, or testing its recall, or doing different things in between presentation and recall. What H.M. can and can't do tells us some of the especially useful subdivisions of memory.

Remember that H.M. had the inner portions of both temporal lobes removed, including the front two-thirds of the hippocampus on both sides. H.M. remembers who he is, where he went to school, where he lived years before the operation. So that type of memory is intact.

"Those are long-term memories?"

That's as good a name as any. It's a very resistant type of memory, in the sense that temporarily interfering with brain functions doesn't seem to do much to long-term memories. They are there after recovering consciousness from a severe brain injury, or after the brain is short of oxygen or nutrients for awhile, or after seizures that interfere with brain electrical activity. And they are there after the inner surfaces of both temporal lobes are gone.

"So they weren't stored there—or at least, not exclusively in the temporal lobe. Sounds like those memories must be fixed in concrete—but somewhere else."

We call it consolidation. Long-term memories probably are fixed in some structural change in neurons, such as synapse size. But H.M. doesn't have all his memories from before the operation. He has lost most of them for the several years preceding it, and he doesn't seem to have made many new ones since the operation.

"So one thing the temporal lobe must be good for is making new permanent memories, and that must take quite a while—days to years."

That's okay as a first approximation, but nothing about memory is that simple.

"That's been the story of our conversations," Neil chuckled. "Nothing about the brain is ever simple, although you keep telling me that memory matters are even worse."

Take distractions, for instance. Parents seem to know instinctively how to distract children from unpleasant things, and how that makes them less likely to recall them tomorrow. Distraction turns out to make a big difference in how well memories are stored. H.M. can still hang on to memories if he devotes all his attention to the matter. If you give him a string of six or seven numbers to remember and don't disturb him, he'll be able to tell you the numbers even after fifteen minutes.

So that's another type of memory that seems to be intact after losing both temporal lobes. It's often called "working" or "immediate" memory.

"Sounds like a memory for phone numbers to me. I can remember them long enough to dial them—so long as someone doesn't ask me something in the meantime."

Although H.M. can remember the numbers if you don't distract him, the moment you ask him to do something else for a moment, the memory of the numbers vanishes. What doesn't work in H.M. is a "recent" or "short-term" memory that is "post-distractional." That is, the defect is evident only when something has to be stored over a distraction, and it isn't evident if the memory can be continually rehearsed without distraction.

"That explains why the memory test I had to do during that Wada test was constructed the way it was. I named an object, then read a sentence, and then when the neuropsychologist yelled, 'What was it?' I was to tell him the name of the object that I had to keep in memory while I read the sentence."

That sentence serves as the distractor, to make it a test of post-distractional memory.

"Clever. I guess that test was to make sure I didn't turn out like H.M., making my living as a subject for the neuropsychologists' memory tests. Does post-distractional memory ever fail after anything except loss of function in both temporal lobes?"

Sure. We call it concussion. Football players who are concussed during a play also demonstrate this distinction between an immediate and a post-distractional memory. When they are flat on their backs on the field, and again when being helped off, they can often tell the team physician that the play they were running was "Twenty-three Tango"—and be correct.

You initially think that their memory is okay. But within a few minutes, the player has no recollection of those events. Both immediate and short-term memories are pretty labile and easily disturbed by such things as a concussion. Or a shortage of oxygen in the brain, or anything like a seizure that interferes with the ongoing brain electrical activity. But the post-distractional recent memory seems to be the most labile and easily disturbed of all, and it's the one that seems to slip away with aging.

"So are there two memory defects when both temporal lobes don't work? One for your post-distractional memory and the other for making new long-term memories?"

Probably not, only one for post-distractional recent memory. It just seems as if new long-term memories have to first survive post-distractional recent memory first. There's no separate path into long-term memory, only the one through short-term memory. So H.M.'s short-term memory deficit accounts for his long-term one, too.

There's also a temporary version of H.M.'s problem that strikes some people. They can't remember what's happened in the last hour or two: they know who they are, they probably know where they are—but they don't know what they're doing there, or how they got there. They're confused, but all their reasoning ability is working except for their ability to remember what's happened recently. Still, they can tell you what they were doing last night, or discuss local politics. Then the problem clears up later in the day and, except for having a permanent gap in their memories of an hour or so, they're normal again. It's called transient global amnesia. No treatment is needed—except reassurance—and many people never have another episode of it.

"A little stroke?" asked Neil.

Probably not. The current thinking is that it is more like a migraine with much reduced blood flow—just involving a less common location, the inner faces of both temporal lobes. So short-term memory stops working well until full blood flow finally returns.

"So far, at least, memory seems a lot easier than you led me to believe," Neil said. "It seems a lot like my computer. There's a buffer that acts as your immediate memory, such as the type-ahead buffer for the keyboard. My computer's random access memory acts like your post-distractional memory, always being overwritten with new stuff. And then there's my hard disk, once the information has gotten through the two previous stages, buffer and RAM. Once written to disk, the records survive even power failures."

"Although," Neil said, amused, "I'm not sure I'd think much of a computer that took years to get things from RAM to the hard disk. But what's so complicated about it?"

CLASSIFYING MEMORY SEEMED SIMPLE, back when H.M. was first studied in the 1950s. But then it was found that H.M. can remember some types of new information acquired after his operation.

He was taught to draw, while only being able to see his hand and the paper via a mirror. And he learned to trace a maze. Although he doesn't do these perceptual-motor tasks quite as well as normals, he shows definite improvement, getting through the tasks more rapidly from day to day. Of course, if you ask him whether he had ever been taught these skills, he would deny it. He doesn't mostly remember the act of being taught, although he seems to recognize the test apparatus, and he definitely has maintained his skill, being able to do the tasks quickly that had once been difficult. So his post-distractional memory for some types of information, such as motor skills, is intact. But that for other types, the particular episodes of yesterday and today, is defective.

Memory for motor skills is often called procedural memory. There are other types of "unconscious" memory, too. One is called priming, in which subsequent memory performance is changed by information encountered just previously. H.M. has intact priming, too. So he has more than just procedural memory intact—it's an "implicit" unconscious memory that is intact. What he's lost is the memory for the events of today, sometimes called declarative memory or explicit memory.

"A different RAM for each type of memory," Neil said. "That will make my computer a bit more complex. I do wish they'd settle on one name for each type of memory."

Sorry, no industry standards in the human memory field yet. But more subdivisions. Explicit memory seems to have two parts: *semantic* for general principles, facts and associations—the words of your vocabulary, for example. And *episodic* for unique, personally experienced events. H.M. has trouble with both—he hasn't learned very much new vocabulary since his operation, for example. But other patients with temporal lobe damage seem to have much more trouble with "episodic" memories than with the semantic ones.

And when Brenda Milner began to study patients who had temporal lobe removals on only one side, she found that they sometimes had subtle memory defects on her sensitive tests—and they differed, depending on whether the operation was on the right or left side. Left-side memory defects were mostly for words. Patients with right-sided removals had minor troubles with some kinds of spatial information.

"Those crazy, jumbled figures they asked me to remember?" asked Neil.

I think they must make those figures by photographing a pile of coat hangers on the floor. And then mixing them up and photographing them again. The folks with right temporal lobe removals have more trouble recognizing whether they'd seen the picture before. But these right side memory defects are for only some types of spatial information, not all types. And, of course, the problems are seen only after a distraction.

"In all these examples, the memory seems either to be there, or not to be there. Yet I seem to have a lot of fuzzy memories, half remembrances. Do they ever test for them?"

They're one of the first things discovered about the psychology of memory. The nineteenth-century German psychologist Hermann Ebbinghaus memorized lists made up of three-consonant combinations that weren't meaningful words. Then, sometime later, he retested himself and found that he retained few if any of the three-letter combinations—but he relearned the list faster than he had the first time. That suggested that something remained in his head, even if he couldn't recall it.

"Just like I relearned Spanish pretty quickly a few years ago, when we first started doing business in Latin America. And before I started taking lessons, I didn't remember any Spanish words—even though I spoke Spanish in first grade when I had a lot of Hispanic classmates. My instructor said it's pretty common for students like me to relearn it quickly. So some of my Spanish was there all along, but I couldn't make use of it until my refresher course."

What you are "conscious of" may be just the tip of the iceberg. There are other unconscious memory effects, too. One memory may inhibit a second memory. Proactive inhibition is when, in trying to recall a person's new phone number, the old number gets in the way. Retroactive inhibition is when, in trying to recall the old number, you keep getting the new one instead.

"Sort of the way I'll see someone across the room," Neil observed, "and tell myself that it's Jane Doe. And then realize that it really isn't Jane Doe but someone else I know. But I can't come up with Betty Smith's name because Jane Doe's name keeps getting in my way."

Until a half hour later, when Jane Doe's name has faded and the right name finally pops to mind, unbidden.

"Exactly. With all these interactions, I'm surprised anybody remembers anything with any accuracy."

OUR MEMORIES AREN'T AS RELIABLE as we'd like to think. The problem is especially serious for an episodic memory, which is a unique category that ties together a series of elements.

Everyone thinks that recall is especially good for "flashbulb memories," like the Kennedy assassination, but it isn't. The morning after the disastrous explosion of the space shuttle *Challenger* in 1986, the psychologist Ulric Neisser asked the students in his freshman psychology class to fill out a questionnaire asking where they were when they heard the news, what they were doing at the time, who they were with, and who first told them the news. He then filed them away for three years and contacted the students when they were seniors, got them to answer the same questions again—with one additional question, asking them how sure they were of their answers.

At least a quarter of the students were completely wrong in every major detail. Only about one in ten remembered the events the same as on the morning after.

"They were the ones who were pretty sure of themselves?"

Being positive that you're right isn't, alas, very reliable. The students who got things wrong in every major detail were just as likely to be confident of the accuracy of their recall. They were quite puzzled when shown the original questionnaire—in their own handwriting, furthermore.

SEQUENTIAL EPISODIC MEMORIES seem to be the hardest to correctly recall. You have to remember not only a certain set of elements, such as the who-where-what of the space shuttle explosion news, but also the order of the elements.

Sometimes, as in the case of remembering lunch yesterday, we have a mental script that helps us: it's like a "lunch form" to be filled out. The only three mandatory items about lunch are *where, when,* and *what—* and some of those may be standard. But there are optional boxes for the common additional elements: *with whom* and *conversation topic.*

Other episodes may not have this crutch, and often there is no standard script for the conversations we may experience in the course of a morning.

The most common error, in real life as well as after brain injury, is to get the elements a little out of order. We might try to report accurately who said what at a particular committee meeting, but unless we have taken notes, the order of speakers is likely to become jumbled.

"Eyewitnesses to a car accident are supposed to be especially unreliable," nodded Neil.

Yes, but that's for an additional reason. Episodic memories also turn out to be easily changed afterwards, not remaining permanent as in a recording. A lot of experiments have been done by psychologists on that very topic, usually using undergraduates as research subjects. For example, Elizabeth Loftus and her colleagues staged a fake accident and videotaped it—just a simple matter of a car slowly turning a corner and bumping into a pedestrian. There were several other cars in the picture, and several other people. There was a stop sign visible. The experimenters show this tape to the subject, followed by a short quiz.

During the weeks that follow, the subject is again asked questions about the videotaped episode. How many vehicles, how many people, and so forth. But there were also some misleading questions that incorporate a passing reference to a nonexistent yield sign, such as "Did another car pass the red Datsun while it was stopped at the yield sign?" The next time the subject is asked what he originally saw, the answers favor the yield sign—even though it was really a stop sign. About 80 percent of normal subjects make this error. And this happens the next week as well, even without any additional misleading information, even with warnings that some misleading information was introduced. More than 90 percent of these subjects correctly identified it as a stop sign just after the original videotape viewing. But that correct memory is no longer recalled.

"Ouch! It makes me worry, all those leading questions with hidden assumptions that detectives like to ask suspects. And about the lawyers rehearsing witnesses before a trial."

Maybe the original information is overwritten, maybe it's only hard to access with that misleading information more accessible—the retrograde inhibition effect. I think that we tend, just like the football player with the concussion, to fit together the elements of the story into a reasonable order. Sometimes there is a standard lunchlike script to help us. We usually get the right elements, and often in the right order. But the person with amnesia has a more difficult time getting the right elements; they may substitute yesterday's lunch for today's, and they often scramble the order. Yet they seem sure of it. They're not consciously lying, so we tend to call this confabulation. In our nighttime dreams, elements and order are really scrambled but may seem quite real to us at the time, just as a delusion does to the psychotic patient.

WHERE IN THE BRAIN do memories reside? As Neil observed, with all the different types of memory, a lot of different brain areas must be involved. He couldn't believe it was just a matter of the temporal lobe, or only a part of it like the hippocampus. Too big a job for one structure, he said as we walked around the campus in the summer sunshine, carrying our coffee cups.

Right. There are different places involved, more subdivisions to learn.

"I'm not sure I want to know any more divisions of memory," Neil groaned.

Suppose that I ask you to silently recall some facts from history, say of the American Revolution. That seems to activate the cerebral cortex in the parietal lobes more than in the frontal lobes. But if I ask you to silently recall an episode from childhood, perhaps a vacation trip, that will instead increase the activity of the frontal lobe. Events in which you were a participant are part of episodic memories, but things you've learned more generally are part of semantic memories, just as vocabulary is.

But the big subdivisions aren't places in the brain. They're the different parts of the memory *process*. There is a difference between memory acquisition (sometimes called encoding), memory storage, and memory retrieval. Probably the easiest way to illustrate the relationships between different brain areas and these different aspects of memory is to describe some of George's stimulation mapping studies.

George used a memory test like the one during the Wada test, which I also mentioned back when we discussed stimulating the thalamus. It's a measure of—let's see if I can remember all the qualifiers—post-distractional, recent, explicit, episodic memory. It's that test which uses sets of three slides. The first just shows the object to be named. Then there is a distractor slide, a sentence to read during which the memory of the object name must be stored. Finally there's a retrieval slide, a cue for the subject to recall the name of the object in the first slide.

Sometimes George stimulates the brain during the first slide as the memory is being acquired, sometimes during the distraction slide, and sometimes during the recall attempt. But he's always looking at how well the object name is retrieved from memory.

The first thing he found was that this memory performance is altered from different cortical sites than the naming sites.

"So if the naming sites are semantic memory," observed Neil, "maybe these other sites store episodic memories?"

Perhaps. The next thing George found was that stimulating temporal lobe sites tended to interfere with memory most when applied during the first or second slide—during acquisition and storage. Stimulating during retrieval didn't much affect performance. By contrast, frontal lobe stimulation had effects mostly when applied during retrieval.

"As if," Neil said, "it was just distracting from the task."

Rather unexpectedly, hippocampal stimulation didn't have much effect, unless such large currents were used that small seizures were produced on both sides. Then memory failed, regardless of whether the small seizures occurred with acquisition, storage, or retrieval. But then your memory usually fails when your seizures spread to involve the inner parts of both temporal lobes.

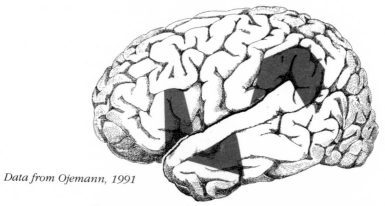

Data from Ojemann, 1991

Zones (arbitrary) where stimulation disrupts
short-term post-distractional memory

"My seizures must be inactivating both temporal lobes," Neil said, "as I'm temporarily like H.M. for the ten minutes or so after a seizure. I sure don't make any new memories then. I never remember what happened during a seizure. From what you described of the stimulation studies, I'd expect memory problems with the temporal lobe, the frontal lobe, and damage down in the depths."

And that's pretty much what we find. The most severe amnesias occur with damage to both temporal lobes, which have something to do with recent post-distractional memory storage. There's still controversy as to exactly which structures in the temporal lobe are most critical to this process, but it's probably both the hippocampus and the cortex.

Certainly the cortex adjacent to the hippocampus is involved—in Alzheimer's dementia, that's where the earliest signs of neuron degeneration appear. And it probably accounts for the early symptoms of recent memory loss in Alzheimer's. But it appears from brain-stimulation studies as if those kinds of memories also involve the evolutionarily newer parts of the cortex, the ones on the side of the temporal lobe.

"The cortex you see during an epilepsy operation?"

Right. Much less severe memory deficits are sometimes seen after removal of the temporal lobe on only one side. As I mentioned before, you see deficits for verbal material after left removals, for spatial tasks after right removals. For example, after left temporal removals, patients may have some difficulties remembering the names of individual people or cities.

"George explained to me the possibility of that type of memory loss after my operation," Neil said, kicking a stone on the path. "But those are subtle problems compared to my seizures. So maybe I'll have to peek in my address book more than other people do."

Memory-retrieval problems also occur with frontal lobe damage, especially when the outer part of the frontal lobe has been damaged on both the left and right sides. You see something similar in Huntington's disease, an inherited defect in which the cells deep in the cerebral hemisphere degenerate and disrupt connections with both frontal lobes.

Severe amnesias also occur with damage to subcortical structures on both sides—such as the mammillary bodies of the hypothalamus. That's a typical location of the damage seen in Korsakoff's syndrome, which appears in alcoholics who have a thiamine deficiency in the diet—which may be largely liquid. They have major problems in forming new memories, as well as some difficulty with retrieving previously formed long-term memories. These are the patients who usually give medical students their first experience with confabulation.

"You'd think that they'd add vitamins to cheap wine," Neil said, "just the same way as they add vitamins to milk. Wouldn't that prevent many cases of Korsakoff's?"

Of course. Getting enough knowledge to act effectively is hard enough. Getting people to care—enough to bother doing something—seems to be the real obstacle. There are a lot of preventive measures that would reduce the number of severe mental problems.

Just look at how long it took to get seat belts routinely installed in new cars, despite what everyone knew about how devastating head injuries are. And then think about how it took another quarter-century to get even half the drivers to wear their seat belts.

chapter 8

How Are Memories Made?

NEIL WAS GOING INTO THE HOSPITAL for a few days for more diagnostic workup. George wanted round-the-clock monitoring of his EEG, needing to double-check that Neil's seizures always began in his left temporal lobe—and not his left frontal lobe.

We were sitting outside in a summer breeze. Neil wanted to get some sunshine while he still had the chance. The first thing to realize about human memory, I said, is that it doesn't work like any known filing system, including computers and videotape. The second thing is to think *process* rather than *place*.

"But I thought the hippocampus was the place?" Neil said. "Not so?"

There are some important places, but they're probably not where the information is really stored in the long run. And the places don't tell you much about the mechanisms.

It seems that the *how* of memory is a layer of mechanism deeper than the *what* and *where*. We backed into the topic by considering the size of the "buffers" and "RAM." There are some interesting clues, just from the size limitations you encounter. The capacity of immediate memory is indicated by the title of the psychologist George Miller's study of it in 1956: *The magical number seven: plus or minus two*. It's working memory, where the subject gets to rehearse those seven items of information.

"Like trying to remember a phone number without writing it down, holding onto it long enough to dial it," Neil said.

Broca's area seems to play an important role in that kind of working memory, I explained. Some people can only hold onto five digits, some can manage nine, but the average is about seven. That's how many we can hold in sequence long enough to repeat them back or dial a phone. Anything longer—and unless part of it is very familiar to us already—we have to use crutches. With perhaps 15 digits to place an international call, we have to do something, such as writing it down and then reading it back digit by digit. Without writing, the common mental trick is to subdivide the problem whenever approaching the seven-digit limit, a process that has become known as chunking.

Most of us can manage longer sequences this way: remembering the international-call access number separately (011), the international dialing code for the United Kingdom separately (44), then the code for Central London (71), and then the familiar prefix (338) at University College London, followed by the four-digit extension. That's eight chunks total, rather than the fourteen separate units stored by the memory phone button.

"So the limitation seems to be on the number of chunks rather than on the total bits of information."

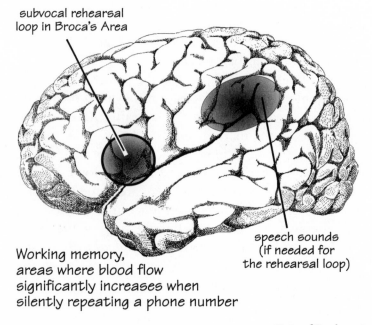

subvocal rehearsal
loop in Broca's Area

speech sounds
(if needed for
the rehearsal loop)

Working memory,
areas where blood flow
significantly increases when
silently repeating a phone number

Data of Paulesu et al., 1993

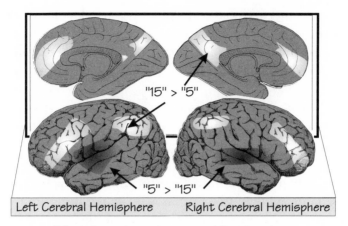

"15" > "5"

"5" > "15"

Left Cerebral Hemisphere Right Cerebral Hemisphere

What learning a long word list involves
(repeat back a 15-word list, minus the
blood flow changes on an easy 5-word list)

Data from Grasby et al., 1993

Exactly. We make the individual chunk represent more, since packaging is everything. That's a lot of what building your vocabulary is all about, making one word replace a longer, roundabout phrase. The linguist Philip Lieberman thinks that efficiencies like that were an important part of the evolution of language from the ape level to the human one, that this limitation on working memory otherwise limits one to saying very simple things.

Suppose I were to read aloud a list of five names, and then ask you to repeat them back in any order. Nearly everyone can do this task. But when the list is fifteen words long, you'd be lucky to get seven or eight. During either chore, many areas of your brain would receive increased blood flow. By subtracting the map for the five-word list from the map for the fifteen-word list, you can get some idea of the brain areas that are involved in trying to chunk.

The frontal lobe is busy on both sides of the brain, as are the posterior parietal areas that are ordinarily involved in visual-spatial tasks. And since the test is all verbal, done with the eyes closed, it suggests that many subjects were making some use of the traditional mnemonic techniques involving imagining a list, or "placing" the items in the rooms of a large mansion.

If each word of a seven-word sentence stands for something very simple, like a digit, then the sentence itself cannot say much. But if each word stands for a whole concept and its many connotations, then a unique seven-word sentence can encompass much. Chunking creates new categories. Some are as temporary as that memory mansion. Other chunks get used often enough to become part of your private vocabulary.

CONTINUOUS NEURONAL ACTIVITY has always been assumed to be the substrate of working memory, what goes on during rehearsal. There isn't much evidence one way or the other for that assumption, although recording of neuron activity in monkeys has shown some frontal lobe neurons that are continuously active between the time a monkey matches two objects and the time the memory of the object is retrieved.

Neurons like that have also been found in the temporal and the parietal cortex, with the temporal neurons active during the memory storage phase of visual cues such as colors, while the parietal neurons were active during storage of memory for sensory discriminations. So working memory may be part of the brain concerned with perception of the material to be remembered—but maybe it's neurons further along in the postsensory areas. In the monkey studies, the neurons changing activity with perception were usually different from those active during memory storage.

"Okay," Neil said, "immediate memory is just keeping the activity going, the perception that noticed the event in the first place. But what happens if I distract you? Prevent you from rehearsing it?"

There might be various scratch pads that you can shift among—but eventually you're going to fill them up and have to overwrite. I doubt this will be as simple as the number of windows you can keep open on a computer screen. Overwriting itself is interesting, as another substrate for post-distractional memory would be lingering synaptic changes from the earlier immediate memory, such as those enhanced releases of neurotransmitter and enhanced postsynaptic responses. From that, you might be able to reconstitute the activity present during working memory.

It's possible to record individually from some of the neurons in the temporal lobe, prior to their surgical removal. We've done this by sneaking up on them with a sharpened needle whose tip is in electrical contact with the tissue. As we get close to a neuron, its impulses can be heard through the loudspeaker.

"That's what you mean by 'wiretapping' a cell?"

Exactly. It's usually called "microelectrode recording." The technique was invented about 1950, and it has greatly increased our knowledge about how the brain is functionally wired up, what neurons are interested in. But it's time-consuming, and so it takes a while to build up a picture of what's going on. We have to pool data from many patients to make any sense of it.

George has recorded the electrical activity of individual neurons in the temporal cortex during the three-slide show. He found that over two-thirds of the neurons increase their activity when a new item of information enters memory. This increased activity continues for some seconds, longer than the time required for any language processing of that information. Activity then returns to baseline while the memory is stored.

"So that's how working memory might look, if you were just trying to keep the activity going after the fact."

The first time this information must be retrieved, the activity again increases—not as much as originally, and not in as many neurons, and not for as long, but nonetheless you can imagine some semblance of the original activity being reconstituted during recall attempts. The second time this item or information is retrieved, after being stored again, even fewer cells are active. The third time it's retrieved, there is even less activity change.

The neuron activity on initial acquisition and retrieval is so great that it may explain why recent memory is so prone to failure with aging, head injuries, brain loss of oxygen, and other conditions where neurons don't work well. For under those conditions, there may not be enough neurons that can function, in this holding-the-information mode, to get the process started.

Studies using blood flow changes in normal volunteers have shown something similar. There's widespread activity when learning something new, such as tapping your fingers in a particular order. But once it's learned, the activity changes seem more circumscribed. The location of the increased activity seems to be different, depending on whether the task being learned is motor or language.

"So it takes less brain to handle something you know well from having rehearsed it," Neil observed. "Which explains why procedural memory works in H.M. when his episodic memory doesn't?"

One can hope. But we've barely scratched the surface of those issues in research. All of that activity in the temporal cortex might not be the

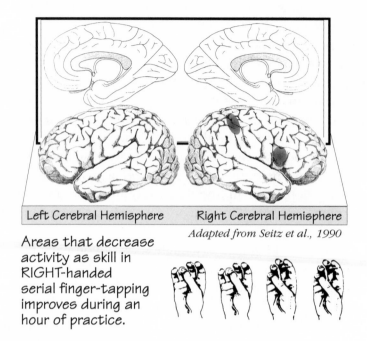

| Left Cerebral Hemisphere | Right Cerebral Hemisphere |

Adapted from Seitz et al., 1990

Areas that decrease activity as skill in RIGHT-handed serial finger-tapping improves during an hour of practice.

actual place of post-distractional, recent, explicit memory storage. It's probably more like a promoter, facilitating change in a much smaller number of neurons that have the synaptic modifications responsible for the real memory storage. It's the sequence of activity in the network of those cells that is probably the neural representation of the memory.

"Yes, but what's the recall of that memory?"

THE NATURE OF THE RECALL is probably the key to the long-term-storage issue, and we don't know for sure what recall comprises. It's reconstitution of some of the original activity patterns, surely, but how extensively? Enough, probably, to somehow trigger the correct motor response, pronouncing the name just as you did during the initial presentation. Pronunciation requires a spatiotemporal sequence of impulses to drive the various muscles involved in saying the word or writing out the response.

"Spatiotemporal sequence? Sounds like reading music."

The standard example would probably be the simple oscillation involved in the muscle commands for chewing or breathing: first, one set of muscles contracts; then those muscles stop and another antagonistic set of muscles starts firing. And it's not just two sets but dozens of different muscles involved in walking. Just imagine shifting from a walk into a run. That requires a spinal cord to produce a different spatiotemporal pattern of commands to all those muscles.

Sometimes it's a one-shot sequence, as when you throw something. That's very much like a player piano, where you are programming 88 different keys at different times in overlapping combinations. Changing the target distance, so you don't overshoot the target on the next trial, requires that you modify the temporal sequence of commands to that spatial set of muscles—and indeed, there are about 88 muscles involved in throwing, making the spatiotemporal pattern for a movement even more similar to the roll on a player piano that houses a spatiotemporal pattern which produces a melody.

"A sheet of music is just the code for recreating a spatiotemporal pattern," Neil mused. "I like that."

Most researchers would say that the evocation of a memory was creating a spatiotemporal sequence of neuron firings—probably a spatiotemporal sequence similar to that present at the time of the input to memory, just shorn of some of the nonessential frills that promoted it. We call it a Hebbian cell assembly. The Canadian psychologist Donald Hebb thought through the problem in 1949, well in advance of the data, even before anyone had started recording from single neurons in a primate brain.

"So it's like one of those message boards in a stadium, with lots of little lights flashing on and off, but creating a pattern. In time and space."

Yes, but I'd modify Hebb's cell assembly in one regard by not anchoring the spatiotemporal pattern to particular cells, to make it more like the way the message board works. There, you can place the pattern of the apple in various parts of the array—or even scroll it along. The pattern continues to mean the same thing, even though it's implemented by different lights. I've even suggested that the basic pattern is contained in a hexagon about 0.5 millimeters across, the equivalent of about 300 unitary elements. And that the pattern can clone itself—but that's another book's worth of explanation.

"A half millimeter is like a thin pencil lead. That's small, all right. How many cells does it take to make a Hebbian cell assembly for some memory? Say, a word? Or someone's face?"

Maybe only several dozen, judging from some of the work on temporal lobe neurons involved in face recognition. But that's several dozen being active, with hundreds of others remaining relatively inactive at the same time. Lack of response is also part of the cortex's representation of the message. It's just like that message board: several dozen lights can trace out an apple, so long as the others stay dim and don't confuse the sketch.

Remember that the intermediate stored pattern may be pretty abstract, looking nothing like the input pattern. Or even the output spatiotemporal pattern that drives all those muscles. Just think of the cerebral code for "apple" as one of the bar codes on a grocery package. It may not look anything like an apple, but it serves to represent the apple.

Neil considered this. "So learning a new item might involve creating a *novel* spatiotemporal pattern? That's a new code?"

Yes, and some regions might be particularly good at recording novel spatiotemporal patterns. You've got to hang onto some kinds of information for a while, just in case subsequent events prove that they were important.

"Of course, you can make a lot of mistakes doing that. It's one of the famous fallacies, assuming 'after this, therefore because of this.'"

Even slugs do that, and I think that we have some even fancier ways of committing that fallacy. The input patterns that need saving are likely to be from the various specialized neurons that analyze the visual

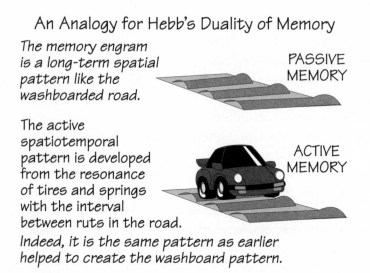

An Analogy for Hebb's Duality of Memory

The memory engram is a long-term spatial pattern like the washboarded road.

PASSIVE MEMORY

The active spatiotemporal pattern is developed from the resonance of tires and springs with the interval between ruts in the road.

ACTIVE MEMORY

Indeed, it is the same pattern as earlier helped to create the washboard pattern.

From Calvin, 1992

image. Saving those for an hour may be important when there are delayed consequences—say, getting sick from an unripe apple that you ate and wanting to avoid it next time. And we have much fancier versions, recognizing as familiar a face we first saw a week ago, even though we only saw it that one time before and we weren't trying to memorize it.

"So memories are made of spatiotemporal patterns like those on message boards. But they're stored forever in a different form? The synaptic strengths?"

A DUAL TRACE MEMORY system seems to be required, just as Hebb also pointed out in 1949—something like active and passive versions that are implemented in different ways.

The active memory—that spatiotemporal pattern of activity—needs to create another pattern, a purely spatial pattern of synaptic strengths, with no explicit time component to it—after all, coma can silence most of the neuron firing in the brain but it doesn't wipe out all those long-term memories. The pattern just lies there like the ruts in a washboarded road, waiting for something to resonate with it and recreate an active spatiotemporal pattern.

You can imagine the hippocampus giving the cortex permission to modify its recently potentiated synapses, or spending a few days rehearsing the cortex to engrain those new memories in the manner of habits. When the memory is reliable, the synaptic strengths successfully recreate the right spatiotemporal pattern.

"So now the problem is down to how to make those changes in synaptic strengths permanent?" Neil said. "Cast them in concrete. Pardon my construction analogies—I've been remodeling my house—but didn't you say earlier that the short-term process created the forms for the later concrete? But the forms themselves are thrown away after the concrete has set up properly?"

It may be more similar to the way that petrified wood is created. It's as if the wooden forms became petrified, because the decomposable wood was gradually replaced by hard minerals that endure. For example, whatever temporarily enhances the synapses could serve as a stimulus to growth for the next few days, and so their standard amount of neurotransmitter release would become greater, more like the synapse released after the original experience during the temporary enhancement. Instead of growing larger, maybe the axon would bud off some more axon branches or create additional synaptic sites where there were none before.

There is good evidence for that as part of a simple learning task in sea slugs. Further evidence that growth of synapses or formation of new synapses is important to forming long-term memories is the observation that drugs that block production of new proteins, the building blocks of new tissue, interfere with long-term memory formation. Indeed, recent research into memory has been directed at many of the same questions as research into the causes of cancer: what regulates cell growth.

Certainly the number of synapses per neuron increases considerably in the cerebral cortex of a rat when the rat is learning a lot, as when given enriched environments to explore. In the enriched rats, there are 80 percent more synapses than in the rats housed in individual cages, and considerably more than in the rats that merely exercised on boring treadmills rather than exploring. The ability to increase the number of synapses, when going from a basic to an enriched environment, lasts throughout a rat's lifetime. But the ability to correspondingly beef up the blood supply doesn't.

In addition to such use-dependent changes in synapses, there is evidence that simultaneous use of several different sets of synapses can enhance their synaptic strengths. Associative learning, as in Pavlov's dog salivating at the sound of the bell, might use this type of synaptic modification. It was also predicted on theoretical grounds back in 1949.

"Hebb again? The Hebbian synapse?" Neil asked, and I nodded. "So is there something they could give me to make my memory better? Anything that helps set up the cement? Or vitamins for the Hebbian synapse?"

DRUGS TO IMPROVE MEMORY have long been sought, but seldom found. If memory involves a step of synaptic modification, you'd think that the various synapse-modifying drugs would make memory better. Or even worse. But specific actions on long-term memory recall are hard to find, even though there are various "anesthetics" that will prevent short-term memories from ever being established as long-term memories.

There are two chemicals that seem to have important roles in memory. One is acetylcholine. Drugs that block acetylcholine interfere with memory. Neurons that use acetylcholine as a transmitter influence activity in the hippocampus and are among the early cells lost in Alzheimer's disease. Unfortunately, giving drugs to increase the supply of acetylcholine doesn't improve the memory of Alzheimer's patients.

The other chemical is glutamate. While it's one of the amino acids and widely used for building proteins everywhere in the body, it is also used as a neurotransmitter. The excitatory synapse of cerebral cortex where glutamate is the transmitter is, so far, the best candidate for a synapse that encodes memory, for a memory mechanism at the cell membrane level. There are at least two types of postsynaptic channels that open up when glutamate binds to their receptor molecules. One is pretty ordinary, as excitatory synapses go. It allows sodium ions into the dendrite, which raises its voltage temporarily.

The other type of glutamate channel—named "NMDA" for reasons that are arcane and irrelevant—allows some calcium ions to enter the dendrite as well. But what's really extraordinary about the NMDA channel is that it won't open unless it has two signals at the same time: it takes both the right voltage and the right neurotransmitter to open up. That's like a locked entrance door that requires a valid keycard to be stuck into a slot—but also requires that the power for the latch's electronics be on.

Until the discovery of the NMDA channel, all channels had been operated either by voltage alone (as in the sodium and potassium channels for the impulse) or by neurotransmitter alone. And certainly not both in combination, which allows it to detect near-simultaneous arrivals of inputs to the dendrite. That's considerably more interesting than merely the combination of keycard and power.

In an NMDA pore, there is a plug. Typically a magnesium ion diffuses into the channel and gets trapped, unable to go all the way through. When a neurotransmitter binds to the channel's receptor molecule, the gate may open, but no sodium or calcium flows through because of the magnesium ion plug.

"So the channel opens, but that doesn't do any good because it's plugged? How do you unplug it?"

That's what's so interesting. If the dendrite has received an input elsewhere, its voltage change may prevent the plug from getting stuck in the NMDA channel. And so, if the NMDA synapse is now activated by neurotransmitter, positive ions flow into the dendrite, creating a synaptic potential to add atop the original one. This is what is so exciting to neurophysiologists—the calcium entry points to a mechanism for short-term memory spanning many minutes. In the hippocampus (an old part of the cortex with a simpler layered structure), long-term potentiation sometimes lasts for days, and part of the reason for LTP is the NMDA business.

"Do you suppose that NMDA also has something to do with my epilepsy?"

When the NMDA channel is open for a long time—as in the early part of a seizure—a lot of calcium leaks through it into the cell. That may make for a strong synaptic change—unfortunately, making a memory of the spatiotemporal patterns leading up to a seizure.

"And maybe making another seizure more likely?"

That's one worry. The excess calcium entry has another consequence. A lot of calcium is toxic to cells—it can even kill them. That's a major way that lack of oxygen kills cells, in the hours following a stroke, by opening up the NMDA channels and allowing calcium in. So overstimulating NMDA receptors may damage neurons in the long run, one reason that repeated seizures may be bad for you in a way that a single seizure isn't.

Seizures that are repeated might also tap into a repetition mechanism that the brain uses to make weak memories more secure, to promote their retention in the long run. Repetitions, as in a child practicing handwriting, are what distinguish procedural memories from episodic ones. It's why you remember a new name better if you repeat it aloud after being introduced to someone.

"So the brain might beef up an episodic memory by automatically recalling it a few times while it's fresh?"

For example, your hippocampus could trigger your cortex to run through some of its recent routines, and thereby solidify them. This refresher course might never reach the level of any conscious awareness, although I can imagine it showing up as a nighttime dream.

"Trigger? How so?"

Just imagine the hippocampus playing back a partial spatiotemporal pattern to the cortex—maybe a fragment of something from the previous week. If the cortex resonates to that pattern and isn't busy doing something else, then it might wind up filling in the complete spatiotemporal pattern—rather in the way that, upon hearing the first few notes of a melody, we can fill in the rest of the stanza. I'm just guessing now, but hippocampal priming is a way that the cortical pattern could be repeatedly exercised, and perhaps increasingly embedded into the synaptic strengths—just as procedural memories are probably created, without hippocampal help.

"So that's why the hippocampus is essential for creating new episodic memories but isn't essential for creating procedural-type memories? One part of the brain is just rehearsing another, to get the episodic stuff embedded?"

That's how I piece together the present-day evidence—but it's surely not the only important thing the hippocampus is doing. One of the nice features of such a model is that rehearsal occurs when the cortex is not otherwise occupied, which provides an important role for sleep in the scheme of things; we've long wondered why lack of sleep interferes with memory consolidation.

"You mean there's finally a reply to that child's unanswerable question, 'Daddy, why do I sleep?'"

Not so far, but you can see some testable ideas starting to appear—it's another one of those "tune-in-next-year" topics.

The sequential episode—your memory of a car accident, or of a snatch of conversation you overheard—is a hard case for memory mechanisms, since it doesn't repeat, and so it may need the offline rehearsal more than the other types of memories. The sequential episode may be difficult, but it's not impossible. Indeed, language is all about constructing unique sequences, and so is planning ahead for tomorrow. We humans do those things better than the other primates, so I'd expect to see a brain specialization for handling the episodic sequence.

chapter 9

What's Up Front

THE ROUND-THE-CLOCK EEG monitoring had resolved George's doubts about whether the frontal lobe might be contributing to the beginnings of Neil's seizures. So George finally made the decision to offer the temporal lobe operation to Neil, and Neil was quite relieved—so relieved he plunged ahead in his brain reading and discovered that something was missing.

Piecing together a picture of how the brain works was beginning to intrigue him, as I discovered the next time we met in the cafeteria. He was in rare good form for a little verbal fencing.

"This is like the killer crossword puzzle on Sunday," he reported in mock despair. "Clues everywhere. Even some intersecting words, already. But where's the *real me?*"

A question that's been puzzling philosophers for at least 2,500 years, and you expect an answer after only half a book? If the problem were that easy, someone would have solved it long ago.

"You don't get off that easy. You still haven't said where the executive suite is. Just a lot of departments that don't always work so well. How do I—you know, *Neil*—make those decisions about what to do next? Why do I say *this* rather than *that?* Who's running this show, anyway?" he said, tapping his head.

A collective of "intelligences"? The self that "emerges" from the parts? You're permitted to fill in your favorite platitude temporarily, because science hasn't provided a firm answer yet. But seriously, don't expect an executive suite or a chain of command.

For a century, we've been searching for places in the brain that are absolutely central to that higher-order consciousness involved with deciding what to say next, or planning for tomorrow. I didn't save up those places for a grand finale. There simply aren't any.

More than a century of careful neurology, and no stroke or tumor patient has shown up with such a devastating executive disorder, localized to a particular place. Sure, there are lots of disturbances of decision making, but no one site. You have to lose lots of frontal lobe, or lots of language cortex.

While there isn't a special site, I like to think that there is an executive *function*—what you might call "The Narrator." It's always telling itself stories, construing what's happened so far, or speculating about what might happen next. Analyzing the past, forecasting the future. The narrator function can probably be performed by many regions of cerebral cortex, often in some sort of committee fashion.

"But I don't feel like a committee. Well, maybe while I'm fixing breakfast, feeding the dog, getting the kids off to school, reading the newspaper while keeping one eye on the stove, and listening to the radio. But there are times, I assure you, when I have a *unity of purpose,* all focused on asking you just the right question."

I'd say that is because there's a winner, one story made up by your brain that won out in a competition, against some other made-up candidates, for what to say next. The also-rans are the subconscious— we see similar not-very-good candidates every night in our dreams when good-enough criteria have been relaxed. Your unity of consciousness is because there is only one winner at a given time. When you move on to think about something else a few seconds later, you're probably using a somewhat different area of cerebral cortex: it now dominates the competitors.

"This is beginning to sound like some kind of war in the Balkans. You mean that the real me is just—what's that word—*hegemony?* The current winner that can temporarily dominate over all the other warring factions? Juggle them somehow, but seldom eliminate them?"

That's the best model we have, at least for creating a new idea, speaking a sentence that you've never spoken before. After all, the darwinian process—variations, followed by selective survival and reproduction, repeated many times—nicely explains how new animal species arise over a timescale of millennia. And how your immune system creates better and better antibodies in response to a new foreign molecule during the course of several weeks. We know a lot about how fancy results can emerge from those simple-minded darwinian processes, repeated over and over.

Your mind probably goes through the same darwinian process when creating a novel sentence to speak or deciding what to buy for dinner tonight. In other words, a competition between different possible candidates that shapes up a better and better sentence on a timescale of milliseconds to minutes. Usually within a second or two, enough generations have passed so that you consider it good enough to let out of your mouth.

"So it's a *process* and not a *place?*"

Yes, and it needs to be a process that produces something useful in only a second or two. Individual neurons work in milliseconds, a thousand times faster. So perhaps it can, with time for a few generations in which the spatiotemporal patterns can evolve, shape up new

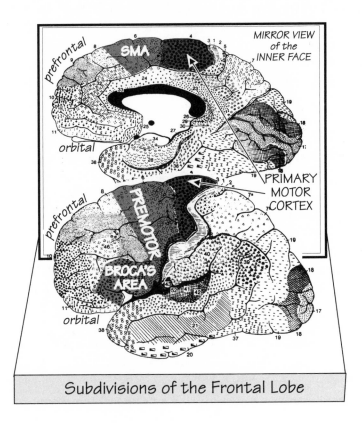

Subdivisions of the Frontal Lobe

mental images within the time frame on which our narrators seem to function. Maybe even shape up mental images that guess what might happen next, forecast the future.

THE FRONTAL LOBE is where forecasting-the-future abilities might be housed, since that's where movement planning seems to be. And the motor strip is part of the frontal lobe, forming its rear border with the parietal lobe.

Just in front of the motor strip is another "premotor" strip, all movement related. Broca's area (or its parallel structure on the right) is at the bottom, the premotor cortex lies in the middle of the band, and the supplementary motor area starts near the top in the view from the side and continues down on the midline face of the hemisphere until stopping before the cingulate gyrus.

But the functional map in this premotor strip does not parallel the head-to-hand-to-foot sequence of the motor strip. There are multiple maps of the body in this band, with the arm in front of the leg in each case. The left premotor cortex has the reputation of controlling both sides of the body to a much greater extent than the right premotor does. The premotor cortex has extensive connections to the parietal lobe and all its egocentric neurons, as well as to the thalamus (and

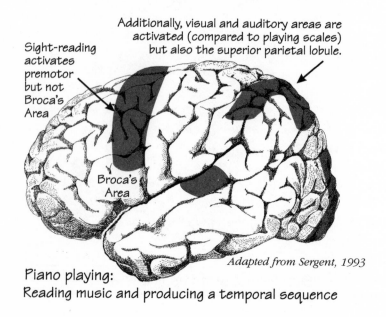

Sight-reading activates premotor but not Broca's Area

Additionally, visual and auditory areas are activated (compared to playing scales) but also the superior parietal lobule.

Broca's Area

Adapted from Sergent, 1993

Piano playing:
Reading music and producing a temporal sequence

thus the basal ganglia, another major component of the movement-control system), that the motor strip doesn't.

When brain activity imaging is done on someone who is mentally rehearsing finger movements (but not actually moving), the supplementary motor area appears to work harder than the rest of the brain. As I mentioned before, Broca's area plays a role in holding onto telephone numbers until they can be dialed. When playing the piano (and sight-reading music), the premotor cortex (and posterior parietal) is working hard, compared to just playing scales.

The neuropsychologist Alexander R. Luria discovered a number of the more subtle aspects of movement planning when dealing with Soviet soldiers injured during World War II. Premotor problems show up, not in individual movements like putting a key in a lock, but in sequences of actions, as when you turn the key, rotate the doorknob, and finally push open the door. Patients with damage to the left premotor cortex have trouble chaining the actions together into a fluent motion, what Luria called a kinetic melody.

To tap your fingers rapidly is a typical request made by a neurologist who wants to check out premotor performance, as speed requires a lot of coordination of the movement commands. Patients with premotor problems may not be able to easily change from one rhythm to another. If asked to draw a sawtooth line but then change it to a wavy snake, the patient may be able to do each pattern separately, but not switch back and forth between patterns. The premotor cortex is all about chaining movements together, and musicians make much use of it when sight-reading, as they have to produce an unfamiliar sequence of hand and finger movements.

The prefrontal cortex is in front of that premotor strip of Broca's, premotor, and supplementary motor areas. Humans have a lot of prefrontal cortex, compared to dolphins, whose motor strip is far forward in the brain. Prefrontal cortex has a lot to do with maintaining a mental image of something in its temporary absence; monkeys with prefrontal removals will have trouble remembering where they saw their keeper hide food if they're forced to wait more than a few minutes before being allowed out of their cage to retrieve it.

Another prefrontal function noted by Luria is contingencies. Suppose that a prefrontal patient is in bed with his arms under the covers and you ask him to raise his arm. He doesn't seem able to do so. But if you ask him to remove his arm from under the covers, he can do that. If you then ask him to raise his arm up and down in the air, he does it all correctly and smoothly.

So in prefrontal problems, there is no motor-strip-like paralysis, and no difficulty with stringing together the modular movements, as the premotor cortex does for musical performance. There's just a difficulty in planning the overall sequence, as in getting stuck on the condition of working around the obstacle of the confining bedcovers. Contingency planning, which unfolds a proper sequence of actions, is part of the role of the prefrontal cortex. At its worst, the loss of this ability after major frontal lobe damage shows up as "perseveration," continually repeating the same action over and over again, apparently unable to shift to a new movement pattern.

THE FRONTAL LOBE is about the closest thing to an executive department in the human brain. Yet it has many reciprocal connections to the temporal lobe and the parietal lobe, big pipelines through the white matter. They're so extensive that a better analogy might be to the three lobes as an executive committee.

"A troika, as the Russians might say? Leaving the occipital lobe as the only part of cerebral cortex not involved in the executive?"

Touché. And that's not the only problem. Figuring out frontal lobe functions has been quite difficult. Small strokes of frontal lobe seldom come to the attention of neurologists. The symptoms are so ill defined that patients may not seek medical attention. Head injuries often produce diffuse injuries with disorderly symptoms—often these patients merely cannot plan ahead very well. Tumors of frontal lobe often grow so slowly that the functional problems are assumed to be part of aging or of a mild mental illness.

One classic story is about Wilder Penfield's sister. He operated on her for a rather large right frontal lobe tumor. Apparently she had been one of those cooks who could spend four hours preparing a five-course Christmas meal and have everything ready to come off the burner or out of the oven just when it was needed. But she lost this ability. A family dinner distressed and confused her because she could no longer get properly organized.

"She couldn't plan ahead anymore?"

Or she couldn't maintain the plan "in mind" or couldn't monitor its progress. There's a fascinating study of patients who had epilepsy operations on the frontal lobe because of cysts or tumors there. All the neurologists did was to ask them to count a series of clicks or taps on a finger. If they presented them at a slow rate, once per second, the patients couldn't count them very well, but they did fine if the presentation rate was much faster. It's totally counterintuitive. Once per second seems to require vigilance, while seven per second doesn't. And vigilance uses the right frontal lobe, up in front of the motor strip for the left arm.

Or Penfield's sister might have had an ability to make plans but couldn't make up her mind about which alternative was best. The neurologists talk about an accountant with a large tumor involving the base of his frontal lobes. Six years after the operation that removed the tumor, this guy exhibited a high IQ and did quite well on a battery of neuropsychological tests. Yet he had big problems in organizing his life—got fired from a series of jobs, went bankrupt, had two divorces in two years.

He was often unable to make simple, rapid decisions about what toothpaste to buy or what to wear. He would instead become stuck making endless comparisons and contrasts, often making no decision at all or a purely random one. Relatively simple decisions could take hours. Going out for dinner required that he consider the seating plan, menu, atmosphere, and management of each possible restaurant. He'd even drive by them to see how busy they were, yet continue to be indecisive, unable to come to a decision about where to eat dinner.

"He sounds compulsive. Like those people who keep washing their hands over and over. Compulsive contemplation."

That same region his tumor damaged—the base of both frontal lobes—sometimes lights up in the brain imaging of the people with obsessive-compulsive disorder, although other evidence suggests that their trouble may lie primarily in the basal ganglia.

"So what's the difference between obsessions and compulsions?"

Thoughts versus actions—it's probably all the same disorder, but the splitters won out over the lumpers. The common obsessions are recurrent, persistent thoughts that seem intrusive and senseless, such as excessive concern over dirt, germs, and toxins. Or thinking that something terrible is about to happen. Or perhaps an obsession with symmetry, order, or exactness.

The compulsions are repetitive, purposeful behaviors that the person knows are really not necessary—such as rechecking to see that the door is locked when you've just done it ten minutes earlier, and ten minutes before that as well. Sometimes compulsions are in response to an obsession, sometimes they just seem to be a preoccupation with rules—such as counting to four, over and over again. And we're now starting to recognize some minor compulsive symptoms, such as in patients who are constantly combing their hair.

Fortunately, three of the many antidepressant drugs turn out to be effective for many of those people (they even work for some pets that constantly lick themselves). The effective drugs differ from the antidepressants that are ineffective for obsessive-compulsive disorder in only minor ways, sometimes just a single atom in the whole molecule.

"I don't think I've ever met a full-blown compulsive. Although we're always kidding our accountant, it doesn't sound like he's going to qualify. He *knows* that it's necessary to go through the figures three times, because he's often found errors the second or third time through. Nothing unnecessary about it."

Right. These patients know it's unnecessary—they have insight. The obsessive-compulsives seem to be rare, but that's because they are so secretive—many of them lead secluded lives and never even seek medical help. It now looks as if they are several percent of the population, even more common than epileptics or schizophrenics. With an effective drug treatment available, perhaps more of them will venture out of seclusion.

ADAPTING TO A CHANGING ENVIRONMENT is an everyday problem. Individually, we have to adapt to changed circumstances, such as taking the bus if we can't find a taxi. The frontal lobe has a lot to do with developing strategies for various contingencies, with monitoring the progress of things, and switching to an alternative tactic when necessary.

"Left frontal lobe, right, or both?"

Both. And for a long time, we thought that both frontal lobes had to be damaged before any symptoms occurred. We now know that damage to only one frontal lobe can be detected by certain sensitive neuropsychological tests. One is called the Wisconsin card-sorting task, which requires the patient to sort a special deck of cards into two piles.

"I had that one. All cards with red symbols were supposed to be placed in the right-hand pile, all other colors in the left-hand pile."

But of course the patient has to figure this out from the responses elicited from the neuropsychologist. The patient is not given any specific instruction. He just starts sorting the cards into two piles and the neuropsychologist says *yes* or *no* after each card, depending on whether the correct criterion for sorting was used—in the example, *yes* if a card with a red symbol was placed on the right pile. Patients catch on to the criterion after a short while and soon are hearing a *yes* after each card. But that's not the hard part.

Partway through the deck, the neuropsychologist changes the criterion without any warning. Now it's *yes* if cards with three symbols are placed on the right pile, regardless of color. Since the neuropsychologist doesn't mention that the criterion has changed, the patient's only clue is hearing *no*. Over and over. A normal person soon realizes that the rules have changed and tries another sorting pattern and eventually discovers the new criterion by a string of *yes* responses.

"So that's what was going on. It was rather fun, actually. But maybe that's because I caught on each time she changed signals on me."

The patient with damage to one frontal lobe catches on to the original sorting strategy and gets the string of *yes* answers. But, when the needed strategy changes, he keeps on sorting the cards the way he started out, red on right, despite the string of *no* answers that this elicits. He seems unable to adapt his behavior to the new game. So it's the same problem as in Luria's patients, an inability to adapt behavior to contingencies.

"So I guess I passed the test."

With more extensive damage the ability to abstract is lost. Neurologists often test this by asking patients to explain proverbs: "What does it mean when I say, 'People who live in glass houses shouldn't throw stones'?" After frontal damage, the patient may just paraphrase the proverb. With more extensive damage he will just repeat the proverb—one example of what is called concrete thinking. As frontal lobe function deteriorates further, the patient repeats actions over and over. We call that perseveration. And ultimately, he may become an akinetic mute, just sitting there awake, but not doing or saying anything.

"Sounds like a little problem in those selective attention circuits you told me about, a while back."

Certainly this frontal lobe role in adaptive behavior is linked to the mechanisms of selective attention. The interaction back and forth between frontal cortex and thalamus selects from those sensations that are germane to the individual's present situation and plans. Thalamic activity increases the probability that the significant sensory cues will be retained in memory, becoming part of "conscious experience." Failure in this frontal-thalamic link accounts for loss of interest in the surroundings after frontal lobe damage. The inner and under surfaces of the frontal lobe seem to be particularly important to this link; extensive damage there is most likely to lead to that akinetic mute state.

"Sounds like depression to me. But when I'm depressed, it's not lack of interest, but a black pit, a real emotional change that I can't seem to control. Is that frontal lobe?"

One PET study showed decreased metabolic activity in the frontal lobes during depression, particularly in the left one, but whether that's cause or effect isn't known. Patients with frontal lobe damage also show a reduction in emotional responsiveness. George tells the story of a patient named Tom with a large tumor pressing on the inner sides of both frontal lobes. Not only had he lost interest in his former activities and surroundings and had signs of concrete thinking and perseveration, but he had lost much of his emotional responsiveness. He didn't care about the effects of his behavior on his surroundings or on the people about him. Nor did he show any emotion when George told him about the tumor and that he'd need a major operation. Fortunately, George says the operation went well, with the tumor completely removed. Tom is apparently back to his old self now, including showing emotions.

"What about sociopaths? They sure show little concern over how much they distress others."

Ah, yes—what in the nineteenth century was called "moral insanity." They're now called people with antisocial personality disorder—but sociopathic personality and psychopathic personality are still common names. They're estimated to include about 3 to 5 percent of men and 1 percent of women—and that's by a definition that requires that the behaviors have been present in youth as well as adulthood.

There are reports that some of these people don't have the same autonomic reactions to disturbing pictures that normal people do. The areas of brain where damage alters emotional responsiveness also are concerned with visceral function: regulation of heart rate, blood pressure, respiration, digestive activity, and level of various hormones. As George likes to say, there really is a relation between emotion and butterflies in the stomach.

"Gut feelings?"

We even know one place they're likely to come from—which is important, because that makes it a possible site for psychosomatic diseases. This link between emotion and visceral function is present at several levels in the brain and provides a basis for identifying the most emotionally responsive parts. But the overlap of frontal lobe sites for emotion and visceral function is particularly promising because of the link to the higher cognitive processes—spinning all those *what-if* scenarios that contribute to anxiety, worry, and suffering.

Regulation of visceral functions depends on two systems. One is called the sympathetic nervous system. It prepares the body for fight or flight, raising the heart rate and the blood pressure, making your hair stand on end—and decreasing digestive activity, since its blood flow is needed elsewhere. The parasympathetic nervous system does the reverse, preparing the body for more vegetative activities.

The head offices for these two systems are located in the hypothalamus, the piece of brain immediately below the thalamus and just above the pituitary gland. The hypothalamus really is the head office for regulating visceral functions, not only through the sympathetic and parasympathetic pathways but also by regulation of hormones, through its control of the pituitary gland activity.

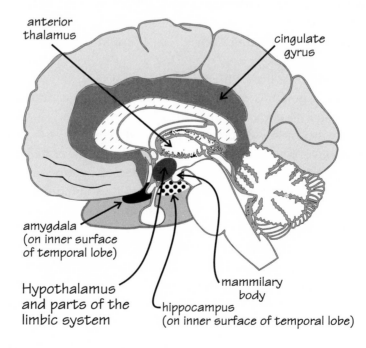

Damaging the hypothalamus in experimental animals not only disturbs the regulation of their visceral functions, but alters their emotional responsiveness. When a small area of the outer part of the hypothalamus is destroyed, cats change from being easily handled to responding with blind rage to all contact. Cats with damage a few millimeters away, in inner parts of the hypothalamus, never show rage. They become placid and fat.

There are a few patients with tumors or small strokes in the different parts of the hypothalamus who had the same types of symptoms. The hypothalamus is also a major site where electrical stimulation seems to produce quite pleasurable feelings. Given a choice of food, water, sex, and a bar to press, animals will press the stimulating bar to exhaustion.

"So 'mean and lean' and 'fat and happy' might be due to what kind of hypothalamus you have. Isn't that what's supposed to be different in the brains of homosexuals?"

There's one report of a difference in the size of one of the clusters of nerve cells in the hypothalamus, known as AH3. In that report, male homosexuals have the cluster size that's associated with normal females, at least in this one region. A difference in the hypothalamus would not be totally surprising, though, since it has a major role in regulation of levels of the various sex hormones throughout life. But no one knows yet whether this is cause—as everyone seems to assume—or effect. It could be the atrophy of the unused.

"Well, I can see how differences in function of the hypothalamus can change a person's emotions," Neil said. "But isn't the cortex the real boss when it comes to emotions?"

At least the more integrated emotional behaviors—hypothalamic behaviors are pretty raw and unrefined. At the hypothalamic level, emotions of rage and pleasure are little altered by any environmental stimuli. It's at the cortical level where that interaction between environment and emotions seems to occur.

The primary areas where emotional expression and visceral functions can be altered by damage or electrical stimulation are the inner surfaces of the frontal and temporal lobes. These areas have connections with the hypothalamus; together they are called the limbic system. Extensive damage to the temporal lobe portion of the limbic system on both left and right sides can lead an animal to be more likely to respond to any environmental stimulus with rage. The same thing is seen in some patients with such bilateral damage. Damage to the frontal lobe portion of the limbic system leads to placidity and indifference—as in George's patient, Tom.

"So emotionally, the real me is in my hypothalamus and limbic cortex?"

There's more. Wide areas of cortex interact with the limbic system. The mix of emotional character and thought that results is our personality. The right temporal lobe discerns the emotional coloration of faces, and emotions are more expressed on the left side of the face. Laughing and smiling, unlike other sequential face movements, are more readily disturbed from the right brain than the left. And, of course, injuries to the temporal lobe can cause someone's personality to change.

"In what way?"

On Saturday morning neurosurgery rounds, I once saw a man with a head injury. The nurses had posted a handwritten sign on the door to his room: "Do not give this patient matches!" He had been mischievously lighting matches and throwing them around the room. Nothing lethargic about this guy. He didn't want to be in the hospital. He was bright-eyed, aggressive with the docs, teasing the nurses, and generally acting like a sailor in port, looking for a good time. If he could have walked, it would have been with a swagger—however, his leg was injured also.

The next Saturday, there was another temporal lobe contusion patient. This man was meek, most hesitant in his dealings with the staff, usually averting his gaze when talking with someone—totally different from last week's patient. I didn't realize, until we were talking about him afterward in the hallway, that this was the very same patient I'd seen the previous week.

"But which was his real personality?"

The second one. His family had been rather perplexed at the fun-loving sailor. Which warned the neurosurgeons that the temporal lobe's limbic circuits were probably getting injured by brain swelling. And that they needed to do something quickly to shrink the brain a little. That usually means giving diuretics and the like, to reduce the amount of water in the uninjured regions of the brain. You can sometimes "buy time" that way.

"Good thing he didn't walk out of the hospital. God knows what he would have gotten into."

Into a coma, most likely. And an even more serious brain injury. I have a feeling that the chief resident decided that this patient's minor leg injury required an extra-large cast. As an anchor. The cast was certainly gone at the time of my second visit. I don't even remember seeing bandages on the leg.

Some changes in temporal lobe function may be more permanent. Patients with right temporal lobe epileptic foci are said to have personalities that are more likely to show emotional responsiveness, sexuality, concern for detail, and helplessness. These patients tend to underrate their deficiencies and overrate their abilities.

"Image polishers," observed Neil. "I can hardly wait to hear about left temporal lobe epileptics. But tell me anyway."

Patients with left temporal foci—on average, and not reliably—are said to have somewhat different personalities, at least in some studies. The patient with a left temporal lobe focus more often has a moralistic, religious, rigid, sober, self-deprecating personality, tending to emphasize the personal significance of events, and often writing down all that personal significance in great detail. Both Dostoyevsky and Rasputin are thought to be examples of the left temporal lobe personality.

"That left temporal epileptic personality bit is only half right for me," reflected Neil. "Like most averages, I suppose. Sober, yes. Self-deprecating? My wife would never believe it."

It does give rise to another one of those "I can spot a case of *that* from across the room" stories that doctors like to tell each another. George says he can always diagnose a left temporal focus when, at the first clinic visit, he sees a patient approaching with a thick manuscript describing all his symptoms.

chapter 10

When Things Go Wrong with Thought and Mood

Throughout history, it has been known that melancholics, though they have little energy, use their energy well; they tend to work hard in a focused area, do great things, and derive little pleasure from their accomplishments. Much of the insight and creative achievement of the human race is due to the discontent, guilt, and critical eye of [melancholics].

The psychiatrist PETER D. KRAMER, 1993

In a sense depression is a view of the world through a glass darkly, and mania is a shattered pattern of views seen through a prism or kaleido-scope: often brilliant but generally fractured. Where depression questions, ruminates, and is tentative, mania answers with vigor and certainty. The constant transitions in and out of the constricted and then expansive thoughts, subdued and then violent responses, grim and then ebullient moods, withdrawn from and then involving relationships, cold and then fiery states—and the rapidity and fluidity of moves across and into such contrasting experiences—can be painful and confusing. Such chaos, in those able ultimately to transcend it or shape it to their will, can, however, result in an artistically useful comfort with transitions, an ease with ambiguities and with life on the edge, and an intuitive awareness of the coexisting and oppositional forces at work in the world. The weaving together of these contrasting experiences from a core and rhythmic brokenness is one that is crucial to both the artistic and manic-depressive experience.

The psychologist KAY REDFIELD JAMISON, 1993

TRUSTING WHAT YOU SEE AND HEAR isn't just a matter of judging the reliability of other people. For some patients, "Did it really happen?" refers to the sensation itself—was it real or imagined? I hadn't wanted to bring up Neil's hallucinations so soon after we discussed the important issues of muffins versus scones, latté versus cappuccino—but Neil reminded me of that odor of burning rubber that sometimes preceded his seizures.

"And, of course, no one else smells it. Are hallucinations always a sign of schizophrenia or temporal lobe epilepsy? I'd always thought," he added, "at least, until my neurologist straightened me out on the matter, that hallucinations were what defined schizophrenia—which had me more than a little worried."

According to the picture that is emerging of post-traumatic stress disorders, hallucinations are not even necessarily a sign of a serious mental illness. Quite a few people have probably had an occasional hallucination—for example, after the death of a pet dog or a close relative. And stress disorders are surprisingly common, what with people and pets dying, car accidents, burglaries, divorces, and the like.

A San Francisco psychiatrist, Mardi Horowitz, likes to tell the story of his quickest diagnosis and course of therapy, five minutes start to finish. Over the years, he tended to have conversations with an elderly neighbor over the back fence, often about this guy's hip replacement or his prostate troubles or his cataract surgery. But this time, the neighbor happened to mention his handgun.

This seemed out of character, so the psychiatrist gently asked, "Are you having thoughts of suicide?"

The neighbor said that he could put up with all those medical problems of the past, but he wasn't going to let his mind go, not without doing something about it while he still could.

The psychiatrist asked, What sorts of new problems?

Hallucinations. He keeps seeing his dog (who died of old age three months earlier) out of the corner of his eye, sometimes hears her bark.

The psychiatrist replied that he'd bet it happened most often about the time of day that the dog had been fed.

Er, yes.

The psychiatrist explained that people who are grieving often suffer hallucinations. [That's presumably why the word *ghost* had to be added to our dictionary—because so many people have shared a similar experience.]

The neighbor thought he was being humored. So the psychiatrist asked if he'd believe it if he saw it written in a book. Well, maybe. And so the psychiatrist went into his house and returned to the backyard fence with the textbook and showed it to the neighbor.

Yes, said the neighbor after reading the page—but those are *people* they're hallucinating—dead wives and husbands and children. This is a *dog* I'm hearing.

Well, the dog meant a lot more to you than most people, right?

Psychiatrist recommended a new dog. Neighbor got new dog, lived happily ever after.

"Let's aim for one of those 'lives happily ever afters' for my story," Neil said, amused but serious.

And then he continued. "From what you've told me, I gather that hallucinations don't necessarily mean an 'organic' psychiatric illness. Does this mean that they can be a mind problem, rather than a brain problem? So what psychiatric disorders are brain problems?"

Ahem. All psychiatric problems are brain problems, and the psychiatrists are changing their classification scheme to try and avoid that cartesian dichotomy. *Organic* has tended to mean obvious damage of some sort, producing psychiatric symptoms. As from head injuries, strokes, and tumors.

But it doesn't have to be easily visible damage produced in reaction to something external to the brain. Focal degeneration is sometimes seen—Maurice Ravel's inability to compose during the last four years of his life is thought to have been due to a degeneration of cortex in the lower part of his left parietal lobe. And, of course, degeneration includes Alzheimer's dementia, the most common organic disorder, 4 million cases in the United States alone due to more widespread degeneration of the brain.

"That's really brain rot?" Neil asked.

Well, not the whole brain, but crucial parts of it. Alzheimer's disease is a condition in which neurons wither up and die, often in the cortex along the inner side of the temporal lobe, such as in the hippocampus. Initially the result is a loss of recent memory, but it's followed by loss of other functions as the degeneration extends to other brain circuits. They lose long-ago memories as well as failing to store new memories. Eventually even vocabulary and skills are lost—they'll fail to recognize a knife and know what it's used for. The degeneration is associated with the accumulation of an abnormal protein, amyloid, in a characteristic pattern called senile plaques, although the cause of the Alzheimer's degeneration is unknown.

You can also get brain damage from substance abuse, such as all those cases of instant, and permanent, Parkinson's disease in young people who took the street drug MPTP. Adolf Hitler abused psychostimulants for years, and some psychiatrists think that an organic delusional syndrome might have caused his delusions of grandeur and persecution. Sometimes delusions persist long after amphetamine abuse ceases.

"I've always wondered about whether there's an organic cause for arsonists," Neil said. "Not the professional arsonists—but the ones who like the thrill of it all."

Those serial arsonists are a surprisingly well-defined group of people—and yes, there's some evidence of an organic basis for their behavior. To everyone's surprise, they're not psychotic—in other words, they don't have delusions and hallucinations. They're nearly all male—and alcoholics. They seem to have a more general disorder with serotonin and blood sugars. They're generally coming off a binge when their blood glucose levels plunge and their brain serotonin levels change. In this state, they seek excitement by setting fires.

"Sounds like mania."

No, they don't share most of the other symptoms experienced by the people with mania. Fitting the same syndrome as the impulsive fire-setters, however, are those who impulsively attempt to kill someone.

"What do you mean by impulsive? No obvious premeditation?"

When the police said that the victim was unknown to the assailant and didn't do anything to provoke the attack. Furthermore, the police couldn't see that a robbery motive was involved. These people are also at risk of doing violence to themselves, many of them once having been hospitalized after attempting suicide. And they aren't characteristically violent, or setting fires, while in prison—where alcohol is generally unavailable.

The manslaughter-or-arson disorder, whatever you want to call it, doesn't fit very well into our usual subdivisions—few of them, for example, fit the usual diagnostic criteria for major depressions, despite all those suicide attempts. It could easily be a metabolic disorder involving some of those lawn-sprinkler neurotransmitters such as serotonin.

"So is this a thought disorder? A mood disorder? I'm confused."

You're not alone—it's hard to tell how they'll classify it. Mood disorders such as mania and depression involve inappropriate emotional responses. Thought disorders involve inappropriate thoughts. Schizophrenia, delusional disorder, and a few minor ones constitute the thought disorders—but let's stick to mania for a minute.

In mania, you see excessive excitement and a lot of impulsive behaviors, but when the mania is mild, such people can be very energetic and get a lot done. Still, they get into trouble from hypersexuality, inappropriate laughing and joking, buying sprees, and reckless driving. They tend to get disorganized as the mania increases, and even more prone to poor judgment. Their speech becomes pressured and they may answer questions at great length. They sometimes even keep talking after their audience has fled the room. Virginia Woolf, when becoming manic, would talk almost without stopping for two or three days. For the first day, she made some sense, but by the third day she was totally incoherent. That's back before lithium salts as a treatment for mania; schizophrenia and mania used to be confused with each other, especially in the United States, until the response to lithium treatment served to better define the two patient populations.

The euphoria and the sometimes infectious cheerfulness of mania is confusing, but the psychiatrist can usually tell manic euphoria from a genuine "good mood" by other symptoms that are clearly pathological, such as uncharacteristically poor judgment and extreme grandiosity.

And, of course, mania usually alternates with depression, to form a bipolar disorder. Mania's association with depression was first noted 1,800 years ago. The bipolar patients are not continuously abnormal, being quite functional in the periods in between their manic and depressive phases—indeed, they may get a lot done. But there is a lot of alcoholism and drug abuse associated with manic-depressive illness.

More often, depression comes by itself. Depressed people sleep poorly (or too much) and feel fatigued, they get little pleasure out of daily activities, they have difficulty concentrating, and they may feel worthless or guilty. A depressed mood might be an appropriate emotion after death of a loved one, but not as a response to the only sunny day of the month in Seattle.

Depression can be very profound, preventing the patient from doing any activity and with a significant risk of suicide. The lifetime rate for attempted suicide in individuals with no history of mental disorder is 1 percent, but for the depressed it is 18 percent, going up to 24 percent in manic-depressives. And 70 to 90 percent of all suicides seem to be in people with mood disorders.

"Depression is what they used to call melancholy?"

That's the Hippocratic name for it, 2,500 years ago, and Aristotle thought that "those who have become eminent in philosophy, politics, poetry, and the arts have all had tendencies toward melancholia." But mood disorders can be traced back 10,000 years to King Saul in the Old Testament book of Samuel. Saul developed periods of severe depression, guilt, and incapacity; later he became psychotic and attempted to kill his son Jonathan along with David, nemesis of Goliath.

"Hamlet?"

There are lots of examples—St. Augustine, John Keats, William James, Leo Tolstoy, Ernest Hemingway, Sylvia Plath, John Berryman, Ann Sexton, Winston Churchill—quite a few politicians, actually. Poets seem to have the highest rates of mood disorders and suicide. The psychiatrist Nancy Andreasen, who started out as a professor of English literature, did a study of creative writers using modern psychiatric criteria for schizophrenia that showed that the writers had three times the expected rate of mood disorders, and none had schizophrenia; their parents and siblings also had the same rate of mood disorders. Other studies show artists, poets, and writers with eight to ten times the major depression rate for the general population and ten to forty times the rate for manic-depressive illness and its milder variants. So perhaps Aristotle was right.

"So are there really more depressed women than men?"

About twice as many, for depression by itself. But manic-depressive illness is an equal-opportunity disease.

Mood disorders and schizophrenia are relatively common. About 4 percent of the population is suffering from depression at any one time, with about 10 to 20 percent of the general population experiencing an episode sometime during their life. Schizophrenia has a lifetime prevalence between 1 and 2 percent, with about a tenth of the schizophrenics in the hospital at any one time and many of the rest unemployable—so it's expensive, something like $73 billion annually in the United States alone.

INHERITANCE HAS A LOT TO DO with both schizophrenia and mood disorders. A major way to sort out environmental influences from biological ones is through the study of twins separated at birth by adoption into separate homes. If one identical twin has schizophrenia, there's about a 50 percent chance that, when the other twin is located, he too will be schizophrenic. For fraternal twins, the chances are only those of siblings in general—about one in six. The incidence of schizophrenia in the adoptive parents has little influence. The data is similar, though not as strong, for mood disorders.

However, a genetic predisposition does not seem to be the only factor that accounts for these disorders. Even with the identical genetic makeups of identical twins, about half of the identical twins of schizophrenics never develop the disease. So the environment, the accidents of upbringing and exposure to viruses, make the difference between having the genetic predisposition and actually coming down with the disease.

The importance of some environmental factor in these illnesses is particularly apparent for mood disorders, because something seems to have changed after about 1940. Most of the people who are going to get a manic-depressive disorder will have gotten it by age 30, if they were born after 1940. But for people who were born before 1940, it took several decades more to develop. Relatives of patients with mood disorders born after 1940 are also more likely to have the illness than relatives born before that date.

The environmental factor is unknown. One way of looking at these disorders is that they change the way the brain responds to novel environmental cues and are thus less evident in a stable environment.

"Which our current times certainly are not," Neil added.

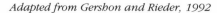

Adapted from Gershon and Rieder, 1992

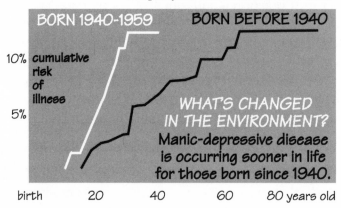

The first clinical episode, in both the thought and the mood disorders, often occurs in adolescence. It may appear suddenly, seemingly triggered by an inconsequential event. Both thought and mood disorders tend to wax and wane during life, with episodes becoming more frequent as the patient gets older. Schizophrenics usually do not recover completely between episodes, while those with mood disorders often function entirely normally in the intervals between exacerbations. However, patients with either type of illness can lead productive lives.

One of these days, we'll consider them organic psychiatric disorders but, despite extensive research, the brain abnormalities in both disorders are not completely known. In each type, abnormalities seem to be present in multiple brain areas, suggesting that the defect is in a broadly-based brain system—such as those lawn-sprinkler systems using serotonin and norepi coming up from the brain stem— rather than a specific anatomic area. Moreover, the most effective drug treatments for each disorder tend to affect systems of nerve cells that use particular transmitters. For mood disorders, it's the neurons that use norepinephrine, dopamine, and serotonin (collectively called the monoamines) as neurotransmitters. For schizophrenia, the effective drugs relate to neurons that use dopamine and glutamate.

Or maybe the problem is in neurons downstream from them. There are many different postsynaptic receptor types for each of the neurotransmitters, such as those ordinary and NMDA receptors for glutamate. The same key fits several locks, in other words. And only some of the receptor types seem to be involved in the disease. In mood disorders, effective drug therapies seem to alter a class of receptors that are linked to a specific substance in the cell's cyclic adenosine monophosphate, decreasing the amounts of that intracellular "second messenger." In schizophrenia, the balance between nerve cells using dopamine as a transmitter and those using glutamate may be the important factor, with excessive dopamine levels or inadequate glutamate levels the likely problem.

Although these abnormalities in systems of nerve cells using specific transmitters have effects throughout the brain, different parts seem to be more affected in one type of disorder. Temporal lobe abnormalities seem to particularly characterize schizophrenia. More patients have both schizophrenia and temporal lobe epilepsy than would be expected by chance, although most patients with temporal lobe epilepsy are otherwise normal.

"So you can operate on the temporal lobe and cure schizophrenia, just as with my type of epilepsy?"

Unfortunately, no. Curing the epilepsy in these patients doesn't help schizophrenic symptoms if they are already present, nor prevent their later appearance. One investigator, however, reported that schizophrenia is more likely in patients whose epilepsy was associated with a specific anatomic change in the temporal lobe, known as "hamartomas." They are little pockets of nerve cells buried in the white matter where they don't belong, evidently because of a developmental misstep during gestation. That finding hasn't been confirmed, but magnetic resonance imaging of patients with schizophrenia alone has shown changes in the temporal lobe—for example, a 20 percent loss in gray matter volume and atrophy of the hippocampus.

Sometimes the hallucinations associated with small seizures in the temporal lobe have characteristics suggestive of schizophrenic thought, especially paranoia. George told me about one such patient of his, who had a paranoid experience upon stimulation of the surface of the temporal lobe.

"I thought you said they didn't operate for paranoia?"

Not by itself—this guy had a brain tumor. He had been referred to a psychiatrist because of increasing suspiciousness and unusual thoughts over the past few months. He even occasionally heard voices talking about him. The psychiatrist thought he "looked organic" and so ordered an MRI. It showed a tumor in the frontal lobe in a very awkward place: close to the motor strip and language areas.

So that operation involved stimulation mapping with the patient awake, similar to the mapping that is needed during epilepsy operations. The operation for this tumor was going very smoothly. The patient had cooperated completely with all the testing, and George had identified the face motor area, as well as the frontal (Broca) language area. The tumor was just between them. Then George applied the stimulating current to the temporal lobe, just below the motor and speech areas.

And the patient unexpectedly said, "I hear people outside talking about me." George chatted with the patient for a moment and went on to test more of the frontal lobe. The patient performed the tests with no other comment—until the temporal lobe site was stimulated again without warning. The patient immediately asked, "Is the radio on? I hear something on it about me." Later the temporal site was stimulated a third time, and again he volunteered that he heard voices saying things about him.

"I remember that you said something about Penfield's patients, that they often reported unidentified voices offstage. If that's the most common kind of experiential response, suppose that the temporal lobe is the scene of the crime in paranoia?"

That's not clear yet. The blood flow to the tip of the temporal lobe does increase in studies of anticipatory anxiety. Usually anxiety doesn't go away when one temporal tip is removed in epileptics—although, if there is any consistent personality change after that operation, it is in the direction of being less anxious.

Actually, contrary to popular belief, hallucinations were not part of the original definition of schizophrenia. Eugen Bleuler, a Swiss psychiatrist of Freud's generation, coined the term. He thought that hallucinations, because they were so often seen in manic-depressive illness, were secondary to his "four *A*s" of schizophrenia that were taught to generations of psychiatrists: affective blunting, association disturbances, autism, and ambivalence (by which he meant indecisiveness). But these days, the criteria for schizophrenia emphasize prominent hallucinations and bizarre delusions.

DELUSIONS are also a thought disorder, as opposed to a disorder of perception. Together, hallucinations and delusions are known as psychotic symptoms.

"And the psychotic symptoms are most commonly seen in schizo-phrenics?"

While they're seen in all schizophrenics, it's actually the people with mood disorders who have more psychotic symptoms. That's why it's important to distinguish between the psychoses—the psychiatric diagnoses, such as manic-depressive illness—and the psychotic *symptoms.*

Only half of the manics and a fifth of the depressed have psychotic symptoms—but mood disorder patients are many times more common in the population than are schizophrenic patients. Needless to say, it sometimes confuses the diagnosis. In any event, if anybody you know has a psychosis, it's more likely to be from a mood disorder than from a thought disorder.

There are also people who primarily have delusions, but none of the functional deterioration and bizarre delusions that characterize schizophrenia or the mood swings that characterize the other major source of delusions. The delusional-disorder patients mostly have delusions—but occasional hallucinations as well. What they *don't* have is the gradual deterioration seen in schizophrenia, which makes the disorder especially devastating.

Delusions are firmly held beliefs that are both untrue *and* contrary to what the patient's culture provides in the way of explanatory metaphors. Thus, magical thinking might be delusional in a college kid from the white suburbs, but it may be just cultural if the patient is a ghetto kid whose parents are from Haiti.

The common delusional-disorder patients are the paranoids, the pathologically jealous, the persons with grandiose delusions about their special relationship to a celebrity such as John Lennon, the people who think they're the devil and are condemned to burn in hell. Some have somatic delusions—maybe they are absolutely sure that some part of their body is shrinking over time.

But people with delusional disorder aren't disorganized the way schizophrenics tend to become. They have well-preserved personali-ties and they have rationalized their symptoms to the point that they have an answer for everything odd they experience. They seldom need hospitalization. And they usually can stay employed.

"Right. As leader of the Third Reich. Or of the Branch Davidians."

Yep. Hitler, David Koresh—they had good sales and leadership skills, in addition to delusions. The delusional can be so sure of themselves, so certain they are special, that they can attract followers who will do almost anything. And with their occasional hallucinations, the delusional may have some interesting visions to report—which, of course, they weave into their well-rationalized explanations of conspiracies afoot and revelations to come.

"So what defines a schizophrenic, then? Their hallucinations and delusions are simply more bizarre?"

Their delusions are indeed more bizarre, such as thoughts being broadcast into their heads or being controlled by men from Mars. But what defines any psychiatric disorder is the *combination* of symptoms and how long they last, not one particular symptom.

It can be terribly confusing on slight acquaintance, as you focus on one symptom, see it in yourself perhaps, and worry. Just think of all those middle-aged people who worry that their "memory problems" constitute a slippery slope into Alzheimer's dementia—not realizing that the folks who are alert and lively at 92 have also been complaining about their difficulty remembering people's names for the last 45 years.

The combination of symptoms that provide the diagnostic criteria for schizophrenia include prominent hallucinations and bizarre delusions for some period of time, not just as a drug reaction. The diagnosis assumes you've ruled out a mood disorder first. And the diagnostic criteria emphasize a deterioration of functioning—in work, social relations, self-care—that isn't seen in the other thought disorders. Both schizophrenia and mood disorders show evidence of decreased activity in frontal lobes and abnormal function of the system for directed attention. Mood disorders also show abnormal function in the hypothalamus, particularly in the regulation of the hormones involved in responses to stress.

THE DEVELOPMENT OF DRUGS altering transmitter levels has allowed many patients with these conditions to function normally, or nearly so. However, a few patients do not respond to drug therapy. In the 1920s, physicians observed that mental patients who also had seizures were, paradoxically, better after a *grand mal* seizure, especially in their mood. This was the basis for electroconvulsive therapy for depression, a treatment valuable in depressed patients not responding to drugs, and which also seems to produce the same changes in neurotransmitter receptors as do many of the effective drugs. Unfortunately, there remain a few patients with severe depression whose symptoms persist despite drugs or electroconvulsive therapy.

"What do you do for them? Surgery?"

That's an option. Psychosurgery is still alive and well after fifty years, although one would think, from popular belief—even among some psychologists, who should know better—that it was some sort of discredited mutilation from a mad-scientist age of psychiatry and neurosurgery. In the mid-1970s, the critics of psychosurgery helped persuade the U.S. Congress to establish the National Commission for the Protection of Human Subjects of Biomedical and Behavioral Research. And to charge it, among other things, with evaluating psychosurgery.

Needless to say, prominent critics of psychosurgery were represented on the commission. But when the commission issued its report in 1976, it turned out to be surprisingly favorable, concluding that the operations were useful in selected cases, provided that the patient is competent to give informed consent. It concluded that legislation wasn't needed after all, that the regulation of psychosurgery could be left to the medical profession. Which goes to show that people shouldn't get their medical information from novelists trying to create dramatic stories about Orwellian nurses dealing with troublemakers.

"So it's still an option for severe depression?"

At least the kind that doesn't respond to drugs and induced seizures. Modern versions of psychosurgery also help with obsessions and phobias, and it seems to have helped some schizophrenics. But the typical psychosurgery patient and typical brain lesion created is illustrated by someone like Edmund.

He was an honor student in his final two years of high school. Nobody noticed anything wrong until he tried to kill himself—except, of course, Edmund himself, who had started noticing something wrong months earlier. Schoolwork wasn't worth doing. Tennis wasn't fun any more—he dropped out of that with an excuse about an injured knee. He didn't have enough energy for anything. He felt he wasn't "good enough" for his girlfriend; he saw her less and less. By the time he took all the sleeping pills, he was sure that life wasn't worth living.

Edmund's psychiatrist started him on one of the newer antidepressant drugs as soon as he recovered from the overdose. That usually works, but for Edmund it didn't—he just felt sleepier. There were therapy sessions with his parents, with his brother and sister, but Edmund continued to feel that he wasn't "worthy" of them.

Eventually, every possible drug having been tried without success, the psychiatrists recommended a series of electroshock treatments to induce seizures. These usually help, but Edmund was again the exception—he continued to feel that the only way to get rid of that awful blackness, the pain and unworthiness, was to die. While being walked around the hospital grounds, he broke away and jumped in front of a speeding car. Luckily, he got out of that with just a broken leg, and while he recuperated, there were more therapy sessions, more drugs, more electroshock. Still, nothing helped. He still felt empty and rotten inside, wanting to die.

Now if our Edmund had lived in Great Britain, the next step would have been referral to a specialty center where psychosurgery is done. Several British centers have reported extensively on their experience with operations that destroy a small region on the inner face of the frontal lobe. This provides complete relief from depression in about half of the patients like Edmund; another third of the patients improve, although they do not get complete relief. In the British experience, the improvement lasts for five years or longer, with side effects in less than 2 percent of the cases.

"Are any of the drugs for depression better than that?" asked Neil.

No. Such modern psychosurgery is certainly an effective treatment for that small group of severely depressed patients like Edmund, who prove, for unknown reasons, to be unresponsive to drugs and electroshock. Despite this favorable British experience with modern psychosurgery, Edmund would probably not be treated with such an operation in the United States—even though there would seem to be no other options except waiting, with its hazard of suicide.

"But why not treat them?"

Because there are still too many people who would question the judgment of the clinicians involved and say that "everyone knows" that psychosurgery is "bad." Nonetheless, the operation does get performed in the United States, but there are still many remaining pockets of ignorance-but-strong-opinion.

The history of prefrontal lobotomies has a great deal to do with political controversy over modern psychosurgical operations. The original operation was also controversial in its day, even though it too marked a major advance for the treatment of the mentally ill and reduced the mortality from suicide. Cutting some of the connections in the white matter running between the front of the frontal lobe ("prefrontal") and the rest of the chimpanzee brain was associated with more docility and placidity. These results were presented by the American neurophysiologist John Fulton at an international physiological meeting in 1935, where they came to the attention of an inventive Portuguese neurologist, Egas Moniz. So Moniz tried the same thing in humans.

This innovation had many effects. The Moniz medical practice was disrupted by demonstrators opposed to psychosurgery. But, for the first time, a treatment was available that allowed some of the severely mentally ill to leave the asylum and return to society. Patients with depression, phobia, and obsessions were helped the most, patients with schizophrenia not as reliably. Indeed, the prefrontal lobotomy was so highly regarded that, in 1949, Moniz (but not Fulton) won the Nobel Prize for Physiology or Medicine.

The medical profession soon recognized that this treatment was imperfect. Although the patients could leave the asylum, they often demonstrated some personality changes. Like George's patient with the big tumor pressing on the inner sides of both frontal lobes, some lobotomized patients were uninterested in their surroundings, as well as unconcerned about the effects of their behavior on others.

About this time, a French naval surgeon by the name of Laborit made an important discovery in the course of using chlorpromazine to treat sailors for worm infections. He noticed that his schizophrenic sailors with worm infections not only lost their worms but that the drug had a side effect: it calmed the mentally disturbed sailors. Now there was an alternative to psychosurgery, and many different drugs affecting dopamine receptors were tried. In animal research, it became apparent that the better a drug bound to the D2 version of the dopamine postsynaptic receptor, the more effective it was therapeutically in schizophrenics. Effectiveness had no relationship to binding to the D1 receptor type.

Schizophrenia wasn't the strong suit for psychosurgery, in any event. And there were still lots of severe cases of depression, obsession, and phobia—so the psychosurgery operation was refined. Essentially, a much smaller lesion works just as well as the earlier ones but has many fewer side effects. In the modern operation, only selected areas are destroyed by using a small probe inserted through a small hole, in exactly the same

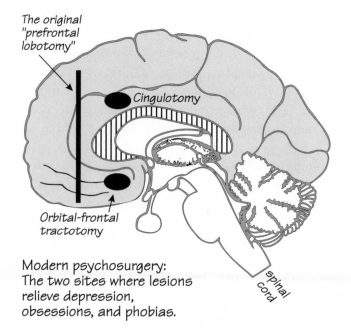

The original
"prefrontal
lobotomy"

Cingulotomy

Orbital-frontal
tractotomy

Modern psychosurgery:
The two sites where lesions
relieve depression,
obsessions, and phobias.

spinal
cord

way as the thalamotomies for Parkinsonism are done—just in a different place. The areas destroyed are on the inner face of the frontal lobe, usually on both left and right sides. In one operation, called a cingulotomy, a portion of the cortex just above the front end of the corpus callosum is destroyed. In the other effective operation, some white matter at the base of the frontal lobes is destroyed instead.

In these modern operations, the change to an "uninterested" personality does not occur. And just as in the original operation, there is great improvement in the symptoms of depression, phobias, and obsessions, with schizophrenia not helped as much. These behavioral improvements occur only if the correct location is destroyed, not if the lesion is made nearby. There seems to be something specific about that portion of the brain for these mental disorders, especially depression, suggesting that the original operation destroyed far more brain tissue than was needed to get the desired relief. That specificity is very important, as one part of the debate over frontal lobotomy was how specific the treatment was.

"Specific? How so?"

Both foot amputations and insulin injections are treatments for diabetes, but only the latter is specific to the disease process. Physicians had worried, quite reasonably, that psychosurgery wasn't specific enough.

"So why all the fuss about lobotomies? Is it just a question of bad press?"

The debate over psychosurgery was clouded by the failure of critics to distinguish between the modern operations, with their more specific criteria for operating on a patient and their infrequent side effects on personality, with the original Moniz operation, which made a much larger cut in the white matter and had the unfortunate side effects. That's like criticizing modern jumbo jets using the crash record of airplanes built in 1936.

Of course, with the development of better drug treatments in psychiatry, the number of patients with persisting illness also decreased to the point that a psychosurgical operation is now warranted only for the very occasional patient, perhaps a few depressed patients in a thousand. But for that rare patient such as Edmund, the operation may be lifesaving. Unsuccessfully treated severe depression is a disease with a mortality rate similar to that of cancer.

CAUSE AND EFFECT IN THE MENTAL DISORDERS isn't a simple matter. Asking *why* someone is depressed, for example, may be relevant if you're dealing with depression following a post-traumatic stress disorder, because it's useful for planning treatment. But what happened before an episode of manic-depressive illness may be quite irrelevant: the cause lies elsewhere, at a different level of brain organization.

"I was getting a little concerned, because we've been talking only about the organic psychiatric problems. I was about to ask you what in psychiatry *isn't* organic?"

A problem doesn't have to be organic to be real. *Organic* just means damage that can be seen in the brain with current neuroanatomical techniques. Probably half or more of psychiatric problems surely aren't organic, at least not at the beginning.

Take the problem commonly seen in treating couples. Both husband and wife are undecided and somewhat ambivalent about having a child, or buying a house. One, for the sake of argument, will indirectly say, "Let's do it." And the other, mistrustful of making a decision just yet will, for a better defensive position, take the opposite stance rather than continuing to sit on the fence.

This artificial creation of opposition, where both are really ambivalent, creates all sorts of trouble as positions harden and the problem festers. The undecided middle ground is where the doubts can be talked out. Going to extremes, however, has a certain amount of stability to it that maintaining the middle ground doesn't. And so once you slip to extreme positions, it can be hard to get out.

All it takes to fall into that trap is a normal brain. But the festering problem may have *effects* on the brain, just as it can elsewhere in the body. Stress reactions are bad for the stomach, leading to ulcers. And, because of the adrenal stress hormones stirred up, it's bad for the brain in the long run. Stress may damage neurons in the hippocampus and set you up for memory problems later—converting a mild psychiatric problem into a rather different organic one.

Both kinds of problems are "real"—and so are those in-between conditions that we have such difficulty labeling, the ones that look like neurological "hardware" problems but which we can't yet see in the neuroanatomy. You don't need to get wrapped up in the nomenclature difficulties to realize that psychotherapy can prevent more serious, expensive problems—such as broken homes.

MANY OF THE ANXIETY PROBLEMS that psychiatrists treat are probably of that same stuck-in-a-rut nature. But not all. And a newly recognized disorder serves to show how one comes to be recognized amid the psychiatric morass.

Sometimes a psychiatrist, having been reminded of seizures or the behavioral tics of Tourette's, will wonder if there is a subgroup of anxiety patients who really are different—the patients who say they have shortness of breath, break out in a sweat, tremble. Or maybe it's flushes and chills accompanied by dizziness. And it happens for no good reason, just all of a sudden.

Yet it lasts for as little as five minutes and seldom as long as a half hour—it's not a fluctuating problem like most anxiety and most headaches. So it's really an episodic thing, like seizures and tics, but involving autonomic symptoms.

And then he remembers that these are things that the base of the frontal lobe might regulate. The psychiatrist asks herself, Could "panic attacks" be the medium-sized seizures of that part of brain? Or the *petit mal* of the more visceral parts of the thalamus? Or tics without the rest of Tourette's?

"Are they?"

Ask next year. It's another of your unfinished crossword puzzles. Certainly about ten percent of the population has suffered at least one panic attack. Two to three percent of women suffer from recurrent panic attacks, and maybe a half percent of men—they usually visit at least ten physicians before it gets properly diagnosed. Late twenties is the age when it usually develops. It often runs in families, being seen in about 20 percent of the patient's first-degree relatives.

Antidepressant drugs often help, although these patients usually aren't depressed. And this same group of patients, it now turns out, are the ones who tend to suffer from fear of public places. About a third of panic attack victims also experience agoraphobia.

"I bet they don't want others to see them when they're having a panic attack. I sure don't want people to see me when I'm having a seizure."

I think you're right. They've probably seen themselves in a mirror when having a panic attack, and know how they look to others. When they do go to a meeting or concert, they sit close to exits, so as to readily escape to a restroom where they can sit out the attack in privacy. They come to dislike situations that limit their flexibility, such as standing in a line or having to keep an appointment—especially getting their hair cut, where they're trapped in a chair with someone working on them in a public place. Once you understand the panic attack problem, these particular fears of public places make perfect sense.

There are patients with agoraphobia who don't have panic attacks, but some of them are surely organic—maybe they have had a little right parietal stroke affecting their spatial orienting abilities, and so feel disoriented when they get away from familiar surroundings, worrying that they won't be able to find their way home. So they refuse to travel without a companion, and hesitate to explore new places—all perfectly reasonable, once you understand the parietal lobe aspect, and quite different from the panic attack variety of agoraphobia. With an MRI brain image, the psychiatrist can often spot where the gray matter is missing.

"So what about those people who are very shy?" asked Neil. "Kids seem to be born that way, while others are so bold as to worry their parents."

Maybe 15 percent of kids are at those shy-or-bold extremes as preschoolers, but it's only several percent by the time they're adults. And, of course, some people may become inhibited in dealing with the world because of some traumatic experience. What's been surprising psychiatrists is that these personality disorders—which traditionally have been difficult to treat successfully—are responding to some of the newer drugs that selectively inhibit serotonin reuptake. It's long been thought that those lawn-sprinkler systems for the monoamines might provide the bias that makes a person happy or sad, bold or shy, and so forth. But the downfall of those theories was that the earlier antidepressant drugs affected both norepi and serotonin—yet rarely affected "personality traits." And the effect of some of the antidepressants isn't simply to make people less shy. We're still trying to figure it out.

Psychiatrists get most of the leftover problems no other specialty can diagnose or treat, and so psychiatrists need a considerable tolerance for ambiguity and uncertainty, as well as a vast knowledge of medicine. But they're on the frontier—occasionally they recognize some order amid all the individual variability and discover a new "neurological" disorder.

chapter 11

Tuning Up the Brain by Pruning

NEIL HAD BEEN PRUNING his apple trees, taking out his frustrations (or so he said) with a little hard labor. Even though the decision to operate had been made, the surgery schedule was filled for months ahead. But since he lived nearby, there was a chance Neil could take advantage of another patient's cancellation on short notice. All it took for elective neurosurgery to be postponed was someone catching a substantial head cold.

Pruning, I explained, also goes on inside the brain. Exploration and pruning are two major principles that he needed to understand if he wanted to appreciate how the brain operates in the real world. They determine which memories are stored, and what decisions are made.

WE EXPLORE OUR WORLD, seeking sensations. Some come to us unbidden, such as the sound and sight of lightning. Others we seek out by touching or tasting or smelling, just as we strain to hear a faint sound or move our head and eyes to get a better view.

"I'm glad to hear that sensation-seeking is normal," Neil said.

We can ignore the movements and just talk about "sensations" and "inputs" to the brain, but movement is really an integral part of sensation. If forgotten too long, it can lead you into an overly abstract notion of a little person inside that receives the inputs and decides on the outputs. In reality, outputs are being produced at a number of stages of the analysis. But, despite the hazards, let's stick to the input path for a moment, the passive sensation side of things.

The input path always has a series of stages. The interface with the external environment is a sensor that converts some form of energy into the electrical signals that the nervous system uses for comparisons. We're always comparing. We have sensors buried in our muscles and joints that tell us where our arm is currently located. Although bending a single hair on your wrist will produce a sensation, hairs are seldom bent one at a time. It's the comparison with neighbors that enables you to discern whether the sensation is produced by a breeze, a pencil point, a shirtsleeve, or a wristwatch.

For our skin sensations, this comparison is not done in the skin. Rather, the axons of the sensory neurons carry impulses back into the spinal cord. Neurons there do the comparisons. Or at least they start the job—they are the second neurons in a chain of analysis that extends to a third neuron in the thalamus, a fourth one in the sensory strip of cerebral cortex, and even more in other "association cortex" areas. Of course, it's not a real chain of neurons but rather a web.

"Association cortex? Doesn't all the cortex make associations?"

Indeed, all of the brain and spinal cord. That's an old name for all the neocortical areas exclusive of the primary sensory cortices and the motor strip. Terra incognita, at the time.

"So how's the comparison done? Bigger versus smaller?"

Inhibition serves to subtract one input from another. If you were to listen in on a spinal cord neuron, you would discover that it was excited by a small patch of skin, but inhibited by an even larger patch of skin surrounding the excitatory patch. From the one neuron's point of view, the world consists of two areas of skin that contradict one another. In the business, their combined skin area is known as the neuron's "receptive field."

"That's something like a city's watershed, up in the mountains?"

I nodded agreement. And for a neuron back in the spinal cord or brain, the watershed has two antagonistic regions, one sending hot water and the other cold water, mixing in the neuron to determine how hot it acts. So any one neuron to going to have a limited knowledge of what's happening out on the skin. Collectively, a number of such neurons can form a committee that says "Watchband" from the temporal and spatial characteristics of their activity.

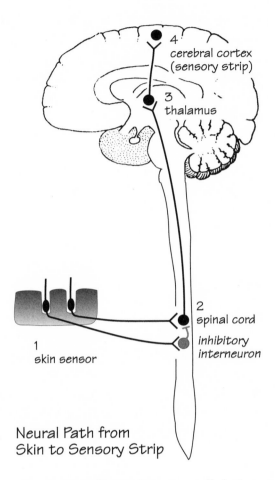

4
cerebral cortex
(sensory strip)

3
thalamus

2
spinal cord

inhibitory
interneuron

1
skin sensor

**Neural Path from
Skin to Sensory Strip**

Sensory neurons are usually excitatory at all their axon terminals—but some end on inhibitory neurons that, in turn, connect with the neuron doing the comparisons (making it both a second-order and a third-order neuron; the convention is to name it for the shortest possible path from the sensors). Each sensory axon from the skin has—at a minimum—tens of thousands of axon terminals.

Since a neuron has a threshold for initiating impulses, it may be quite silent unless the excitatory input starts to considerably exceed the inhibitory input. If it is only inhibited because the skin stimulation avoids the excitatory patch, the neuron doesn't pass on the information.

"So the uniform pressure of a wristwatch band may be ignored by many neurons in the spinal cord, simply because inhibitory patches cancel out the excitatory ones?"

Doesn't cancel out in all of them. A dull pencil point, however, would keep lots of them active. And would likely result in a sensation being transmitted to higher brain centers, perhaps eventually reaching a level where it could be talked about.

But, of course, a decision to act can be made by your spinal cord before the brain even knows what's up. The neurons down there, on their own, are likely to command some muscles as a result of the sensory information—without waiting for the "higher centers" to comment. A quick withdrawal from a threatening stimulus is underway even before the brain knows about it, as when you step on a thumbtack. And the many modifications of routine body movements for walking or maintaining posture are made by the spinal cord without much need for involvement by higher centers.

Similarly the second neuron in the pathway from the ear, located in the brain stem, may command protective reflexes against loud sounds without awaiting cortical intervention. But the reflex pathway always involves a round trip into the brain or spinal cord and then back out.

"You mean that a muscle doesn't contract because a local sensor directly commanded it? Why's that? Seems it would be faster."

Faster, perhaps, but full of problems. Invertebrates sometimes use local circuits in the periphery, but many actions demand an integrated response of many parts of the body. Even if you step on a thumbtack, you may not want to withdraw that leg.

"Why ever not?"

Suppose that your other leg wasn't on the ground at the time. Initiating leg flexion in that situation would cause you to collapse—indeed, toward the source of the pain. Giving autonomy to the local sensors and muscles, to make their own decisions, can be dangerous. And so most reflex paths are more roundabout, the decision-making abilities concentrated in the central nervous system (a collective term for spinal cord and brain). But yes, that does indeed slow down reaction times.

Let's take some high-end sensory abilities. Sound and sight are the most varied of our sensations. Language, invented sometime in the last few million years, involves some really fancy abilities for categorizing sounds.

But fancy visual abilities have been important for much longer, and it shows. The visual pathways in the brain seem to have elaborated and streamlined in ways that have no counterpart in the hearing pathways. Our primate ancestors of 40 million years ago may not have needed to read, but they needed to look up at the top of a tree waving in the breeze, causing patches of bright sky to flash on and off, and nonetheless spot the little dark patches of fruit amid the dark leaves.

Having identified the form of fruit, they needed a sense of color to judge whether the fruit was ripe enough to make it worth climbing up to the top of the tree.

"I certainly climbed an apple tree a few times when I was a kid, only to discover that the apples at the top really weren't ready to eat. Now I just wait until they're surely ripe."

But you probably don't have other primates raiding your apple trees. The monkey needs a fine sense of color, capable of discerning almost-ripe fruit. If the monkey waits until it's unequivocally ripe, some other monkeys will have picked the tree clean in the meantime.

Life in the trees also shaped up our abilities to operate vehicles. Swinging through the trees produces a visual stream rushing past on both sides of your head. And so does riding a bicycle, with many protruding branches to track and avoid. Some objects move faster than the average visual stream, and so are judged to be closer—or perhaps even moving themselves, such as other monkeys in the trees.

We largely owe our excellent visual abilities for judging form, color, distance, and motion to the monkeys of long ago. Whenever we drive a car or read a book or admire a sunset, we are using neural machinery that was honed on the difficult task of finding ripe fruit amid clutter and confusion.

Yet this neural processing is imperfect: we sometimes see things that are not there, sometimes fail to see things that are really there, and often distort things. Our visual system is not a video camera.

"Of course, at first glimpse, our eye is rather like a camera."

Yes, in the sense that the lens produces an inverted image of the world on the back of the eye. Rather than the little silver grains of film that turn black when light strikes them, our retina has a great mosaic of 100 million photoreceptors that change their voltage, not unlike those in a very-high-definition television camera. But the analogies stop there. Our visual system is in the business of taking apart the visual image, not preserving it for some little person inside the head to view.

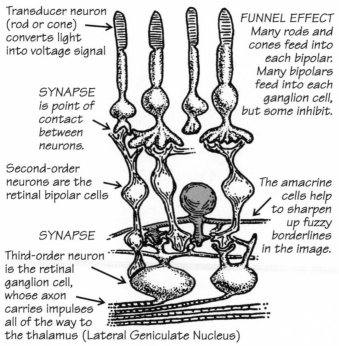

Transducer neuron (rod or cone) converts light into voltage signal

FUNNEL EFFECT
Many rods and cones feed into each bipolar. Many bipolars feed into each ganglion cell, but some inhibit.

SYNAPSE is point of contact between neurons.

Second-order neurons are the retinal bipolar cells

The amacrine cells help to sharpen up fuzzy borderlines in the image.

SYNAPSE

Third-order neuron is the retinal ganglion cell, whose axon carries impulses all of the way to the thalamus (Lateral Geniculate Nucleus)

Modified from Dowling and Boycott, 1966

UNLIKE MOST OTHER SENSES, the comparisons between neighbors in the visual system start right out next to the sensor layer.

"I thought you just said that comparisons are always made in the central nervous system."

Quite right. But the eye's an odd exception because the retina is part of the central nervous system, just as the spinal cord is. The brain actually grows out into the eye during fetal development. The optic nerve is really only an honorary nerve—properly speaking, it is part of those internal tracts that make up the white matter of the brain.

Each of the third-order neurons in the retina, whose axons make up the optic "nerve," receives input from thousands of photoreceptors but never directly, only via intermediate cells called bipolar cells and amacrine cells. It's like a funnel that collects raindrops from a wide area and concentrates them into a narrow stream. There has to be some funneling, as there are about a hundred photoreceptors for each axon going back to the brain.

"Sounds like the visual system discovered what, in computer design, is called a preprocessor. They're handy to reduce the amount of information that must be transmitted over long distances. So they do a preliminary analysis and only ship out the results."

The funnel isn't quite the right analogy, actually. It isn't a matter of a hundred photoreceptors connecting to each ganglion cell. Messages from thousands of photoreceptors are funneled into each ganglion cell, except some cancel out the actions of others. That's because each photoreceptor contributes to hundreds of ganglion cells—there's a spreading out as well as a funneling. There's a hundred funnels beneath each photoreceptor.

FROM EYE TO BRAIN, the route goes through the thalamus, whose lateral geniculate nucleus is an elaborately layered structure. Surely, everyone thought, something fancy happened in those six layers, all of which send axons to the visual cortex. Three layers receive inputs from one eye and three receive from the other.

"Why?"

It still isn't known. But let me try asking a question that eye surgeons like to pose to medical students: What is the most important reason to save a damaged eye?

"Wider field of view with two eyes?"

But that surely isn't the most important reason, as we can get around pretty well with one eye patched. There is a crescent-shaped region seen by one eye that is not seen by the other. We just have to turn our head or good eye a little to see it, if missing the one eye.

"The range-finder effect, comparing the view from the two eyes to judge how far away something is located?"

While we obviously improve our depth perception with the range-finder effect, that too can be mimicked by moving the head sideways momentarily, as when we shift our weight from one foot to the other. That gives us two views to compare. There are various other indicators of an object's distance as well, such as how much surface detail you can see. No ability is really lost when we lose one eye.

Here's the answer to this Socratic question about saving a damaged eye: *In case the remaining eye is damaged at some future time.* Blindness is a very serious business. Any threat to the vision in one eye is far more serious than the immediate problem. And sometimes the threat doesn't involve overt damage to the eye, just lack of sufficient experience.

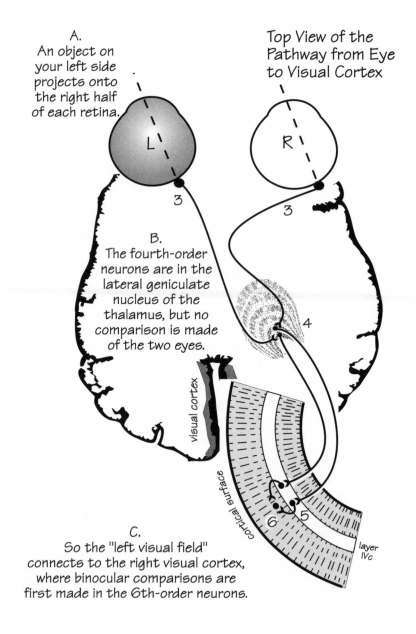

A.
An object on your left side projects onto the right half of each retina.

Top View of the Pathway from Eye to Visual Cortex

L

R

3

3

B.
The fourth-order neurons are in the lateral geniculate nucleus of the thalamus, but no comparison is made of the two eyes.

4

visual cortex

cortical surface

6   5

layer IVc

C.
So the "left visual field" connects to the right visual cortex, where binocular comparisons are first made in the 6th-order neurons.

For example, I saw a boy named Ross in one of the teaching conferences. A nice six-year-old who is very cross-eyed. And now he's almost blind in his right eye. The eye wasn't damaged—it's just that his brain ignores anything coming from his right eye and relies totally on the left eye instead.

"But why?"

That's not known. Unfortunately it's now too late to do much about this "amblyopia." Cross-eyed babies who see doctors earlier in life get sent to see the eye surgeon, as doctors know that the child is very likely to become functionally blind in one eye or the other. Fixing the squint (usually in the first year) prevents the loss of vision in one eye or the other.

Lack of regular well-baby checkups is not the only reason that Ross is now blind in one eye. His mother also thought of correcting crossed eyes in the same cosmetic terms as fixing a crooked nose. A perfectly understandable common-sense notion—but wrong. There are critical periods in the development of the brain where the right experiences are needed, or things get set up wrong—and then get set in concrete, as it were.

"And normal depth perception is one of them?"

Well, maybe not depth judgments using the two eyes—maybe just the two eyes getting used to working in tandem, so you can fuse the two images.

That one shouldn't wait around with a cross-eyed baby, or bandage an eye for very long, were just empirical facts in medicine until the 1960s, along with the fact that nothing terrible happened if you patched an adult's eye for equally long. Empirical just means, "Don't know why, but that's what happens." There was something different about

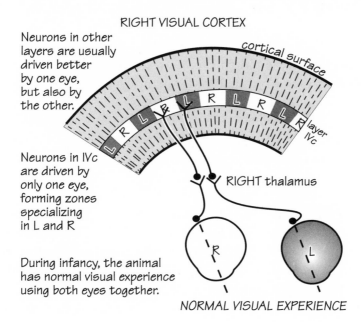

RIGHT VISUAL CORTEX

Neurons in other layers are usually driven better by one eye, but also by the other.

cortical surface

layer IVc

Neurons in IVc are driven by only one eye, forming zones specializing in L and R

RIGHT thalamus

During infancy, the animal has normal visual experience using both eyes together.

NORMAL VISUAL EXPERIENCE

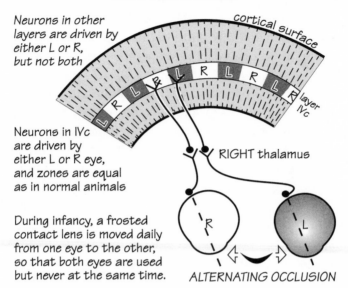

RIGHT VISUAL CORTEX

Neurons in other
layers are driven by
either L or R,
but not both

cortical surface

layer IVc

Neurons in IVc
are driven by
either L or R eye,
and zones are equal
as in normal animals

RIGHT thalamus

During infancy, a frosted
contact lens is moved daily
from one eye to the other,
so that both eyes are used
but never at the same time.

ALTERNATING OCCLUSION

infants. Finally, research on kittens and infant monkeys advanced far
enough to show us some reasons.

The two eyes seem to need experience working together at an early
age. Now you've got to know at what level in the visual pathway the
neurons begin comparing the slightly different view from the two eyes.
It's not until the sixth-order neuron. The fifth-order neurons—the ones
in cortical layer IVc which receive the lateral geniculate inputs—are
still "monocular," just as were all the neurons in geniculate: if the
neuron responded to the right eye, it wouldn't respond to the left eye.
But when recording from sixth-order neurons in the layers above and
below the fourth layer, many neurons are found that respond to both
eyes. Usually the receptive field for the left eye is similar to that for
the right, but the response is usually stronger for one eye than the
other. For some sixth-order neurons, the right eye is the "stronger"
one, and for others the left eye has the most influence. Only a few are
strongly biased toward one eye and ignore the other.

But in infant monkeys wearing an opaque contact lens, this changes.
Suppose the opaque contact lens is switched every day from one eye
to the other, so that both eyes get visual experience during the first
year of life—but never together. Recordings made from the brains of
these animals are very different from normal ones. Now the neurons
have strong preferences for the left eye or the right eye, with very few

neurons paying attention to both eyes. And even if the contact lens is then left off for many months, so that the two eyes get a chance to work together, this bias tends not to reverse: few of these biased neurons drift into comparing the two views.

"So the bad eye has been disconnected?"

That's probably too strong a way of expressing it, since drugs that block inhibitory synapses can temporarily reveal some underlying connections from both eyes. But for all practical purposes, the *functioning* of the visual system seems to have been permanently altered by this abnormal early experience.

"But what causes a critical period?"

Probably a lot of disconnections. Even in normal people, a progressive reduction in synaptic connections occurs with age, all over the cerebral cortex—it seems that things are connected up somewhat indiscriminately to start with, then refined. You had the most synapses per neuron that you'll ever have back when you were eight months of age. After that, it's all downhill—you lose a third to a half of cortical synapses during childhood.

"That's amazing. We're *losing* connections while we're storing additional vocabulary, accumulating more memories?"

Yes—at least, on the average. In addition to detaching synapses, reduced connectivity also occurs by neuron death in some cortical regions. A monkey's motor cortex loses a third of its neurons during infancy and the juvenile period.

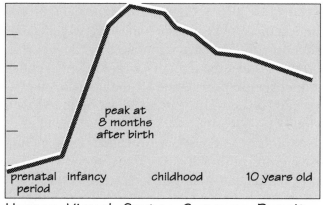

Human Visual Cortex Synapse Density

Data from Huttenlocher, 1984

RIGHT VISUAL CORTEX

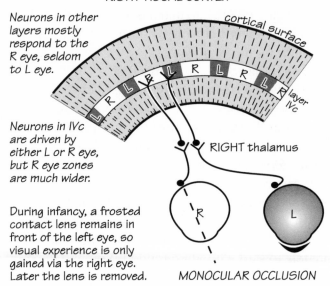

Neurons in other layers mostly respond to the R eye, seldom to L eye.

Neurons in IVc are driven by either L or R eye, but R eye zones are much wider.

During infancy, a frosted contact lens remains in front of the left eye, so visual experience is only gained via the right eye. Later the lens is removed.

RIGHT thalamus

MONOCULAR OCCLUSION

"They eliminate the clumsy ones?"

That might be a good pruning principle. In any event, relatively few cortical neurons are lost after reaching adulthood. The current thinking about pruning principles is that there is elimination of the less active connections during this "sensitive period." That you retain those synapses that you use a lot.

A good example of this activity-dependent pruning principle is seen in layer IVc where the geniculate inputs terminate. Normally, there is a zone about 0.5 mm wide that is exclusively left eye, flanked by right eye regions that are also 0.5 mm wide. Suppose the opaque contact lens remains on the left eye, rather than being switched back and forth daily, so that only the animal's right eye sees the world normally.

What happens is that the right eye zones in visual cortex's layer IVc *expand* at the expense of the zone for the unused left eye. And again, this is not readily reversed by leaving off the opaque contact lens once the critical period is over.

"Sounds as if those exercised neurons had won a competition."

Yes, "use it or lose it" is still our best theory for why there are critical periods in development. And why kids such as Ross still can't see in one eye, even when their squint is belatedly corrected.

NEIL WAS VERY INTERESTED in the notion of synapses being pruned, presumably using some pruning principle fancier than the one he used on his apple trees.

"So are synapses being made and broken all the time?" he asked.

Probably, although surely there is a core of fairly stable synapses. Remember all those experiments with rats living in enriched environments? They increased their number of synapses per cortical neuron by 80 percent. That shows you that the rate of creating synapses sometimes exceeds the rate of breaking them.

The average decline with age, after eight months of age, shows you that the rate of breaking can predominate in the long run. But we don't know if 10 percent are turning over every week, or every year. Until our research methods improve, we just know the results of the average differences in the rates of making and breaking.

"It all sounds like economic theories, you know. And speaking of pruning, Joseph Schumpeter—an economist of about a half century ago—used to emphasize that 'creative destruction' was needed on an ongoing basis by society."

Certainly our memories are malleable enough to suggest that true events can be overwritten by false ones, like those eyewitnesses who came to believe they saw a yield sign rather than a stop sign. Year after year, we add more memories atop the old ones—and our brains aren't like a file room that fills up and has to be cleaned out occasionally, but some different kind of memory system that carves a new pattern atop the old carvings. Occasionally the old patterns get pretty hard to see.

"It's like a sculptor getting carried away with details. If you carve away for too long, nothing's left!" smiled Neil.

But then he frowned. "Does that mean there's a limit to how much our brains can store? If we live too long, do we run out of brain to carve patterns into?"

Brains aren't inanimate raw material like wood and stone. They renew themselves by making new synapses. And it's the pattern of those synaptic strengths that seems to be the long-term memory trace. The question is whether you'll continue to be able to retrieve some of the rarely used records, whether they'll get overwritten so thoroughly that retrieval takes too long to be useful.

Perhaps the most exciting possibility . . . is the extension of this type of work to other systems besides sensory. Experimental psychologists and psychiatrists both emphasize the importance of early experience on subsequent behavior patterns—could it be that deprivation of social contacts or the existence of other abnormal emotional situations early in life may lead to a deterioration or distortion of connections in some yet unexplored parts of the brain?

The neurophysiologist DAVID HUBEL, 1967

chapter 12

Acquiring and Reacquiring Language

Normal speech consists, in large part, of fragments, false starts, blends and other distortions of the underlying idealized forms. Nevertheless . . . what the child learns is the underlying [idealized form]. This is a remarkable fact. We must also bear in mind that the child constructs this [idealized form] without explicit instruction, that he acquires this knowledge at a time when he is not capable of complex intellectual achievements in many other domains, and that this achievement is relatively independent of intelligence . . .

The linguist NOAM CHOMSKY, 1969

STILL NO WORD of a cancellation on George's surgical schedule, so Neil was biding his time, reading and taking advantage of the good weather while he could.

One day he offered to pick me up in his boat, from the waterway in back of the medical school. I waited out at the end of the seaplane dock and swung aboard his sailboat as it drifted into the dock. So our conversations about language took place to the background music of sails luffing, punctuated by the occasional bong.

"If you listen carefully, that aluminum mast sounds like a whole set of wind chimes," Neil remarked.

All I heard myself were muted gongs—all of the same monotonous note, not multiple ones. Undoubtedly, I told Neil, this was a matter of categorical perception—and he could hear more categories than I could. Remember, I asked him, telling your foreign language instructor—after she'd corrected your pronunciation—that you *were* pronouncing the word as she did?

"Must have happened a dozen times."

The instructor could hear differences that you couldn't. She had classification categories for sounds that you didn't have. Newborn infants are also better at hearing subtle differences, compared with adults. Just like your language instructor, they can detect the slight differences between certain speech sounds that adults will insist are identical.

Babies may not be able to tell you which pronunciation is correct, but they can tell you whether a sound has changed from its previous repetitions.

"How does anyone know that? The babies can't talk, after all."

The child psychologists have gotten very clever. Babies get bored when hearing the same sound over and over, but they'll perk up if you introduce a little novelty. They'll get quite good at detecting subtle shifts in the repeated syllable if you reward them with a brief glimpse of a dancing bear. When they hear the sound change, they'll turn to look at where the bear will briefly appear—that's how you tell they heard the sound alter. And so you have the speech synthesizer vary the sound timing a little, perhaps exploring the range between /pa/ and /ba/. Newborns seem to detect the sound changing—in other words, they perk up and watch expectantly for the bear's appearance—when older children or adults are insisting that nothing changed.

We adults hear the sound suddenly switch from /pa/ to /ba/ in the middle of the timing gradations—in other words, we create a dichotomy where none existed. Such categorical perception is often shaped by experience, and newborns are without much experience.

"Don't they hear sounds in the womb?"

Yes, but only low frequencies—the higher frequencies are filtered out, just as they are from the sounds of your neighbor's hi-fi. The walls only let through the low stuff, the boom-boom. And the fetus hears lots of pulsations from the mother's heart, or gurgling from her gut, that may interfere with concentrating on external sounds.

Our sound categories are formed from experience listening to parents and siblings and television audio. The baby literally tunes itself up to the peculiarities of the language that it hears. In particular, he learns to deal with the variations between speakers in how they pronounce those sounds by creating broad categories. In the process, the baby loses the ability to detect subtle differences in speech sounds ("phonemes") that he could earlier perceive. He forms mental models of the phonemes and ignores any slight variations.

"Is that why the Japanese have so much trouble in pronouncing R?"

Having sound categories can create some problems when hearing a language that you weren't raised with. In Japan, for example, babies learn a phoneme that is midway between /r/ and /l/. Forming such a category means that you learn to ignore variations around this phoneme. So, when exposed to an English /r/ or /l/, the Japanese tend to hear that in-between Japanese phoneme.

"So they think that the two English phonemes are the same thing."

They are, after all, both captured by the same mental category. Most of us can't hear the difference between similar Hindu or Portuguese phonemes either, thanks to our upbringing. If we can't hear the difference, we can't correct our own pronunciation. Eventually we become the somewhat defensive student who complains at the language instructor, unable to hear a sound difference that we could have detected as a newborn baby.

After this tuneup period of infancy for the locally used speech sounds, various aspects of language develop.

"Such as babbling, which is what my youngest is now doing."

But soon she'll be building a basic vocabulary, and going on to the two- and three-word sentences in her second year. Then she'll acquire syntax and fancier sentences in her third year. And develop a fascination with stories and other sequences, then learn to read.

"So the language cortex is self-organizing around the natural categories of what it hears? Does it reorganize the same way, after damage?"

Cortical map of the hand's surfaces is never this orderly.

Exercising only the third finger enlarges its territory but also rearranges all other fingers and the thumb-face and hand-wrist borders.

Of course, sometimes the cortex can't effectively reorganize, such as after those critical periods for using both eyes together. But clearly some cortical areas are very good at reorganizing, even in adults. There aren't many studies from hearing or speech, but there are some wonderful reorganization stories from the sensory strip.

THE HAND'S MAP IN THE SENSORY STRIP is not fixed but subject to considerable rearrangement. The boundaries between finger representations in the cortex move by millimeters on a timescale of days to weeks—and this is in an ordinary adult monkey who is merely getting a little exercise of one part of one finger for several weeks, touching a bumpy surface.

"Something like a blind person 'reading' braille?"

Exactly. Someone has even mapped the sensory strip in blind people and shown that their finger areas are larger than average. In monkeys, you can see how it happens.

Even without such obvious exercise, the thumb-face boundary in monkeys moves by about a millimeter over a period of several weeks. Some neurons that were responding to a patch of skin on the face will stop responding to it—and begin responding to a patch of skin on the thumb. This back-and-forth, for no apparent reason, suggests a continuous dynamic retuning during the monkey's life.

"It sounds like a boundary dispute. Just like the province of Alsace on the French-German border, which has changed nationality four times since 1871."

And so has a composite character, just like those neurons that represent the thumb one week and the face the next.

"Use it or lose it" may overstate the issue, but these studies of the sensory strip in adults certainly suggest that competition is alive and well in the cerebral cortex. Before that discovery, the adult primate brain was considered rather inflexible, with only young brains capable of such substantial rearrangements of function.

"But how radical can this reassignment be?"

It seems quite variable: more in juveniles than adults, more for skin sensation than for vision. And there are preferences: if an arm is lost, its space in the sensory strip seems to be taken over entirely by the lower part of the face, mostly the chin and jaw. The chest representation, on the other side of the sensory strip from the vacated area, doesn't invade at all.

FOR LANGUAGE, there are no detailed studies of the kind possible in experimental animals, but there are many clues from how infants compensate for severe damage to their brains. Things can go wrong with the usual developmental sequence, and some of them teach us about the child's changing brain organization for language.

Certainly the most dramatic clue comes from a rare congenital malformation, called the Sturge-Weber syndrome, where abnormal blood vessels occur over one side of the brain during fetal development. In such arteriovenous malformations, much of the oxygenated arterial blood is shunted directly into the veins without ever traversing the capillaries. Thus the neurons are not properly nourished. The brain under these vessels develops severe seizures, is stunted in its growth, and becomes essentially useless.

That's bad enough. But the seizures spread to affect the other side of the brain as well, preventing it from getting on with development. The malformed blood vessels of one side of the brain essentially put both sides of the brain out of commission. For decades, neurosurgeons have treated babies born with this problem: they remove the abnormal blood vessels and the cerebral cortex it supplies, leaving the subcortical structures that get their blood supply from elsewhere.

"And these poor kids get along on only half a brain? I sure didn't, back during the Wada test."

Well, actually the baby has more than half a brain, as the cerebral cortex isn't everything. These kids only have half as much cerebral cortex as is normal. Surprisingly, they grow up without being paralyzed on one side of the body, or blind in half of their visual world, as you might predict. Evidently the remaining half can run the same side of the body as well as the opposite side. Sometimes the malformation is on the right side of the brain, leaving the baby with only a left cerebral cortex.

"So they can talk okay?"

Yes. But sometimes it's the left cerebral cortex that has to be removed, and that leaves the baby without the structures thought to underlie language. Now, if development of language were totally dependent on wiring in the left brain, language shouldn't develop in such right-brain-only kids.

Yet it does. When examined years after such an operation, children with left-hemisphere removals have useful language, although they are often considered to be rather quiet children. The right brain evidently can support language, even though it doesn't normally.

However, this language is not quite normal. Testing these children at about the age of ten, the psychologists Bruno Kohn and Maureen Dennis found that the children with left-brain removals had many more problems using complex grammatical constructions than children with right-brain removals, even though both groups seemed to be of similar intelligence.

"Differ? How?"

Children with left-brain removals tend to talk in the present tense, finding the future tense somewhat difficult. There appears to be some wired-in mechanism in the left brain that allows for the full expression of language, a mechanism the right brain cannot completely support. The linguist Noam Chomsky suggested that because all real human languages use a finite set of construction rules, out of the infinite set imaginable, there must be a biological basis for syntax and grammar. The remaining language in the Sturge-Weber children suggests that only the left brain has the full set of neural structures needed for language.

Although in infancy, the right brain could mostly compensate for loss of left-brain language mechanisms, adults are not so fortunate. A large left-brain stroke usually results in a permanent loss of most

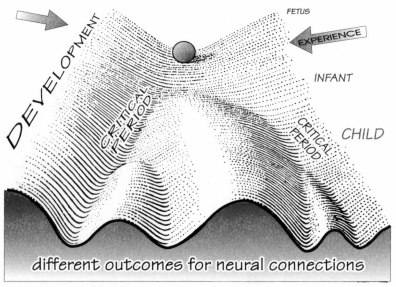

The downhill epigenetic landscape
and the "winds of experience" that
bias outcomes during critical periods

Modified from Waddington, 1956

language functions, just as in Broca's patient, "Tan-tan." The right-brain compensatory ability seems to be lost for most of us sometime in the preschool years.

Most children suffering major left-brain injury before the age of two seem to develop useful language. Permanent language loss begins to appear when such injuries occur at age 6 or 7. Children suffering left-brain injury between ages 4 and 6 are left with severe verbal learning deficits, even though they retain most of their previous language abilities.

"Can George study kids in the operating room?"

Not usually. While they sometimes have epilepsy that cannot otherwise be treated, the neurosurgical approach often used in adults, recording and mapping in the operating room, requires an awake, cooperative patient under only local anesthesia for part of the operation. That's a bit much to ask of children or of adults with mental retardation. For them, a different technique is used, although it is considerably more expensive and somewhat riskier than the adult procedure. Under general anesthesia, a sheet of electrodes—called a "grid"—is implanted so that it rests atop the cortical surface, with the wire brought out through the skin incision. Mapping and recording in these children is then done during the following week.

"That's what George said I might require, if the round-the-clock EEG didn't resolve the frontal- versus temporal-lobe issue."

Grids are quite wonderful, as the child's language organization can be discovered during brief testing sessions in the days that follow implantation, when the child is awake and cooperative. The youngest child studied with such grid-based stimulation mapping during naming was four years old. The naming sites were nearly dime-sized, much as they are in adults. Multiple naming sites in the same lobe have not been identified before the age of eight.

While the data from children are limited, they certainly raise some interesting questions. Might the development of localized naming sites correspond to language becoming "set in concrete," an indication of the loss of an ability to shift it to the other hemisphere?

HOW CHILDREN LEARN LANGUAGE is a favorite subject of many a parent and teacher. Many "stages" (albeit, overlapping) of language development have been postulated by both linguists and developmental psychologists.

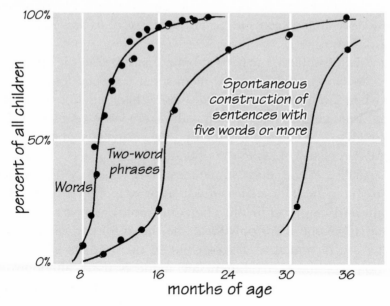

Data from Lenneberg, 1967

"My daughter's still babbling. But we're trying to teach her Mama and Dada."

Parents and teachers assume that children would never learn language without their constant assistance. But it is fair to say that language is not taught so much as it is acquired willy-nilly, that children would probably learn language even without prompting and correcting.

"That'll surprise a lot of parents."

While children would surely learn language more slowly without help, most children would discover the word meanings for themselves in the preschool years. What is so important is *hearing* the sentences, seeing what people do in response to them, and then learning to influence the people around you by producing word strings yourself.

Unlike the apes who have acquired useful vocabularies of a few hundred words, the preschool child is enormously acquisitive of words, adding a half dozen new words to its growing vocabulary every day. Some are simply acquired through observation, not the pointing-and-naming route; parents are sometimes surprised at a few words that their child picked up by listening in the months before beginning to talk.

And acquisition by trial-and-error observation is particularly true for syntax—what's called grammar in popular usage. They're the rules that we use to interpret strings of words. Did you teach your older children syntax?

"Are you kidding? I barely know the rules. I couldn't possibly have taught them. I only know when something is wrong, and try to point out the correct usage."

You do know the rules—you demonstrate that with every sentence you speak. You just can't articulate them. And even linguists have trouble explaining them. So how did all of us ever learn English syntax?

Children learn sentence construction rules by mere observation. Between about 18 and 36 months of age, children seem especially acquisitive of the structural rules underlying the sentences that they hear spoken around them. They may not be able to describe the parts of speech, or diagram a sentence, any better than their parents—but they act as if such knowledge was becoming embedded in their brains.

This biological tendency is so strong that children can even invent a new language. Deaf playmates have been known to invent their own sign language ("home sign"). The linguist Derek Bickerton has shown that children can invent new languages out of the pidgin protolanguages that they hear their parents speaking. Pidgins are shared vocabulary used by traders, tourists, and "guest workers" (and, in the old days, slaves)—the words are usually accompanied by much gesture, as when I attempt some tourist Greek. It takes a long time to say a little, because of all those circumlocutions. A proper language allows you to pack a lot of meaning into a short sentence.

Creoles are proper languages with their own syntax, capable of quickly conveying models of "Who did what to whom with which means" from one mind to another. The children of pidgin speakers seem to take the shared vocabulary they hear and create a syntax for it, although not necessarily the syntax from their parents' native language. They invent, willy-nilly, a proper language. That's the best evidence that the child's brain is really predisposed to syntax.

Compared to pidgins, a proper language can convey such complicated concepts using relatively few words. That's because they have elaborate rules for interrelating the words to achieve additional levels of meaning.

"Syntax, I gather, is what separates a protolanguage from real language. It's what allows you to understand more than just the meaning of the individual words, standing alone?"

Not quite. The real test of language is *constructing* sentences using the rules, not understanding them. It's much easier to understand a fancy construction of someone else's, simply because you can guess so well. When I was a visiting professor in Jerusalem, knowing hardly any Hebrew—maybe a hundred words of vocabulary that I could use with shopkeepers—I was at a faculty party when some long and heated exchanges took place, all in Hebrew. Noticing that I was concentrating on the discussion, a woman across the room abruptly asked me—fortunately in English—if I understood what they were saying. This brought the discussion to a complete stop and everyone turned around to look at me. I replied that I understood some of it. Well, she then asked me—in front of all those people—to describe what they'd been talking about.

"That sure put you on the spot. So what happened?"

I briefly said that they'd been discussing the peace treaty with Egypt and the loss of the settlements near the Gaza Strip, the loss of the Sinai Desert air bases, the political problems of relocating people. And it turned out I was right! Despite being unable to speak anything fancier than three-word sentences using my hundred-word Hebrew vocabulary, I'd guessed my way through complicated sentences to a general understanding of the topic.

Speaking a novel sentence yourself, using the rules, is what's so hard. Yet children find it easy to pick up new sets of rules—they can *speak* second languages easily, once they've learned one. Unlike their parents.

Of course, some children never learn a first language's syntax.

"How's that? You just said they pick it up, even without anyone teaching them."

If they're deaf, they don't learn the words or the rules by listening.

CRITICAL PERIODS IN LANGUAGE DEVELOPMENT are a serious matter for the one child in a thousand who is deaf (or nearly so) from birth—at least for those not exposed to a conventional sign language. Most hearing children are speaking single words by 12 months, form simple two-word sentences between 18 and 24 months, and start getting the word endings for past-present-future and for singular-plural between 30 and 42 months.

Deaf children of hearing parents are doing little of this. In the United States, they aren't even identified as hearing impaired until they are nearly three years old, on average. Meaning, of course, that many are identified even later.

"How's that possible? Surely the parents noticed something wrong before that."

Indeed, they were probably worried about why the baby was a slow learner. But never thought to stand behind the baby, out of sight, and make a loud noise that ought to startle him—if he had normal hearing. Lots of kids never get taken in for well-baby checkups. These days, there are cheap and effective tests you can perform shortly after birth that will detect deafness, before the infant ever goes home from the hospital. They aren't used very widely, but they ought to be—because undetected deafness spells big trouble, thanks to critical periods for picking up the rules that govern sentence construction.

I should start by saying that deaf children born to most deaf parents actually learn language as effortlessly as do most other children, and can readily learn nonsign languages when reaching school age. These deaf kids may have a social handicap in dealing with those who do not use their language, but they don't have a language handicap as such.

And the reason that infant deafness is so serious is also different from the issues of adult-onset deafness, where you're mostly worrying about hearing aids or the paranoia that can develop from social isolation.

If the parents are not fluent in sign language, the deaf child may be unable to acquire a syntax by gradual observation. And this interferes with language skills for life: you can't "make up" for it later. A child not exposed to fluent sign language in the early preschool years may end up with a rudimentary vocabulary and little ability to construct or understand complicated sentences. Or to plan for tomorrow. Or to think before acting and predict why that course of action might distress other people.

It is now clear that a child needs more than words (or signs), more than two- or three-word sentences: a child needs to discover a syntax within its everyday environment. And it needs this experience in its third year of life, not later in school. Learning the syntax of at least one language during its first 18 to 36 months seems to be important for learning another language later, such as lip-reading English. American Sign Language (ASL) has a syntax to discover, and Manually Coded English uses the syntax of English.

"But half of those kids, you said, were discovered to be deaf after 36 months of age."

And so they're really behind, in big need of a crash course. But the parents can't usually provide it themselves, even if the deafness is discovered much earlier. They assume they can "stay ahead" of the child in learning sign-language vocabulary—and don't realize that the real problem is syntax. Unless raised in a deaf community themselves, the parents seldom get good enough at sign language to use signing *syntax,* and so the deaf child can't discover much syntax from watching them.

"So those deaf kids really need to be in a deaf preschool, with fluent signing all about."

Exactly. But a few hours a day in such a preschool may be marginal, compared to what is experienced by the babies of deaf parents who are surrounded from birth by fluent ASL all day. They, however, are only 10 percent of all deaf children.

"So what's a parent to do?"

I asked one of the experts what she'd do herself if she had a deaf child. And she said that, besides having the whole family learn ASL as quickly as possible, she'd supplement the deaf preschool by hiring a deaf baby-sitter for the rest of the day. That certainly sounds like a more optimal strategy for the hearing parents of a deaf child, and it's perhaps an essential strategy when the child's deafness is discovered after much of the normal language-acquisition period has already passed.

Time's just too short after the discovery of the deafness, and so most parents don't get their act together before the window closes. In many places, community resources don't kick in until school age. So another child loses out on its proper human heritage, language, all because the community didn't try to head off trouble with free well-baby clinics and outreach programs.

"At least they're better off than those 'wolf children,' the kids supposedly reared by wild animals."

They're a particularly dramatic example of an abnormal upbringing, but they usually have multiple medical and social problems that interfere with an analysis of their language learning deficits. The deaf children of hearing parents are almost normal in comparison, having everything except language experience.

There are some intermediate cases around, such as Genie. She's the girl brought up by a mentally ill father who locked her in her room. Until she was discovered at age 13, the only human voices she encountered after the age of 18 months would have been heard through the walls of her room.

Although said to be of normal intelligence, Genie has never developed normal language, despite intensive therapy provided after her discovery and release from her secret prison. After passing through the pre–two-year-old stages of language acquisition, she remains stuck at a level of language exemplified by such utterances as "Applesauce buy store."

Most sensory systems do not develop properly unless there is exposure to appropriate sensations during a particular phase of development, what we call the "critical period." Genie, those deaf children reared without syntax to discover, and the brain-damaged children—all suggest that there is a critical period for language in the preschool years. Without appropriate experience, then, language—in the beyond-the-apes sense—becomes impossible. Such language-deprived children will likely, like Genie, remain stuck at the level of protolanguage. For them, the "window of opportunity" may be past, and we can only try to prevent other children from suffering the same fate.

This is not to say that intensive instruction may not be helpful to the many children who were not totally isolated from language in the preschool years. A child's hearing loss may gradually develop, so the child has some syntax experience before becoming deaf. Developmental abnormalities that limit social interactions—such as the autistic children that talk very little—may give the appearance of lacking language, but such children may have gotten enough listening experience to acquire language during the critical period and thereby benefit from therapy later.

"What about critical periods for the chimps that have been learning sign language? Is that why some chimps have failed to learn syntax?"

It's not really sign language, in the ASL sense, although some early studies were indeed done with ASL. But manual signing is so hard to teach apes that not enough words can be learned in the time available.

What the experimenters now do is to use symbol boards with hundreds of arbitrary symbols, just like the ones used with retarded and autistic kids. The teachers point to the symbols as they talk aloud, and the apes—unable to talk very well—learn what symbols correspond to what objects, what foods, what actions, which people. And so they themselves point at a series of symbols to construct their own sentences.

It's much more natural, very much the way normal children acquire words: observing, learning what the symbol is good for, and then producing. The trouble with teaching apes manual sign languages like ASL is that it's a lot of work learning to produce a sign, and that comes before they ever learn what it's good for—which is not the way to motivate anyone, including apes. The symbol board tries to mimic the customary route by which babies work their way into the world of language: comprehension first, production later.

So far, it looks like there is a critical period for this kind of protolanguage even in the bonobos—even for learning words. The two bonobos exposed to the symbol-board language after the age of three—the mother of the two particularly successful bonobos, and their half-sibling—have not been able to acquire either words or an understanding of syntax, despite lots of effort by the teachers. But two other offspring of the same mother—both Kanzi and Panbanesha started on language earlier than age 3—have learned lots of words.

"I saw Kanzi on TV, doing about as well at carrying out complicated instructions as a little two-year-old girl did. So you've got to get to them while they're still young?"

Right. Whether ape or human. There may be some facet of language that is innate, but "language is innate" tends to gloss over the fact that the capacity needs to be developed during a sensitive period of early childhood.

REACQUIRING LANGUAGE AFTER LOSING IT is, of course, the big problem that stroke patients may have. Although most adults with large areas of damage in the left brain will have permanent language deficits, those with smaller areas of injury may recover. They may initially have equally severe deficits but then go on to recover some or all language functions over a period of months to years.

"So speech therapy works for stroke victims?"

Although there is some evidence that this recovery is hastened by speech therapy, it may also occur without any therapy. *How* this recovery occurs is an important question, for it can give us some idea of the extent of "plasticity" of the adult brain. And maybe help us design a really effective speech therapy for aphasics.

"So does the right brain start helping out, when the language areas of the left brain are damaged by a stroke?"

Occasionally. In a few patients, the right brain seems to have a basic vocabulary, as shown by an ability to point at objects whose names they have heard. These abilities have been most clearly shown for some epileptics whose corpus callosum has been severed. This bundle of connections represents the major path for the cerebral cortex of the left brain to connect with the cerebral cortex of the right brain, and so cutting it can prevent the spread of left-sided seizures into right brain as well. In some (but by no means all) of these "split-brain" patients the isolated right nondominant hemisphere seems to have some understanding of the meaning of simple nouns.

The trouble is, this basic vocabulary of their right brains may represent rearrangement rather than intrinsic right-brain language abilities, just as in the Sturge-Weber children with left-hemisphere seizures, where some left-brain language functions emigrated to the right brain before the surgery that cut the connections. Most of the famous split-brain patients also had seizures from early childhood. In any event, human right-brain abilities seem minor on the scale of chimpanzee and bonobo linguistic achievements—unless language has been totally forced out of the left brain early in life.

"Well, what about rearrangements within the left brain itself, after a stroke? Does that work like those sensory strip monkeys?"

Although relatively few cases have been examined so far, it's not looking like those rearranged finger maps—at least with the techniques suitable for use in the O.R. When patients who have recovered from strokes have electrical stimulation mapping for some reason—usually during surgery for the seizures caused by the stroke—their naming sites are found on the margins of the stroke damage. Yet those sites are within the territory where naming sites can be found in "normals." Were there substantial reassignment, you would expect naming sites in unusual places. That hasn't been seen.

But perhaps there would be a better chance of seeing rearrangements while they are in the process of happening, rather than later, when stabilized. In a few patients with brain tumors near language areas, language has been mapped several times, at different stages in tumor enlargement. As with the epilepsy patients without tumors, the tumor patients have multiple well-localized naming sites when first mapped, at a time when language seems normal. As the tumor progresses and language begins to fail, a patient may undergo a second surgery to remove the resurgent tumor; at that operation, remapping shows that one of those naming sites has been altered.

What happens is that the well-defined boundaries of the naming site seem to be replaced by a more diffuse area where only an occasional error in naming occurs during stimulation. The other naming sites seem to be unchanged. Later, when the patient experiences greater language difficulties, remapping shows loss of additional naming sites. Again, naming sites in unusual locations have not yet been observed in such patients.

These findings are not what one would expect if a lot of rearrangement were possible in the adult language cortex. The substantial rearrangements in the sensory strip's map for the hand and the face in monkeys had raised the hope that the potential for adult rearrangement might be widespread, that the visual cortex was just a "hard-wired" exception. Neither set of observations from naming sites suggest that new ones can develop in unusual cortical areas, although such centimeter-scale measurements with stimulation mapping hardly rule out more subtle sorts of reassignments on the millimeter scale seen in the adult monkey sensory strip with sophisticated eavesdropping on the individual neurons.

"But still," Neil observed, "there are several naming sites. That's redundancy, isn't it?"

Not really. A substantial number of naming sites must be destroyed before language fails completely. But gradual loss of even one site, as by a slowly enlarging tumor, seems to be associated with minor language problems. And sudden loss of one site, as in strokes, is often followed by a severe language problem, lasting for months at least. So that isn't redundancy in the usual sense of the word—like those two backup systems for lowering the landing gear of an airplane, in case the primary hydraulics fail.

"But I've heard that you lose neurons every day of your life. So there must be redundancy, or we'd all become demented."

Yes, there's a slow "normal" loss of neurons in many parts of the brain with age. And when that happens, performance does gradually degrade. It takes longer to do things, and more errors are made.

But generalizations about the number of neurons lost every day tend to obscure the really interesting differences between brain regions in the loss rate. The substantia nigra, in the depths of the brain, has lost half its neurons by age 75 in normal humans, a time when some nearby regions of brain stem still have 98 percent of their neurons. One part of the hippocampus (one of the oldest cortical structures) tends to lose about one-fourth of its neurons by age 75. But nothing so dramatic happens to the neocortex, unless aided by disease.

Even though few (if any) new neurons are formed during life, we can retune many circuits to operate with fewer and fewer neurons. As I noted earlier, it is often said that about 80 percent of any given system can be destroyed before symptoms are noticed, so long as it is done very slowly (as in tumor growth) rather than rapidly (as by a stroke interrupting the blood supply).

"So you can get away with a lot of neuron death in the brain, so long as it happens slowly?"

That's the idea. The issue becomes one of the minimum number of neurons needed before compensation fails. For example, about 70 to 80 percent of substantia nigra neurons are missing in patients with Parkinsonism, a level that ordinarily would not be reached until after age 100. It is presumed that some viral disease earlier in life destroyed some neurons there, but that symptoms don't appear until the age-related decline brings the total to the 70–80-percent level.

More sudden inactivation of neural circuitry, where the system doesn't have time to readjust and reassign functions, may result in obvious problems if as little as, say, 30 percent of a system's neurons are not working well. So this really isn't redundancy in the usual sense of the word, but some form of distributed functionality.

"So what happens when you're getting close to the threshold for trouble? Can you get any warning?"

You start getting some intermittent problems, here today and gone tomorrow. And difficult to identify. But they're more likely to occur at some times of the day than others. When the number of functioning neurons in a brain system gets close to the threshold, then fluctuations in function may become noticeable as the patient tires during a long day. Or in response to unrelated illnesses such as head colds. Arms may get weak, a foot may drag, blurred vision may develop, reflexes may become abnormal, remembering a name may become more difficult than usual—depending, of course, on what system is marginal.

This situation is often encountered during recovery from head injuries or strokes, when patients may have neurological deficits when first awakening in the morning while they are still somewhat groggy. The neurological symptoms then disappear by midmorning. But, as the patient becomes fatigued in the evening, the symptoms reappear. As the system recovers from injury or successfully reassigns function to undamaged brain regions, then the fluctuations in function seldom reach the threshold—and so the symptoms disappear.

"That reminds me of some auto mechanics I know who try to explain to me that the hardest problems to diagnose are the intermittent ones. Sometimes you can reveal them by making the engine labor, going up a steep hill. And sometimes you just have to wait until something thoroughly fails, in order to find the problem."

Brains are often like that, too. That's why intermittent neurological problems often have to be referred to various specialists, who are a bit better at figuring out the mental equivalents of those steep hills—so as to temporarily fatigue the patient, and more clearly reveal the nature of the deficit. And thus figure out the right diagnosis, on the route to a prognosis and treatment.

"But auto mechanics have a big advantage over physicians. They can just try replacing one thing after another until the car stops intermittently failing."

Or until the customer's pocketbook runs dry, whichever comes first.

chapter 13

Taking Apart the Visual Image

What we get on the retina, whether we are chickens or human beings, is a welter of dancing light points stimulating the sensitive rods and cones that fire their messages into the brain. What we see is a stable world. It takes an effort of the imagination and a fairly complex apparatus to realize the tremendous gulf that exists between the two. . . . The coding process begins while en route between the retina and our conscious mind.

The art historian E.H.GOMBRICH, 1959

NEIL HAD JUST GOTTEN the good news, that another patient had to be rescheduled. And so Neil was on the O.R. schedule for the day after tomorrow.

This was going to be his last full day of freedom for a while, but he seemed to have everything under control and wasn't at all anxious to cut short our regular discussion at the corner table behind the espresso cart.

"It's nothing like those patients who are on renal dialysis and waiting for a donor kidney," he said. "Those people are carrying beepers and have to be ready to drop everything and rush to the hospital on several hours' notice. I got two days' notice."

Yes, I said, and they have to live that way for months on end.

"I don't have to be anywhere as organized as they do—nor wait for someone else to make a fatal mistake. Probably one of the seat belt-less."

Hereabouts we have another name for the person who ignores his seat belt: the *multiple-organ donor.*

As Neil had been having some of the usual confusion experienced by neurobiology students, we wound up discussing the nuts-and-bolts aspects of sensation. In particular, how a neuron senses a *pattern* of input rather than just saying, in effect, "Yes, *something* is there." You can't understand it, I explained, except from a single neuron's point of view.

A retinal neuron's point of view is of two antagonistic areas of the visual world. It sees a small round patch but also a surrounding ring. Like the skin comparison neurons in the spinal cord, the center may be excitatory and the surround inhibitory. If there is a line or edge passing through the center of their receptive field (but not covering much of the antagonistic surround), the neuron tends to pass on a message "Light-dark boundary hereabouts."

Just as in the case of skin sensations, adjacent areas tend to contradict one another so that only small discrete lighted areas are particularly effective—for example, a white spot on a darker background. Bigger spots that entirely cover both antagonistic areas may be ignored because the two contributions cancel out each other. Some retinal neurons have a receptive field with an inhibitory center and an excitatory surround, something like an inverted Mexican hat, and so they respond best to a black spot on a light background.

"What happens if the light covers both parts?"

The neuron may totally ignore regions of visual space lacking boundaries. Diffuse light on the retina, like the watchband on the skin, may be too uniform to be an effective stimulus for some second-order neurons.

The antagonistic interactions tend to sharpen up some otherwise fuzzy boundaries, since they serve to exaggerate the differences. And when the boundaries were already sharp to start with, this exaggeration can create additional lines where none exist.

"How's that work?"

I held up my hand toward the ceiling lights and squeezed my fingers tightly together, then tried to peek through the narrow slit between the fingers. Neil did the same.

What most people will see are some little black lines in the middle of the slit. They aren't real.

"They're not diffraction patterns?"

They're a visual illusion, just a consequence of those antagonistic interactions in the retina and others farther back in the visual pathways that serve to enhance transitions between different shades of gray. We call them "Mach bands."

Another stage of comparison is made in the retina before impulses finally get to travel down the optic nerve and into the brain proper. The third-order neuron (the retinal ganglion cell, whose axon is in the optic nerve) compares center and surround.

"Again? Weren't the second-order neurons doing that?"

Yes, but the principle repeats all through the system. One result is that even fewer neurons respond to diffuse light. A small spot confined to the excitatory area causes a few impulses to get sent down the optic nerve ("Light on, here").

In addition to antagonizing the excitatory response when a large light spot is turned on, the inhibitory areas of the receptive field tend

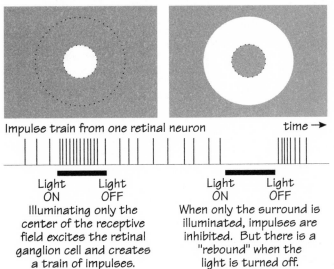

The "receptive field" is the area of the visual world to which a particular neuron is sensitive, responding with either excitation or inhibition. Inhibition is often followed by a rebound, the "OFF response." Here, the receptive field is circular, organized into an excitatory center and an inhibitory surround.

Impulse train from one retinal neuron   time →

Light   Light   Light   Light
ON   OFF   ON   OFF
Illuminating only the   When only the surround is
center of the receptive   illuminated, impulses are
field excites the retinal   inhibited. But there is a
ganglion cell and creates   "rebound" when the
a train of impulses.   light is turned off.

to announce when a light leaves the inhibitory area. There's a brief burst of impulses that says, in effect, "Light off."

"So a burst of impulses from that neuron could either signify the light turning on, or the light turning off?"

Right. This third-order neuron makes, in effect, a temporal comparison in addition to its spatial comparison. Moving the light spot is capable of getting an otherwise silent neuron to perk up and take notice.

While second-order neurons have some tendency to emphasize light-on and light-off, it is the third-order neurons that exaggerate conditions that change in time. Much of this was discovered in the cat retina by the neurophysiologist Stephen Kuffler in the 1950s, building on earlier work by H. Keffer Hartline in the frog retina.

One reason that light-on and light-off is so important is that the visual image is rarely unmoving—it jitters around by the width of a few photoreceptors. So even if nothing is moving in your field of view, everything is in motion on the retina—even when you try to keep your eyes focused on a single point. The visual image is broken up into areas of near-uniform illumination and the boundaries between them. And it's boundaries that activate so many neurons. When you stabilize the image on the retina with a fancy system that eliminates the jitter, parts of the image tend to fade out.

"Really? You mean your view of someone's nose might fade because it isn't moving, but his hair might remain visible because it was blowing in the breeze?"

Yes, a little movement is very important in keeping the brain interested in something. So the system produces some movement,

○ ○ *mild, vigorous response to light being turned ON.*

● ● *mild, vigorous response when light is turned OFF (and inhibition during light ON).*

↕ 1°

Map showing how two retinal ganglion cells respond to small spots of light on a screen

Modified from Rodieck, 1973

even when the external world doesn't have any. Thanks to this micronystagmus, the third-order neurons in a boundary zone between different shades of gray will "see" flickering light—from their point of view, and that's what's important here. Even somewhat fuzzy boundaries are detected by this system. Lines can look sharper than they actually are, because of this. So, even out in the retina, you see both of the major building blocks of visual perception, temporal contrast, and spatial contrast.

THERE ARE FOURTH-ORDER NEURONS back in the brain stem, but the main path to the cortex goes through the thalamus, its lateral geniculate nucleus. The fourth-order neurons there behave rather like their third-order inputs from the retina—at least, when tested with black-and-white stimuli rather than colors. Their receptive fields are the same center-surround doughnut shapes as in the retinal neurons.

"But I thought you expected to see big differences there?"

Yes, it was quite a surprise back in the early 1960s when David Hubel and Torsten Wiesel discovered that the geniculate neurons were so similar to the retinal ones. We'd expected to see major transformations, but things turn out to be more subtle.

The most noticeable difference is that diffuse white light is an even poorer stimulus for geniculate neurons than for the retinal neurons earlier in the path. While retinal neurons often exhibit some net excitation when uniformly illuminated, excitation and inhibition tend to completely cancel out in the geniculate cells.

But that's stimulating with white light or shades of gray. Try out colored lights and something new appears, not seen in the retina. The neuron may be excited by red light over a wide area, and inhibited by green light over that same wide area.

"No more center and surround?"

In some geniculate neurons, the center-surround organization simply disappears. Besides this novelty, the geniculate turns out to have some differences between neurons in the bottom two layers and those in the top four layers. The top four layers have small cells ("parvocellular") and the bottom two layers have noticeably larger cells ("magnocellular"). The magnocellular layers receive preferentially from the larger third-order neurons in the retina.

"So they're the fast track."

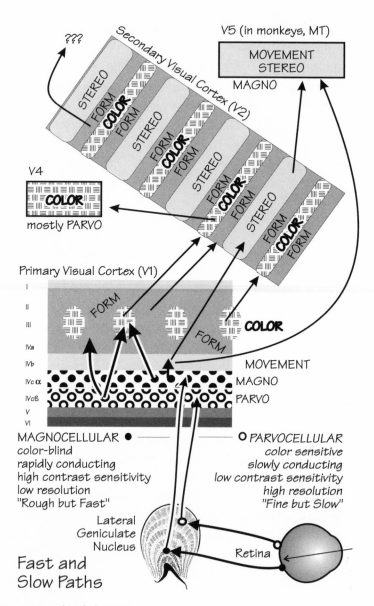

After Livingstone and Hubel, 1988

Not only that, but these magnocellular-layer neurons send their axons to cortical regions particularly concerned with small changes in spatial contrast and small movements. They quickly detect changes in the visual image and tend to exaggerate them.

At least, they do this more than do the neurons of the four parvocellular layers, which receive preferentially from the smaller third-order neurons of the retina and send their axons to regions of the cortex more concerned with color and the more obvious contrast differences.

"Filling in such details can be done more slowly?"

Perhaps. One of the fascinating things is that the parvocellular layers look normal in dyslexic children—but the magnocellular layers look disorganized, their cells shrunken as if neural development had taken a misstep.

STILL FURTHER ALONG, the information from the eyes reaches the cerebral cortex. Here things are really rearranged, with new principles becoming apparent. For example, the cortex pays a lot more attention to elongated objects than it does to isolated spots of light.

The cortex is no relay station in the manner that the geniculate was first thought to be.

"Where did you get that term, 'relay station'?"

It comes from the old Pony Express, in the California land rush days, the places where the mailbags were switched from tired horses to fresh ones—but the messages weren't analyzed or transformed. Geniculate, at first glimpse, is something like that. In the cortex, however, the messages are rearranged to make new patterns.

The inputs to the cortex have those center-surround arrangements but are wired up to a cortical neuron in such a way as to create elongated receptive fields. The optimal stimulus for retinal and geniculate cells is a white spot on a dark background (or in other cells, a black spot on a light background)—always a round spot, although the optimal size varies among cells. In the cortical neurons, round spots might evoke a response, but the optimal stimuli are lines and elongated edges.

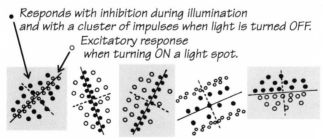

Responds with inhibition during illumination and with a cluster of impulses when light is turned OFF.

Excitatory response when turning ON a light spot.

Maps from five visual cortex neurons, showing how they connect with the projection screen

Modified from Hubel and Wiesel, 1962

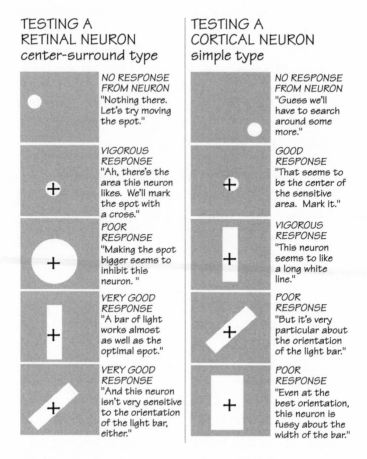

TESTING A
RETINAL NEURON
center-surround type

NO RESPONSE
FROM NEURON
"Nothing there.
Let's try moving
the spot."

VIGOROUS
RESPONSE
"Ah, there's the
area this neuron
likes. We'll mark
the spot with
a cross."

POOR
RESPONSE
"Making the spot
bigger seems to
inhibit this
neuron. "

VERY GOOD
RESPONSE
"A bar of light
works almost
as well as the
optimal spot."

VERY GOOD
RESPONSE
"And this neuron
isn't very sensitive
to the orientation
of the light bar,
either."

TESTING A
CORTICAL NEURON
simple type

NO RESPONSE
FROM NEURON
"Guess we'll
have to search
around some
more."

GOOD
RESPONSE
"That seems to
be the center of
the sensitive
area. Mark it."

VIGOROUS
RESPONSE
"This neuron
seems to like
a long white
line."

POOR
RESPONSE
"But it's very
particular about
the orientation
of the light bar."

POOR
RESPONSE
"Even at the
best orientation,
this neuron is
fussy about the
width of the bar."

"So you've got real line specialists. The frog's eye may specialize in black dots like flies, but our visual cortex likes lines?"

The emphasis on optimal stimuli can be overdone. If the stimulus is a line or an edge, of course, the *inputs* to the cortex aren't firing at their optimum—which occurs with a spot of just the right size for *them*. So they're responding only halfheartedly to the line. Yet a cortical neuron finds those inputs from suboptimally stimulated neurons optimal for itself. And so we have become cautious about characterizing the cortical cells as "optimal for straight lines" when they also respond pretty well to an eyebrow.

Those fourth-order axons coming up to the cortex seem to be arranged so that the cortical neuron sums together the activity of many input cells whose receptive field centers were not all in the same place but rather strung out in a line. And so a white line on a darker background becomes the best way of maximizing the excitation while minimizing the inhibition. An edge (or a very wide line) may also be effective, as only half of the inhibitory flanks are thus stimulated. But diffuse white light that uniformly illuminates the receptive field is likely to cause inhibition to cancel whatever excitation gets through, as even the fourth-order neurons in the thalamus will fail to pass along the information in most cases (unless it's a uniform color).

Some cortical neurons prefer horizontal white lines; others respond best to vertical ones. And there are specialists for the in-between angles as well. As you change the tilt of a line that optimally stimulates a cortical neuron, its response will diminish, disappearing within about 5 to 10 degrees away from the optimal angle. Of course, another group of cortical neurons become active at that point.

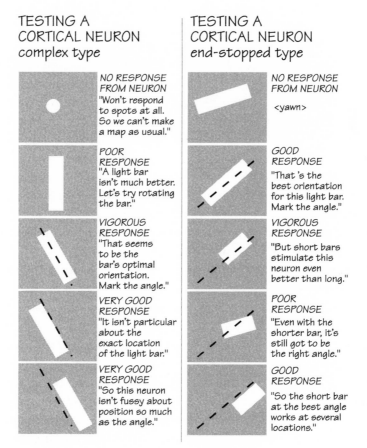

TESTING A
CORTICAL NEURON
complex type

NO RESPONSE
FROM NEURON
"Won't respond
to spots at all.
So we can't make
a map as usual."

POOR
RESPONSE
"A light bar
isn't much better.
Let's try rotating
the bar."

VIGOROUS
RESPONSE
"That seems
to be the
bar's optimal
orientation.
Mark the angle."

VERY GOOD
RESPONSE
"It isn't particular
about the
exact location
of the light bar."

VERY GOOD
RESPONSE
"So this neuron
isn't fussy about
position so much
as the angle."

TESTING A
CORTICAL NEURON
end-stopped type

NO RESPONSE
FROM NEURON

<yawn>

GOOD
RESPONSE
"That's the
best orientation
for this light bar.
Mark the angle."

VIGOROUS
RESPONSE
"But short bars
stimulate this
neuron even
better than long."

POOR
RESPONSE
"Even with the
shorter bar, it's
still got to be
the right angle."

GOOD
RESPONSE
"So the short bar
at the best angle
works at several
locations."

"And I presume that some neurons prefer narrow black lines on white backgrounds."

Yes, as they get their inputs from those inverted Mexican hat receptive field neurons in retina and geniculate whose optimal stimulus is a black spot on a white background. Still other cortical neurons seem to like edges, such as a sky-sea boundary.

The cortical neurons have a lot of variety, but it isn't totally random. Neighboring cells tend to have the same preferences for tilt, until suddenly reaching a neighbor that prefers a quite different tilt. It appears that there is a column of about a hundred neurons in the cortex which are all organized similarly, at least for orientation preference. And that next door, there are adjacent columns interested in other orientations (often the "adjacent" angles, but sometimes jumping to an entirely different orientation). So we began to talk about "orientation columns" in the cortex as key features in the process of taking apart the visual image into important components.

THEN CAME AN EVEN BIGGER SURPRISE: some cortical neurons would respond to the optimally oriented line even when it was moved sideways. For many a lower-order neuron, that maneuver would cause the neuron to be inhibited because the stimulus moves from the receptive field center into a portion of the antagonistic periphery. There was a region perhaps 10 to 15 degrees wide where such a neuron still responded to the line. But only when the line remained at its optimal orientation: try tilting the line away from its favored orientation, and the neuron would stop responding.

"The neuron is sensitive to orientation—but it's independent of where the line is? That's sure odd."

Hubel and Wiesel called these "complex cells" in distinction to the "simple cells" sensitive to orientation but also place.

"So are the complex cells generalizing on the concept of *line tilted at 45 degrees?*"

Psychologists have talked about generalization as a difference between lower and higher animals. Some species will learn to treat an erect and an upside-down triangle as "the same thing." Yet other species will always treat them as different, refusing to "generalize on the concept of triangle." Complex cells are generalizing, not about triangles but about one of the parts of the triangle, a tilted line.

"This is all very interesting," Neil said after finishing off his lemonade, "but it's getting a little abstract. Do you see any patients with such patterning problems?"

Every few years, someone reports a case of an epileptic whose seizures are triggered by patterned light, I told him.

"Flickering lights, like those strobe lights they used to have in discos?"

Sometimes, but in some patients a spatial pattern gives trouble too—as in looking at a screen-wire mesh covering the window or a herringbone pattern in a fabric. There was a case of two brothers who both had seizures triggered by spatial patterns. Their mother would sometimes find one of them frozen in place, staring at a screen door. Sure enough, when hooked up to the EEG machine to record their brain waves, fine repeating patterns would evoke the preseizure waveforms. But only if the lines in the pattern were tilted at a particular angle. It certainly seemed as if their brains got carried away when one type of receptive field was activated.

SO THE VISUAL CORTEX has at least two new building blocks, oriented-line-in-a-place and oriented-line-in-many-places. A third type soon appeared, the "end-stopped" receptive fields where the neuron liked lines, but only if they didn't exceed a certain length at one end. Are there higher-order cells in the brain that specialize in triangles, no matter what their size or tilt, no matter whether black-on-white or white-on-black, no matter whether the center is filled or not? Not so far.

Taking apart the visual image doesn't stop in this first cortical visual area. It continues next door in the second, where specialized subregions emphasize form, color, and distance away. Indeed, there are nearly three dozen "secondary" visual areas so far—and that's in monkeys. No one knows how many there are in humans, whose cerebral cortex is an order of magnitude more extensive than that of the monkeys.

And, if that three-fold variation in size of the human primary visual area is any indication, there ought to be a lot of individual differences in these higher-order visual processing areas as well: inborn differences, plus all the variations due to different early experiences with the visual world.

"But there are no triangle detectors?" Neil teased. "And here I thought that you were going to tell me about the neuron that specializes in my grandmother's face. How are you ever going to get proper names for unique individuals if you can't even get cells to represent common categories like triangles?"

The neuron that is so specialized that it responds only to the sight of your grandmother's face is, alas, a fictitious beast closely related in the cerebral mythology to the boss in the executive suite. We're delighted with all the feature-extracting neurons of visual cortex—but we also doubt that such extreme overspecialization is always needed. If a committee of three generalists is good enough to distinguish between all the colors in the spectrum, maybe a committee of several dozen will suffice for all the faces you know.

The "trichromaticity" committee principle was first discovered by Thomas Young, back in 1802. He was a British physician whose many interests included Egyptology. Then the principle was reformulated by the German physiologist-turned-physicist Hermann von Helmholtz in 1860, and fleshed out by the biophysicists who finally—about 1960—got the techniques to see and measure the three cone types predicted by Young and Helmholtz.

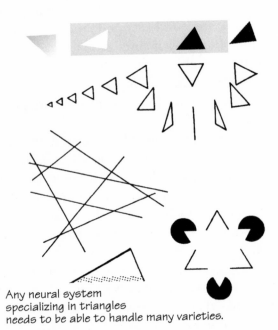

Any neural system
specializing in triangles
needs to be able to handle many varieties.

Adapted from Partridge and Partridge, 1993

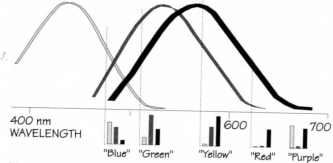

How color judgments arise from combinations
of responses in the three photoreceptor types

"Trichromaticity means that mixtures of red, green, and blue will mimic any color you want?" Neil asked. "The way it works on my color TV?"

Right. One of the photoreceptors is more sensitive to the long-wavelength end of the spectrum—actually it peaks in the yellow-green, not in the red. Another has peak sensitivity in the middle wavelengths near green but has skirts covering the spectrum from blue to yellow. The third emphasizes the short-wavelength end, peaking in the violet but still somewhat sensitive to the yellows.

With only one type, you don't know whether its response is due to a bright yellow light or a dim violet light. With three receptor types, you can sort out this ambiguity. With only two types, as in the common kind of color blindness, you will confuse colors in some situations. With three types of cones, you get a committee judgment that's more reliable.

"Is that where colors like purple come in? Purple isn't in the rainbow."

Purple happens when you get strong votes from the long- and short-wavelength photoreceptors, at a time when the middle-wavelength photoreceptors aren't saying very much. If the middle were to vote equally heavily, you'd see white instead of purple. If the long-wavelength signal were strongest, with the other two very weak, you'd call the light red.

Note that when this happens, we call it red even though the only active photoreceptor actually peaked in the yellow-green. Red is a property of the committee votes in such a ratio, not of any one photoreceptor type. That's why we're so cautious about emphasizing the optimal stimulus shape for those visual pathway neurons. If color is any lesson, the peak sensitivity isn't as important as the spread in sensitivity. And which combinations are activated together.

That's the lesson of color mixing, and we're constantly rediscovering it. Taste works the same way. There aren't any true specialists among the taste buds in the tongue, just four broadly tuned sensor types, all a little different.

"Reminds me of what that gourmet cook is always saying on television, that good taste is a matter of getting the right combination of ingredients. I do wish that cafeteria cooks would learn about those interesting sweet and sour combinations, like strawberries and rhubarb," Neil said.

"I serve on a program committee," he continued, "and I run into some of the same people when I go to a meeting of the fund-raising committee. So you think that, like me, a neuron is a member of a lot of different committees? And that the category is implemented by a committee and not a specialist neuron?"

The Hebbian ensemble notion is that, when you recall a word like *peanut,* you are reactivating that particular committee of neurons. The committee may not look like a peanut, not any more than the bar code on a can of peanuts does, but it serves to represent the cerebral code for the peanut. A proper name, such as your grandmother's, is likely to require a somewhat larger committee, so as to distinguish her from all the other women you know.

"So it might take a dozen neurons to get the category, but another dozen to specify it further, narrowing it down to a particular individual?"

That's the idea, although it might be hundreds rather than dozens. The stroke patient who can't recognize his wife's face, even though he can tell one face from another, usually has a rather large area of damage on the underside of the temporal lobes. And such a patient has just as much trouble spotting a picture of his own car amid a series of photographs of similar cars. It's as if he can't narrow things down further, from the general to the particular.

"But surely it's important to know the basic elements," Neil said. "You can figure out color mixing a lot better for knowing those three cone types. You can't make much sense of purple without them. And as the TV cook says, you've got to know your basics in order to innovate, make the really interesting new combinations."

Yes, and the closer we get to knowing the shapes and colors and motions that the individual neurons like, the better we can understand something like recognizing faces, and why we make the mistakes that we do.

"Mistakes like forgetting my seat belt, fifteen years ago?"

Sorry, we don't know the origins of major mistakes yet. But minor mistakes, such as using the wrong word—*that* we're starting to understand. Tomorrow night, before the operation, we'll give you a preview of the slide show you'll see in the operating room.

"I'll probably make lots of mistakes on that test. George said he could almost guarantee it."

Yes, he can.

chapter 14

How the Brain Subdivides Language

"ESTO ES UN ELEFANTE," Neil says, from under the sterile tent in the O.R. The slide projector advances. "Esta es una manzana," he continues.

Since Neil has been bilingual from childhood, George is going to locate his Spanish naming areas, to see if they differ from the English naming areas. The neuropsychologist reloaded the slide trays in the projector, and Neil was asked to name the pictures of elephants, apples, and other objects, in Spanish this time through. And again the stimulating probe is placed on the same brain areas to determine if any of those sites are essential for naming in this second language.

As Neil's mapping in Spanish proceeds, it becomes apparent that stimulating the earlier naming sites does not always block naming in Spanish. And at some sites where English naming was unaffected, naming in Spanish is disturbed.

YESTERDAY AFTERNOON, after Neil had checked into the hospital room, I went with George when he discussed the details of the operation with Neil.

George described once again why the operation was being done, the probability that it would control Neil's seizures ("operations don't always work"), its risks ("low but not zero"), and the mechanics of positioning and testing and such.

219

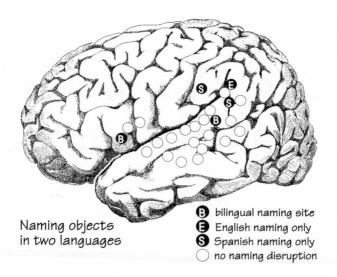

Naming objects
in two languages

B bilingual naming site
E English naming only
S Spanish naming only
○ no naming disruption

"We're going to do some extra testing during the stimulation tomorrow," George said. "Since you use your Spanish in your business, we have to worry about where that's located. And since I hear that your appetite for books is insatiable, I think we'd better do some extra testing of reading localization."

"I hope you'll give me something easier to read in the O.R. than those convoluted sentences that describe brain pathways," Neil said.

"The sentences we use are probably stolen from grade-school textbooks," George said. "Areas for reading are often close to the epileptic area and aren't always in the same place as sites important to naming in English."

"I always suspected that reading and speaking didn't use the same piece of brain," Neil commented. "I once had one of my speeches transcribed, one that sounded pretty good. But it was terrible in the written version. And vice versa—all those prepared speeches that look good on paper—they never sound right when read from a podium. The rules are just different. But different areas for English and Spanish?"

"Well," George continued, "strokes in bilingual patients often cause more problems with one of their languages than the other."

"How's that?"

"Sometimes it's probably because one language had been used more often than the other. If it's the less-used language that's impaired, that's hardly surprising. Or maybe the patient's native tongue is 'better recorded' because it was written on a 'blank slate' of childhood. Perhaps the remaining language is the one used most recently, before the stroke. But occasionally, neurologists encounter a patient whose remaining language abilities can't be explained away by one of these common-sense aspects."

Neil nodded, and George continued. "Following a stroke, someone might speak *only* a language that she learned as an exchange student. Even though she hasn't used it since her teens, that's all she can now speak."

Indeed, I mentioned, the immediate family is quite distressed because nobody knows the language. There's a frantic search to find someone who can guess what language it is.

"Cases such as that have forced language theorists to consider whether second languages are housed elsewhere, not in the same place in the brain as the native tongues. And we think we know why this happens," George explained. "In the dozen or so patients who have had stimulation mapping of two languages, some degree of separation of naming sites in the two languages has been the rule, although there are also sites common to both languages."

"Are naming areas for the second language smaller?" asked Neil from his chair by the window.

"Actually, they're slightly larger than those for the first language," George replied. "In other words, the second language can be disrupted from a nickel-sized site rather than a dime-sized site. It's often hard to separate 'when you learn it' from 'how good you get,' but the first language may be somewhat more compactly organized than later ones—its naming sites are not spread out as widely."

It's rare for a second language to be found in the opposite hemisphere—at least, based on the most reliable methods for establishing such lateralization, judging from the Wada test or the effects of strokes and tumors. Regardless of whether the language is pictographic or phonetic, written or spoken, it usually depends on left-brain mechanisms.

"Even sign languages depend on the left brain, just as do oral languages and reading. A neuropsychologist, Ursula Bellugi, studied the effects of strokes in deaf patients who have communicated with American Sign Language since birth. She found that left-brain strokes interfere with signing, and right-sided strokes do not. Furthermore, stroke location in the sign-language users tends to predict expressive and receptive types of difficulty, just as in the hearing and speaking patient. It shows you that this is a cortical specialization for *language* we're dealing with, not speech or hearing."

Different naming areas can be found for sign and oral language, based on observations in a few hearing patients who learned sign language because of a deaf family member. Just as in the more traditional bilingual patients, mapping shows a partial separation of sites that disrupt signing or speaking the name of the same object pictures.

George then got down to the business at hand. "Neil, each time we have someone awake during one of these operations, we also try to learn a little something more about how the brain works. These are research studies and not crucial to treating your seizures, so we don't have to do them. But awake operations are a unique opportunity to learn more about such functions as language, things that can be studied only in humans."

Neil nodded, and George continued. "So what we would like to do tomorrow, if it's agreeable with you, is a special stimulation study—in addition to the one we have to do to perform your operation safely, localizing your two languages and reading. The only major down side to this is that it will lengthen the operation about 20 or 30 minutes, and you'll be awake that extra time. The extra time probably doesn't change the risk of the operation significantly, except that it might very slightly increase the risk of an infection."

"What have you been trying to find out?"

"Well, we've been looking into the location of different *categories* of names. We've been comparing 'animals' to 'tools'—that's because there are a few stroke patients who can name one of those categories and not another, as if their animal names were stored in the region of cortex that their stroke destroyed. We've also looked at stimulation effects on understanding of speech sounds, and the face and tongue movements you have to make to produce speech sounds. Recently we've been examining the ability to produce verbs from nouns—I say 'bike' and you say 'ride.' It's all the rage in language studies now."

"Sounds like syntax."

"No, that's just the parts of speech and their common partners. The mistakes made when reading seem to involve the syntax of the sentence. These patients make mistakes on verb endings, pronouns, conjunctions, and prepositions—but not on nouns or verb stems."

"Such as?"

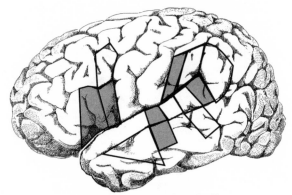

Zones where more than half
of the sites disrupt naming

Data from Ojemann, 1991

"Changing 'them' to 'we' or 'she' to 'it.' Reading 'If my son is late for class again' as 'If my son will getting late for class again.' Things like that."

"My English teacher in high school must have thought I was missing my sites for syntax."

"All in all," George went on, "these studies suggest that language is taken apart by the brain. That different parts of language are processed in different areas, just as the visual system takes apart the visual image into colors and contours and movements using different specialized regions of cortex. But we are only beginning to learn how language

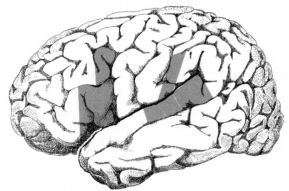

Zones where more than half
of the sites disrupt reading

Data from Ojemann, 1991

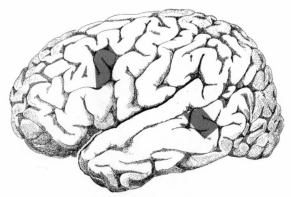

Zones where stimulation produces
reading errors involving syntax

Data from Ojemann, 1991

is separated out. Some of the separations we expected to find haven't proved to be very obvious in the physiology."

Our overall impression from the varied development, stroke, and stimulation studies is that, at the level of the cortex, language is fragmented into many different components, each processed in a separate area, as though there were many different computers running in parallel, each assigned a small portion of a problem. A major question is, of course, how it is all pulled together to speak a meaningful sentence. But perhaps we will first need to discover the sites for nouns and verbs, for adverbs and adjectives, for declarative sentences and questions, for embedded phrases and metaphors.

Yet some caution is in order. Nouns and verbs seem like such sensible categories, but the history of science is full of attempted categories that failed (such as the four humors, or the categories of phrenology). Are we looking for the right categories as we map the language cortex? Is there a different way to slice the speech-and-language pie? Are there more fundamental questions that we should be asking?

"And what's on the research agenda for tomorrow?" Neil asked.

"We'll try to get some more information about a particularly odd finding," answered George. "While it's mostly different places for different things in our language studies, there are two functions that are usually changed from the very same places."

"Which ones?"

"The ability to understand speech sounds, like 'ba' and 'pa'—*and* the ability to move the face and tongue in the sequences of movement needed to produce language. That's what we want to investigate tomorrow—the first is simply a listening task, and the second is a performance task. My technician will come by your room after dinner to rehearse you on the tests that we'll use."

"I thought that speech production and speech understanding were really separated in the brain. Production in the front, and understanding in the rear. And now you tell me they overlap. What about wiretapping some of my neurons? I talked to a couple of other patients of yours who have had operations like mine, and one said he'd participated in a study of individual neurons. And another talked about a brain wave study."

"Yes," George responded, "we've several other studies that try to discern the physiologic mechanisms that generate language. We can't do every study in each patient, because that would take too much time. But I think we'll have time to try some wiretapping on you, if you're agreeable."

"By all means." Neil asked a few questions about this, read over the form asking if he was willing to participate in the research study, and then signed the form.

Microelectrodes are fine wires about the thickness of a hair. They're so fine that they can get close to neurons and record those impulses. But to do that, you have to stick the microelectrodes into the cortex.

"Since we want to preserve any brain that's important to language," explained George, "we can only do microelectrode recordings in brain that we're going to subsequently remove, which means only in areas that aren't essential for language. Even so, those studies have had some very interesting results. In one of those studies, we compared neuron activity during naming aloud to naming silently. And then to matching a spatial feature on the same pictures, such as the angle of a colored line superimposed on the picture. So you see the same pictures each time but pay attention to different things."

"Of course, the spatial thing should be a right-brain function and the naming a left-brain one. Isn't it?"

"When we do those microelectrode recordings from the right temporal lobe of patients who we know are left dominant for language, we find neurons that change activity with naming. Just as we do recording from the left temporal lobe in other patients like you."

"So this is from neurons in cortical areas that aren't close to naming sites—but they still change their activity during naming. Right?"

"About a fifth of the neurons we record from, in either the left or the *right* temporal lobe, get active during naming," George explained. "And the same thing is true for the spatial task. So the special role of the right brain in spatial functions also isn't a matter of having all the active neurons on that side."

"So does anything distinguish the 'dominant' side in these studies?"

"Yes, the changes in activity with language occur earlier in neurons in the left temporal lobe," George continued. "And many more of the neurons show reductions in activity—inhibition—than do neurons on the right. An exactly reversed pattern is seen for neurons active with the spatial measure—earlier activity and more inhibition on the right."

"So the neurons that get there first determine the response? Another survival of the fittest for neuron activity?"

"Possibly," George said. "We think the inhibition is part of an inhibitory surround that helps focus neural activity in the dominant hemisphere. It's interesting that few neurons, if any, seem to be active during *both* the spatial and language measures."

"So it's different neurons for different functions?" Neil said.

"Thus far. Although a few neurons were active with both naming aloud and naming silently, most were active with only one of these, too. We've tested reading aloud and reading silently. And we've recorded a few neurons during naming the same pictures in two languages. The findings are the same. Neurons change activity with only one function."

"And their neighbors do the same thing?"

"Not so far. Once in a while, the microelectrode will record activity from two or three neurons at the same time. Usually each of those nearby neurons will respond to something different. That might be a pretty good arrangement, just to help make associations. Such as having the neurons for naming next to the neurons for reading."

"Is that why this part of the brain is called association cortex?"

No, the name's been around for a hundred years, used for all of the neocortex except for the primary sensory and motor areas. Instead of calling it *terra incognita* like the old mapmakers, they called it the association cortex. Which, in part, it surely is: cortex has the reputation for handling associations. There is thought to be a division of labor with the subcortical regions, which handle the more well-established skills such as riding a bike.

The brain wave studies, of course, can be done from any of the exposed brain surface such as the language areas, not just what is going to be removed later. And so that gives a broader picture without quite as much detail. You tend to judge "getting active" by changes in the EEG of a region, where it becomes faster but with smaller excursions.

"The EEG change during naming, that characterized the naming sites, is called desynchronization," George added, "and likely reflects activity of the selective attention system from the thalamus. That system selects the cortical areas appropriate to the task at hand. For example, all the naming sites become active at about the same time, after the slide comes on the screen—the frontal lobe naming sites aren't lagging behind the temporal lobe naming sites, the way we'd expected."

"On the theory that language involved a serial process," Neil observed, "first decoding in the temporal lobe and then expression in the frontal lobe?"

"That was indeed the guess," George said. "And it was wrong. Our studies didn't find evidence for serial brain wave changes. All sites seemed to be turned on at once, at the beginning of a language event, and they stayed on during the whole event. That's the way many functions in animal cortex seem to be organized, too—parallel activation of dispersed cortical areas."

"And the changes are widespread," George continued. "We found that activation of motor speech areas was present even with silent naming, so our inner speech includes activation of motor systems."

"Whew! My brain as a committee of all these disparate areas still doesn't sit very well with me," Neil said. "And having all the committee members talking at once isn't making it any better. Is there any mechanism to make a particular committee hang together? Or hang separately, as the case may be?"

"We're currently looking for that mechanism in some of our newer brain wave studies. In various animal studies, there is a coherence in the EEG between different brain areas involved in the same task. Sometimes it shows up as a lot more wiggles in the higher frequency range, up around 25 to 70 Hertz. Maybe such a frequency also links together the separate areas for some one language function. That's what we're examining, looking for activity at some frequency in that range that is synchronous at the different language sites during the appropriate language function."

"We certainly haven't found such a frequency yet," George said, "but we're still looking. That's the nature of science. You get an idea of how things work from previous studies, and figure out a way to test it, and sometimes you've guessed right and sometimes not."

LANGUAGE ALSO DEPENDS on several other motor areas of the brain, I told Neil, in addition to the important one surrounding the sylvian fissure. One of these areas is high in the frontal lobe, near the midline, immediately in front of the leg motor cortex. This is a region called the supplementary motor area, a staple of motor organization in many mammals. Especially in the monkeys used in animal research, this area is thought to be important to initiating, planning, and programming of complex movements.

When this area is damaged in the left brains of humans, the effect is initially quite dramatic. The patient is mute, can't speak a word. And he can't move the other side of his body, either. In a few days, recovery begins. At first speech returns—but in an odd way. Initially, at least, the patient's speech is much better when merely talking at random, rather than when speech is requested. The problem seems to be in getting started with movements, including those of speech. George has described it as similar to the car's starter motor being broken.

Recovery continues over the next few weeks and is usually complete. In that respect, the effects of cortical damage to the supplementary motor area are quite different from damage around the sylvian fissure, where the effects may be permanent. Apparently the supplementary motor system on the other side can take over the "starter" function.

The supplementary motor area has shown increased activity during learning of new movements. The cortical region between it and the corpus callosum, the cingulate gyrus, has shown activity with word reading in the blood flow studies on normal volunteers. Stimulation of the supplementary motor area in the O.R. results in movements, usually of a complex nature. In some parts of the supplementary motor area, stimulation will block speech. In monkeys, stimulation in the supplementary motor area and the cingulate gyrus results in vocalization. Monkey neurons in that region change their activity when the monkey hears vocalizations—often selectively, responding only to vocalizations of their own species.

NEIL ASKED ABOUT SWEARING. While it is certainly speech, is it language? Or at least, language of the beyond-the-apes variety?

The brain area immediately below the supplementary motor area, the cingulate gyrus, is part of the "emotional" limbic system. An attractive hypothesis is that the activity of this region in man and monkey is related to emotional speech, especially expletives. Preservation of emotional speech is a characteristic of many patients with aphasia from strokes of the perisylvian region.

Patients who are aphasic are not usually mute. Regardless of how reserved or proper they may have been before the stroke, their limited language is sometimes dominated by swearing. One of many unresolved issues in the brain organization of language is whether this emotional speech is more resistant to the effects of brain damage because it depends on a different brain area, like the cingulate gyrus, or because it depends on the same brain areas as other language but is preserved because of its simplicity and extensive associations.

"Is that where all the swearing comes from in the Tourette's people?"

Impulsive vocalizations, most often grunts, characterize Tourette's syndrome. About 30 percent of the time, these largely involuntary vocalizations consist of shouting words, sometimes obscenities. Except for being interrupted by expletives at points in speech where the rest of us would usually just pause, his — it's males, three to one — language is otherwise normal.

These patients also have motor tics, such as blinking, nodding, tongue protrusion, sniffing, and even hopping and squatting. These usually start earlier in childhood, along with some grunts and barks. The obscenities are added to the repertoire in late grade school or high school.

"Just as in normal youngsters," Neil observed.

Tourette's is highly familial and, in affected families, looks as if it might be a male version of what, in females, turns instead into an obsessive-compulsive disorder. Current evidence indicates disordered function in the motor centers deep in the cerebral hemispheres, another clue that emotional speech and other language may depend on separate brain areas.

The supplementary motor area is the only site where animal and human vocalization can be closely related. Either this region is part of a more primitive communication system than human language, or an example of an evolutionarily older system being co-opted into language. No one has yet produced swearing with human brain stimulation, or even tried a mapping study during emotional speech.

"So tomorrow I'm going to lose some neurons in my left temporal lobe," Neil observed. "Probably even neurons that may be active during naming and other such language tasks—but they're not essential for them? Right?"

"That's why we talk about naming sites as essential sites," George replied. "The other stimulation sites are where naming can continue even though they are temporarily confused by the electrical buzz. The places that are merely active during naming don't seem to be essential in the same way, even though they obviously participate in the process. We can identify them as active using microelectrode recordings, brain wave, and blood flow studies. They're doing something that we don't understand very well. But in epileptics where these areas cause trouble occasionally, we find that we can remove many of them without causing more trouble than we cure."

chapter 15

Why Can We Read So Well?

"YOU KNOW," NEIL SAID, "I've traveled all over the world. But I've never seen an electrical plug like that one. You must have gotten it in Afghanistan."

I was being helpful while George's technician set up the slide projector alongside Neil's hospital bed. I'd tried to plug the power cord into the wall outlet, whereupon I realized that it was one of those old, oversized, explosion-proof connectors used in operating rooms back in the days when volatile general anesthetics were used.

The technician smiled and pointed to the adaptor cord stored on the bottom shelf of the equipment cart. And so I explained it all to Neil while temporarily converting the fancy connector into an everyday three-prong plug. The slide projector lit up quite satisfactorily.

While the technician sorted the circular trays of slides and checked out the equipment, Neil and I talked some more about reading. Neil was still thinking about possible side effects of the operation.

"George said the removal might be close to important areas for reading," he said. "He told me I might find reading a little slow for a while afterwards, but that it ought to return to normal after a while."

"Over dinner," he continued, "I got to thinking about what you'd said about the visual system being mostly evolved so that monkeys could find fruit, high up in the trees amid all the leaves waving in the breeze. How did reading areas get tacked onto that system? Writing was only invented 5,000 years ago, and not that many people have been literate until the last few centuries. That means any hereditary tendencies conserving brain areas useful for reading can't have operated for more than several hundred generations. Which is nothing. So how did we get reading areas so quickly?"

Reading most likely is a secondary use of a cortical area with some other primary purpose, I told him, what Darwin liked to call a conversion of function in anatomical continuity.

No question, though — there are now cortical areas that seem essential for reading, at least in people who have grown up reading a lot. My father once had a bad headache, quite unlike any other he ever had before. But the next morning, he felt somewhat better and fixed himself breakfast, then went out to pick up the newspaper off the sidewalk. Upon sitting down to breakfast and unfolding the newspaper, he discovered to his astonishment that he could not read it. The words weren't blurred. He could name the letters, but not the words.

Later in the hospital, he was asked to write out a paragraph in longhand that was read aloud to him. He accurately wrote out this paragraph, though tending to write all the way over to the right edge of the paper, rather than leaving a margin.

But asked to read aloud from his own handwriting, he couldn't, except for the shortest two- and three-letter words. He would try to piece together longer words but often made errors. His spoken language was normal. He understood everything that was said to him. He didn't have any abnormal blind spots that might interfere with reading. His color vision was normal. He just couldn't read anymore.

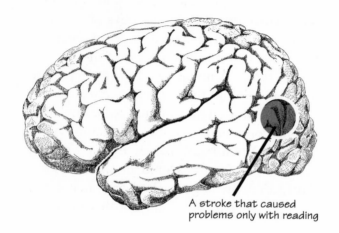

A stroke that caused
problems only with reading

A year later, he had recovered his abilities to read the newspaper, but he still tired easily and wouldn't read for more than twenty minutes at a time. He watched the television news more often.

"Do people often recover like that?" Neil asked.

Recovery of some function is typical of mild strokes. Whatever function is lost — whether reading or muscle control — some lost abilities return in the weeks and months following the stroke. In part, this recovery occurs because, while some brain cells are gone forever, the merely injured cells tend to recover.

Furthermore, the brain's plasticity may allow other areas to do the job instead. This on-the-job retraining depends quite a lot on where the stroke is located, and on the patient's age. For example, soldiers receiving brain injuries at age 18 recover more function than soldiers who are 30 years old and suffer similar injuries.

But, to come back to reading, there are many brain sites that have been identified over the years with alexia — that's just the name for the loss of previously normal reading abilities, without losing much else. Following the disconnection models for the Broca-Wernicke variants, alexia was usually ascribed to disconnection of language areas from visual centers. Indeed, the brain imagery showed that my father's stroke had destroyed a half-dollar–sized area just above and behind his left ear. It was to the rear of the posterior language ("Wernicke's") area, but in front of the traditional visual areas of the brain, perfect for an interrupted pathway between the visual cortex and the language cortex.

"I have a nephew who's dyslexic," Neil said, "smart but he can't read or spell. Is that problem tied in with those same pieces of the brain?"

Dyslexic kids are considered relatively nonverbal and quiet, with their development of reading and spelling considerably delayed, compared to their other skills. Their spoken language may be a little slow too, but they are often smart otherwise. The result, of course, is a major mismatch between the child's delayed reading skills, his other normal skills, and a lockstep school system—one that increasingly relies on reading textbooks in the higher grades to get the lessons across. And so these kids experience a bottleneck, just not being able to absorb information as rapidly as everyone else—even if smart.

"That's my nephew, all right."

Actually, the long-term outlook for his learning to read isn't too bad. Few dyslexics get to the point of enjoying reading, but most can master enough reading to get by. And there's the story of John Hunter who, George tells me, founded surgical anatomy back about the time of the American Revolution. Hunter was born into a wealthy British family that tried to educate him with tutors. They despaired of ever teaching him to read. He didn't learn until he was nearly twenty. But that didn't prevent a later academic career.

"So what's the problem in the brain?"

Many cases of dyslexia are associated with abnormalities in brain development. Some dyslexics seem to have problems in the way the structure of the language areas developed. In a few dyslexics who have died from other causes, the brain shows mistakes in cortical development. The appropriate layering is lost and neurons are in misplaced bundles called "heterotopias."

Dyslexics seem to have less difference in the size of that temporal lobe language region—the planum temporale—that is usually bigger on the left. However, most dyslexics have left-brain dominance for language, just like most of us. There is a suggestion that some male dyslexics may have less strongly lateralized visual-spatial functions than other males. That raises the possibility that visual-spatial functions compete with language for the same left-brain territories. And so the dyslexic kids can't do either job well, neither language nor visual-spatial.

Dyslexics also have problems in processing rapidly changing sensations. The magnocellular pathways that transmit rapidly changing visual sensations are slowed in some dyslexics.

"Is that a consequence of those two magnocellular layers of the geniculate? They got scrambled? No longer the nice layer cake that you told me about earlier?"

Right, the two bottom layers are rather jumbled together. And there are 27 percent fewer neurons in the magnocellular layers than is normal, as if they'd lost a lot of them.

What causes these abnormalities is much less clear. In some cases, the brain changes associated with dyslexia may have been acquired from an event that occurred during development or early life. But more commonly, it seems to be genetic. Dyslexia is more common in males than in females. It frequently runs in families. It's apparently not a matter of just one gene, for dyslexia has been tightly linked to chromosome 15 in one family—but not to that chromosome in other dyslexics. Like reading in general, as we discussed before, there can't have been much natural selection yet to eliminate such variants, given the short time that reading has been important for many people.

And natural selection often can't operate against traits that are linked to other inherited traits. The neurologist Norman Geschwind noted an association between dyslexia and an odd constellation of other abilities. Extraordinarily good mathematical abilities. Left-handedness. Allergies. Not all those have been confirmed by all the later studies, but you can see why things get complicated when there are links.

Several possible explanations for Geschwind's constellation have been proposed. Perhaps there were unusually high levels of testosterone in the mother during the later parts of the pregnancy. Or perhaps it is a manifestation of an autoimmune disease, when the body's natural defenses are turned on its own tissues. In either case, you could get defects in neuron organization in cortex and sensory system relay nuclei. The autoimmune disease suggestion has had a particularly promising spin-off. There is a strain of mice that have an autoimmune disorder. These mice also show disorganized cortex and mouse-learning deficits, providing what may be an animal model for the study of dyslexia.

"Why so much trouble with reading, though," Neil asked. "Especially if the abnormalities are distributed throughout language areas? Why not other aspects of language as well?"

Well, most dyslexic children also had some trouble with speech earlier. It just wasn't as bad as that with reading. George has found that many more neurons change activity with word reading than with naming objects or repeating words. So reading may just be intrinsically harder, requiring more neurons. If there's a shortage of well-organized neurons, it would then be more apparent in reading.

Also, written speech lacks many of the redundant clues present in real speech. When I'm talking, my voice rises and falls, my facial expressions change, I wave my hands and shrug my shoulders. That's additional information. When you're reading, the written word is all you've got.

It seems possible that the major fault was originally not with reading but with listening to speech—detecting the fine timing differences in the sound waves that make a "pa" different from a "ba" (there's a little z-like buzz at the beginning of "ba" because the vocal cords vibrate then, and they don't at the beginning of "pa"). That's again a magnocellularlike task. Yet it might have a lot to do with reading—because learning to read is all about matching up speech sounds with letters, at least in a phonetic language like English.

Since George's studies showed separation between naming and reading for many of the essential pieces of cortex, I suppose that it's possible that the specific system for reading is defective. Nobody really has any information on that in dyslexia.

George also showed a strong association between the location of reading and naming sites and, of all things, that patient's verbal IQ. Presumably that's because verbal IQs measure both reading and other parts of language. So some patterns of location of these functions in the brain are more favorable than others. He found that patients whose sites for reading were in the superior temporal gyrus, with naming in the middle temporal gyrus, had high verbal IQs. And he found the reverse in the patients with low verbal IQs.

Neil seemed puzzled. "I can't see why reading above and naming below should be such a good thing," he said.

We haven't thought of a really good explanation, although people who study how we read emphasize that good reading requires the ability to readily convert from speech sounds to the visual representation of those sounds. And since auditory processing is mostly buried in the great infolding of the sylvian fissure, that might be the reason why having reading nearby, in the superior temporal gyrus, is associated with better function.

"But how does brain development organize all this, if reading isn't specified by the genes?"

Well, the ability to name is learned first. Maybe if the language cortex is innately less efficient in the below-average folks, more patches are needed to do the naming job. When reading is learned a few years after naming, the superior temporal gyrus is—in this theory of George's—overcommitted. And so reading must "make do" with sites in the middle temporal gyrus—a potentially less favorable location, since it is farther away from the cortical area receiving sounds.

So a superior temporal gyrus that can make room for reading at age 5—because naming can be done efficiently elsewhere by then—will be a better home for making the connections between the sounds of words and their written phonetic equivalents. And so a higher verbal IQ results.

Speculations such as these are useful because they suggest new questions: What is the relation between vocabulary acquisition between ages 2 and 4, and the child's reading speed upon reaching age 6, and the verbal IQ even later in life? Can the lower IQ patterns be spotted using functional MRIs early enough in life to do something about them, through intensive reading therapy? And whatever the explanation for the mapping findings, it's apparent that where you have naming or reading located has important implications beyond those involved in planning epilepsy operations.

AFTER REHEARSAL, Neil and I got back into our discussion of brain research, and why there wasn't more of it—all those unanswered questions. My answer to that was relatively simple—four out of five grant applications for brain research are rejected.

"Rejected?"

Approved by the peer-review groups as likely being good science, I told him, but rejected administratively by the National Institutes of Health because of inadequate funds.

"I suppose Congress can't fund everything."

Yes, but the annual costs, in the United States alone, of the major diseases of the nervous system are estimated at $400 billion—which is more than the U.S. defense budget! And even more of a drag on the national economy. The estimate doesn't even include the drug-abuse costs in most cases, which for alcohol is quite high. About $107 billion is direct costs such as hospital bills, and the rest is the disability payments, the lost salary, and so on. About a third of the total is for the 4 million persons with Alzheimer's dementia—and that number has been growing rapidly.

"How many people does this add up to?"

In the United States, about 50 million people with the various neurological and psychiatric disorders.

"So one person in five—one in every family, on average. And the total cost is a few hundred billion. So what's the research outlay—a tenth of that?"

If only. The federal dollars for neuroscience research funneled through the National Institutes of Health and the National Science Foundation—the basic research on brains plus the slightly more applied research focused on the psychiatric and the neurological disorders—add up to about $1.2 billion. Drug company research and private foundation money adds some—but our overall commitment to finding out more about the brain and its disorders is probably less than 1 percent of the overall costs. Development costs by manufacturers adds some more. That's for brains—for health-care expenditures in general, one estimate for 1990 was 3.3 percent for research and development, down from about 5 percent in the 1960s.

"In other words, a drop in the bucket. Peanuts. That's an absurdly low research-and-development percentage even for a horse-and-buggy industry like the utility companies, never mind the 10 to 20 percent for a rapidly changing industry like the one I'm in. And I thought that medicine had a real commitment to changing things."

Curiously, medicine doesn't have much control over its research expenditures. The drug companies are an exception, but most of their research is applied, not basic—and most of their expenditures are more properly called product development. The development costs, just to get just one new drug to market in the United States, are about $240 million. They get their ideas for new products from the basic research of the public sector, and that's the underinvestment problem. Unfortunately, because medical expenditures are so dispersed and so lacking in central authority, there is no way to reinvest a small part of health care expenditures into research for tomorrow.

And so, quite reasonably, it is funded through federal tax dollars—government has accepted the responsibility but continues to fund it at an absurdly low rate. The basic research that eventually paves the way for new drugs and new treatments has to compete for federal dollars with the highly visible, and more easily understood, needs.

"Compete, in other words," Neil interjected, "with the big-ticket items like space stations that provide thousands of jobs in someone's state."

The average brain research grant probably provides two jobs. And, in the United States, over 70 percent of all research and development jobs have been in defense-related industries—compared, say, to Japan where it's about 5 percent. Compared to other countries, we've diverted a lot of our best intellects into arms.

Basic research isn't the sort of thing you can just increase to meet a crisis, the way the shipbuilding industry was built up during World War II. How well we can meet a problem like AIDS infections of the brain—and if you can't fix those, there's not much point in fixing the rest—depends on how much was spent on basic research in prior *decades*. Over the years, the research outlays certainly haven't increased in proportion to the health-care costs.

"What medicine needs," Neil said, "is the equivalent of the highway trust fund, where construction and repair funds are kept proportional to road use via the gasoline tax. Something like a tax on health-insurance premiums ought to assure an adequate research-and-development base. And a few percent of tax is nothing—certainly not when compared to the absurd costs of running that paperwork mill for medical insurance, which has been driving me crazy. Paperwork is supposed to be 25 percent of health-care costs. It's really galling to think that a little creep in the medical costs due to paperwork is the same amount of money that could have doubled our research investment."

LATER IN THE EVENING, I got a phone call from Neil in his hospital room. He'd been thinking some more about dyslexic kids and wanted to talk to me about it, before taking the bedtime pills that the nurse had brought.

"Is there a critical period for preventing dyslexia?" he asked. "I'm thinking of those disrupted layers of the geniculate that you mentioned earlier."

The magnocellular layers in the bottom of the lateral geniculate nucleus, that they found were somewhat shrunken and a little disorganized in dyslexics. What about them?

"Maybe those neurons, being a little disorganized, can't get their act together in time. And so they lose out in the tuneup period. Can you exercise those fast pathways in infants, keep them competitive with the others?"

A Head Start program for magnocellulars? There are certainly neurophysiological techniques, not unlike EEGs, which you could use to test infants for tendencies to dyslexia. They're very similar to the brain-stem evoked potentials that we use to detect deafness in newborns; you could do both tests at the same time. Actually, you don't even have to wait for that. If the father is dyslexic, just assume that the infant is at risk—inheritance is pretty strong for dyslexia.

And you can easily imagine daily exercises, giving the destined-for-dyslexia infant some computer displays every day that are entertaining to look at, and which are jittery enough to exercise the magnocellular paths more than the parvocellular paths. Maybe such compensatory exercise would increase the survival chances of those fast-path connections and prevent them from being eliminated during the critical period. Maybe that would keep the child from having trouble with reading a few years later. A lot of maybes, but such are the ways in which basic research insights suggest suitable strategies for applied research and can carry over into solving practical problems.

"So where do practical ideas like that come from?" Neil asked. "Were people working on the dyslexia problem—or something else—when they discovered this fast-slow distinction?"

Something else, as usual. Although a more subtle version of the fast-slow specializations had been seen in the spinal cord, its exaggerated visual system version was discovered in the cat retina by the neurophysiologist Christina Enroth-Cugell and her student John Robson in 1966, working in Northwestern University's electrical engineering department. No one knew what the fast-slow, transient-sustained business was good for, but it was an intriguing puzzle, and basic researchers persisted. Soon it became apparent that the fast-slow distinction was seen in those layers of the geniculate: the bottom two layers were "fast." And geniculate constituted an even more long-standing unsolved puzzle—those six distinct layers, and no one knew any reason for them.

Like a partially complete crossword puzzle, it was tantalizing. But it was a quarter century, and hundreds of investigations, later before the relevance to dyslexia became apparent. My guess is that it will also prove relevant to clumsiness and verbal intelligence. It certainly shows you how basic research differs from applied research or product development.

"Sounds like a 25-year version of my Sunday crossword puzzle! Well, see you tomorrow, bright and early."

[T]here are three quite different levels of technology in medicine, so unlike each other as to seem altogether different undertakings. . . . Supportive therapy. . . tides patients over through diseases that are not, by and large, understood. . . . [Second are] the kinds of things that must be done after the fact, in efforts to compensate for the incapacitating effects of certain diseases whose course one is unable to do very much about. It is a technology designed to make up for disease, or postpone death. . . .

It is characteristic of [such halfway medical technology as epilepsy surgery or cardiac-care units] that it costs an enormous amount of money and requires a continuing expansion of hospital facilities. There is no end to the need for new, highly trained people to run the enterprise. And there is really no way out of this, at the present state of knowledge. . . . The only thing that can move medicine away from this level of technology is new information, and the only imaginable source of this information is research.

The third type of technology is. . . so effective that it seems to attract the least public notice; it has come to be taken for granted. This is the genuinely decisive technology of modern medicine, exemplified best by the modern methods of immunization. . . and the contemporary use of antibiotics and chemotherapy for bacterial infections. . . . The real point to be made about this kind of technology—the real high technology of medicine—is that it comes as the result of a genuine understanding of disease mechanisms, and when it becomes available, it is relatively inexpensive, and relatively easy to deliver. . . .

It is when physicians are bogged down by their incomplete technologies, by the innumerable things they are obligated to do in medicine when they lack a clear understanding of disease mechanisms, that the deficiencies of the health-care system are most conspicuous. If I were a policy-maker, interested in saving money for health care over the long haul, I would regard it as an act of high prudence to give high priority to a lot more basic research in biologic science. This is the only way to get the full mileage that biology owes to the science of medicine, even though it seems, as used to be said in the days when the phrase had some meaning, like asking for the moon.

LEWIS THOMAS, *The Lives of a Cell,* 1974

chapter 16

Stringing Things Together in Novel Ways

"NEIL, WE'VE COME TO THAT RESEARCH STUDY I talked to you about yesterday afternoon," George says, loud enough for Neil to hear through the sterile tent. We'd just finished the mapping of Spanish. And of reading. A new series of slides was being placed in the projector by George's technician.

"Oh, I'm still here. I thought about going out to lunch, but I decided to skip it today."

"You're not the only one who's hungry," George replies. "And Dr. Calvin is beginning to look as if deprived of his midday espresso. Well, in this next part, just remember that all you've got to do is look at what the model is doing in the slide. And then act out exactly the same things with your face and tongue. Just mimic what's shown on the slide. We'll record it all on videotape."

Neil begins to mimic the slides, puffing out his cheeks three times in response to the first slide, protruding his tongue three times to the next.

Periodically, George stimulates spots on the cortex. Once in a while during stimulation, Neil gets stuck—he can't mimic the movement on the slide. The sites that do that are all clustered together, just in front of the face motor area. It's essentially Broca's area, controlling the movements on both sides of the face that are needed for all speech movements.

The slide tray is changed again. Now Neil mimics the same movements but in sequences of three: puff out cheeks, stick out tongue, clench the teeth. And so on, in various combinations. Stimulation occurs during some slides, but not during others.

And during stimulation of some sites, Neil makes the wrong movements. He adds movements, things that weren't pictured on the slide. Or, during other slides, he produces the movements, but in the wrong order. Such sites disturbing the *sequence* of movements are more widespread, farther forward in the frontal lobe. And there are now some sites in the part of the temporal lobe near the sylvian fissure, others in the parietal lobe around the back of the sylvian fissure. At these frontal, temporal, and parietal sites, the stimulation has no effect on single, repeated movements—it's only disrupting when a *sequence* of different movements must be produced.

Movements are supposed to be a frontal lobe function, but here it is, in the temporal and the parietal lobe sites, as well—all near the sylvian fissure.

"Neil? We're now ready for the other research study," George announces. "This is the one where you hear the funny words—akma, adma, atma—and you tell me if the letter that changed was k, d, t, or whatever."

"All right," Neil says. "That was easy enough, last night."

The neuropsychologist starts a tape recorder. The speaker voice says "akma." Neil says "k." Then "apma," and Neil says "p." And on it goes. George stimulates only when Neil hears the word, not when he's to respond. Since stimulation effects don't seem to outlast removing the electrode from the brain surface, nothing interferes with the response. So the stimulation effects are presumably disrupting the perception of the speech sound.

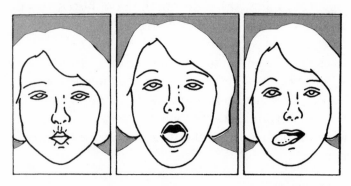

Three oral-facial postures to be mimicked, one after the other

And where are these sites that interfere with sequences of speech sounds? They turn out to be the same sites around the sylvian fissure where stimulation interfered with mimicking face movements, either singly or in sequences. A sensory-sequencing task seems to have the same essential sites as a movement-sequencing task, with 86 percent overlap.

THESE RESEARCH STUDIES in Neil and other patients have provided several further glimpses into the organization of the language cortex. The area of cortex related to motor speech functions turns out to be quite wide, involving most of the brain around the sylvian fissure. This is different from what you'd read in most textbooks, where Broca's area is the only place mentioned in conjunction with motor speech.

Of course, that textbook statement has always been a little surprising, because Broca's actual patient, Leborgne, had damage to the wider area around the sylvian fissure. And it has never been totally clear why Broca focused on just the frontal lobe part of that damage to Leborgne's brain. Indeed, newer studies indicate that a permanent motor language deficit requires a stroke that destroys the whole area around the sylvian fissure, a lot more than just damage to Broca's area. Much of the area of the brain involved in language has a role in the motor aspects of language.

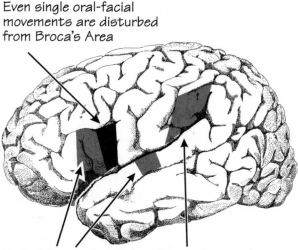

Even single oral-facial movements are disturbed from Broca's Area

Perisylvian regions where stimulation disrupts both phoneme receptive sequences and oral-facial expression sequences

Data from Ojemann, 1991

There are two subdivisions to the perisylvian movement region. First, there is an area involved in the control of all movements of the tongue and face needed for speech, located just in front of the face part of the motor strip in the frontal lobe. Except for the control of movements on both sides of the body from one (left) side of the brain, it is located pretty much where a motor area should be by classical reasoning and labeled with Broca's name.

The second area related to sequencing movements is the one that occupies the much larger region, including parts that classically aren't supposed to have a motor role. This development of the ability to sequence things together seems to be one of the great developments behind the emergence of language on the evolutionary scene in our ancestors, so this is likely a particularly "human" area.

THE EVOLUTIONARY COURSE OF LANGUAGE has, of course, two major connotations—*language* and languages. There's the evolution of *language* per se (syntax, grammar) and the establishment of particular languages (such as the Indo-European origins of modern German).

The latter is easy. We can increasingly estimate the branching pattern for the genealogy of English or French, even use it to infer the migration of people around Asia and Europe. But to go back any more than a few thousand years before written languages developed is quite difficult.

For *language* per se, we know that since our last common ancestor with the chimpanzees, some significant improvements have occurred. We don't know very many details of this route, but one rearrangement stands out very clearly: the wild chimps mostly use 36 different sounds. They mean about 36 different things—the sounds *are* the vocabulary. Humans also use about three dozen different sounds, known as phonemes. And what do they mean? Nothing.

Our phonemes are almost totally meaningless by themselves. It is only in combination, strung together end to end, that most of our speech sounds have meaning. Sequences of phonemes have the meaning of words (easily producing vocabularies of 10,000 words, and more than 100,000 in some individuals). Sequences of words produce word phrases that have an additional meaning, the kinds of relationships between the actor, the action, and the acted upon. Sequences of word phrases (sometimes embedded within one another) produce the infinite variety of our sentences and paragraphs.

Somewhere along the line, during the 6 million years since we last shared a common ancestor with our chimpanzee cousins, our predecessors appear to have minimized a system that assigned meaning to individual sounds—and created this new meaning-from-sequence scheme as an overlay. How and when and where was this conversion done?

That's the big question of anthropology and linguistics. It appears that much of it probably happened in the last 2.5 million years—the ice ages—because that's when hominid brain size and its surface infolding pattern were also changing. Size and infolding changes probably aren't required for brain reorganization, but, just as change is easier in a growing economy than in a steady-state one, so brain reorganization was probably easier during the last several million years than from 6 to 2.5 million years ago when hominid brains remained ape-sized.

So we may not know *when* language abilities changed within that long period, but we surely know a big aspect of *what* changed: sequencing for additional meaning. The combination of chunking and rapid transmission, so that much meaning can be accommodated within the brief span of short-term memory, has surely been important for what can be "held in mind" at the same time. But without the syntax that allows us to make mental models of "who did what to whom," language would lack much of its power. We'd be back to merely using familiar rules of association, as in protolanguage.

STRINGING THINGS TOGETHER is thus likely to be a prime task of the language cortex. And the kinds of studies to which Neil has been contributing show that sequence is indeed a major organizing principle of the language cortex.

During the test of identification of speech sounds, stimulating most of the same areas where motor sequencing was altered also interfered with the phoneme (speech sound) identification. When you hear a speech sound and have to decode it, these areas must be active. But they must be similarly active when you make the sequence of movements needed to make speech sounds.

That finding goes against the traditional teaching, that the brain areas related to speech production are separated from those related to speech perception. That led to an expectation that perception and production met somewhere in the brain at an executive site that analyzed the information coming in and issued the commands going out. Only this site, if it exists at all, ought to be both sensory and motor.

That's one common way of looking at matters, but it is not the view of most modern brain researchers; indeed, the neurologist John Hughlings Jackson, who discovered the motor strip map, warned over a century ago that most cortical areas ought to be both sensory and motor.

And the finding in the O.R. was not totally unexpected, for an earlier investigation in psycholinguistics had suggested the same thing, that there was a common mechanism for speech production and perception. That psycholinguistic finding was an observation about how we perceive speech sounds.

With a synthesizer, speech sounds can be continuously varied between "pa" and "ba." But if you ask a subject to tell you what he hears with those continuously varying sounds, he will report either "pa" or "ba"—not something "in between." This phenomenon is called categorical perception: sounds are heard—or at least identified—as belonging to the closest category. In-between states are assigned to one adjacent category or another. One wonders what the ancient Greek philosophers would have thought of this ideal form in the brain.

The psycholinguist Alvin Liberman proposed that this classification effect is because the decoding process involves creation of a motor representation for how to produce the sound. There is no in-between motor representation, and so it is heard as either "pa" or "ba." Liberman's idea has been called the motor theory of speech perception. Neil's study shows that the decoding of the speech sound and the organization of the motor movements both depend on the same brain areas. So one explanation for Neil's findings would be Liberman's motor theory, that what you can speak helps determine what you can hear.

A second candidate would be the production and detection of precise time intervals. Both speech production and detection are unusually fast processes. Precise timing is needed for both, and as we found in discussing dyslexia, a defect in a fast processing system can interfere with a language function. Precise timing also requires a lot of brain in order to do well, without jitter. So it's also possible that the function common to this cortical area is determining precise timing, whether of movement or of sensation, rather than stringing things together.

The third candidate is that there is some function common to detecting speech sounds and to generating the motor movements for them, one that depends on these brain areas. As we have seen, a cortical mechanism for unique sequences, whether of movements or sounds, is a likely candidate for that common function. Routine sequences probably can be handled subcortically, but unique sequences—as Neil is experiencing in the O.R. tests—may require cortical expertise.

As often happens in neuroscience, further studies indicate increased complexity. In some other patients undergoing operations like Neil's, George used the precious research minutes to record the activity of individual neurons during measures of speech perception and production. Based on the findings in stimulation studies like Neil's, George had predicted that he would find neurons that responded to both speech production and perception, probably in the very same way for the same sound.

Scientific predictions don't always work out. Such common-to-both neurons must be very rare, at least in the areas where George has made his recordings, for he's found only one neuron so far that seems to act anything like what he'd predicted. Most of the neurons change activity to either speech production or perception—but not both. That's actually rather curious, because of the way one study was done: the patient heard words without speaking, and then heard the same words again and repeated them aloud. Neurons were active when the word was heard, spoken by the tape recorder, but those neurons were either inactive or inhibited when the patient spoke the same word—even though, in speaking it aloud, the patient also heard it. So we apparently turn off the temporal lobe neurons that perceive speech sounds for a brief period when we produce speech.

Thus neurons specializing in speech production and speech perception seem to be separate. But they are often nearby, so if you record activity from several neurons at once, the whole population of neurons is active with both speech production and perception. Since stimulation alters activity in many neurons at once, it shows the combined population effect rather than the separate single-neuron effect on both production and perception.

It is certainly tempting to label this large region surrounding the sylvian fissure after the feature in common between the two tests with such near-perfect overlap. In short, "sequencing cortex."

STUDIES OF SEQUENCING OF MOVEMENTS in aphasic patients have also shown deficits, further evidence for the importance of sequencing in language. In one study by neuropsychologists Doreen Kimura and Catherine Mateer, aphasic patients were tested on hand-and-arm movements that needed to be chained together, such as the ones we use every day for putting a key into a keyhole, rotating the key, and pushing on the door. They used tests that were less likely to have become habits—and discovered that, while the aphasic patients could do each movement separately, they had trouble in stringing them together. This is often called apraxia.

Aphasia and apraxia seem to "go together." Sequential movements of the hand and arm seemed to have something to do with language. This set the stage for the kinds of studies to which Neil is contributing: Mateer went on to design the oral-facial sequencing tasks that are used in the confines of the O.R.

Although the single-neuron studies suggest that the relation between decoding speech and organizing movement sequences is a property of nearby networks—and not single neurons active with both functions—the relation has potential implications for therapy of language disorders and for education more generally. For it seems likely that there may be benefits to language from learning other sequential motor activities.

IF SEQUENCING ABILITIES are a major underlying feature of language mechanisms, it may be that they can be exercised by means other than listening and talking (or watching and signing). A game with rules of procedure, for example, might also involve the same neural machinery.

The cortical-subcortical division between novel associations and skilled routine suggests, however, that it may be *discovering* the rules of the game which is more important to developing cortical sequencing abilities than accomplished performance. Learning many new songs might be better than learning to sing one song well, at least for exercising sequencing cortex. If sequence rules could be gradually discovered via increasing success, as they are for many children's video games, the experience might carry over to discovering the syntax of spoken or signed languages—a matter of some importance for the deaf children of hearing parents, who may not discover the syntax game in the usual way. The preschool children taking music lessons are presumably getting to discover a second set of "syntax" rules.

Language, planning ahead, music, dance, and games with rules of progression are all human serial-order skills that might involve some common neural machinery. Hammering, throwing, kicking, and clubbing also belong on that same list, as their sequence of muscle contractions must be completely planned before beginning the movement—feedback is too slow to correct the movement, once underway. Indeed, so many of the uniquely human skills are sequential that it has been suggested that augmenting the sequencer abilities of the ape brain is what human brain evolution was all about.

The sequencing story also reminds us that giving names to things can be dangerous, even when the specialization seems as obvious as that for language. "Language cortex" is only cortex that appears to support language functions, *among other functions.* Defining its function by what stops working in its absence confuses a correlation with a cause. The neurologist F. M. R. Walshe pointed out, back in 1947, that to define the function of a brain region in terms of the symptoms following damage is likely to result in a misidentification of the functions of that brain region. His example was a broken tooth on a gear in a car's transmission, which results in such symptoms as a "thunk" heard once each revolution.

The function of the tooth was not to prevent thunks, and the function of the perisylvian regions is not to prevent aphasia. Language deficits are one clue to the functions of the perisylvian region, strokes affecting hand sequencing are a second clue, and the stimulation mapping of sensory and motor sequencing tasks provides yet another way of inferring the functions that this important cortical region support. "Sequencing cortex" is one way to summarize the results so far.

chapter 17

Deep in the Temporal Lobe, Just Across from the Brain Stem

IT'S QUIET IN THE O.R. during the second research study, the micro-electrode recording. The sequencing study went quickly, so we set up the apparatus that moved a microelectrode in fine increments. Earlier we'd heard the crackle of neurons, their firing sounding like rain on the roof. Irregular firing is par for the course in a cortical neuron, once you find one. But finding one with a microelectrode is very much like fishing, and the fish aren't biting right now.

George is actually sitting down on a stool for the first time in this long day. My back's aching, but then I'm not in practice for this sort of thing. I've been availing myself of the other stool for hours now. The resident still hasn't returned.

"Neil," George asks, raising his voice. "How are you doing?"

"I'm fine, just wondering why things are so quiet."

"We're still fishing for some more single neurons," George replies. "Sometimes it goes a little slowly."

"So what did you find out from all that testing earlier?" Neil asks, sounding much more alert than he did an hour ago.

"We found the language and memory locations. I'm quite happy about that. And the brain-surface recordings we did this morning confirmed that the seizures involve mostly the deeper parts of temporal lobe."

"Are you going to be able to remove all of that epileptic area?"

"Maybe so. Certainly the majority of it. But that ought to do the job pretty well. It's not like a tumor, where you want to get rid of every last bit. We want to eliminate your seizures, but I wouldn't want to remove any brain that is any closer to those language and memory sites than about the width of a finger." George advances the micrometer as he speaks, continuing to fish for single neurons, listening for the distinct crackle they make in the loudspeaker fed by the microelectrode.

Silence returns. No luck. George looks at the clock, stands back up, and starts to remove the apparatus from Neil's head.

"Neil, we're finished with the recording. So it's time for us to start removing that piece of your temporal lobe. We'll let you go back to sleep. We'll wake you up in an hour or so, when we do some more recording to check on how much those deeper brain structures are contributing to your seizures. But you won't have to work at anything. In fact, you'll be awake so briefly that you probably won't even remember it. I'll be seeing you back in your room tonight."

"Fine," says Neil. "See you then."

The anesthesiologist, I see, is filling a syringe with the short-lasting anesthetic. And placing it in the little infusion pump, which slowly injects it into a vein. Soon Neil is asleep again. If the pump is stopped, Neil will wake back up after about 10 minutes, as his body metabolizes this anesthetic very rapidly.

IMMEDIATELY THE O.R. SEEMS to spring back to life. Now there is something for everyone to do, rather than watching us fish. The circulating nurse appears with the fancy headgear, carrying it atop a towel. Rather like, I reflect, a crown of jewels on a velvet cushion.

The scrub nurse holds out a new pair of gloves for George. He slips them on over his other gloves. Then he takes the headgear from the circulating nurse and mounts it on his head, adjusting the headband himself. He swings down the little spotlight, making it point in the right direction. Next he swings down the little magnifiers, miniature binoculars a few inches long that stand outside his everyday eye-glasses. The binoculars are so skinny that he can look past them for ordinary maneuvering around the O.R. But when he looks straight ahead, he gets a magnified view of whatever is at arm's length. The binoculars and the headlamp are for looking down deep, dark holes, and one is about to be created in Neil's temporal lobe.

Headgear adjustments complete, George strips off the now-contaminated gloves, leaving him with his original gloves still sterile. He takes a wet towel from the scrub nurse and wipes them off, just in case any glove powder was left behind. The circulating nurse takes the trailing fiber-optical cable from the spotlight and inserts it into the light source. A uniform spot of light suddenly appears on the sterile tent in front of George.

HALF AN HOUR LATER, the tip of Neil's temporal lobe is gone. George whittled it away, not with a knife, but very gently, using the tip of an ultrasonic vibrator. Any cells it touches turn into a liquid, which is then sucked up along with any blood. This slow sculpturing of the temporal lobe removes the tissue with preseizure activity on the earlier recordings, but stops well short of the tags denoting the language and memory sites on the brain's surface.

As George worked down into the depths of Neil's temporal lobe, he finally opened a hole into one of the brain's natural cavities, the tip of the lateral ventricle, reservoir for cerebrospinal fluid. And some of the clear CSF flowed out.

"Send for the EEG folks again," George says. I see the circulating nurse walk over to press the button on the memory phone that dials the beeper of the EEG staff, who are standing by in their offices. Or

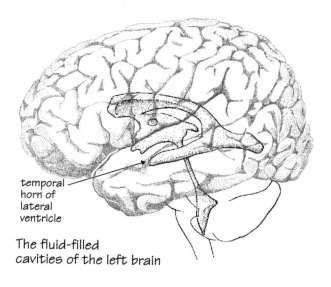

temporal
horn of
lateral
ventricle

The fluid-filled
cavities of the left brain

perhaps snacking in the hospital cafeteria. My stomach reminds me that lunchtime is long past.

The scrub nurse, anticipating, places the little red box of strip electrodes on the front edge of her big tray so that George can reach them. The anesthesiologist reaches over to the infusion pump and, receiving a confirming nod from George, turns it off so that Neil will start to wake up once again.

George picks up a strip electrode. It is a flexible sheet of translucent material about the size of a paper clip, except that it also has a long pigtail of fine wire with a little plug on the end. There are four little silvery patches on one side of this sheet that serve to monitor the voltages on the surface of the brain that they rest against.

This strip electrode is going to be placed against an *inner* surface of the brain. That's the inside surface of the lateral ventricle that is visible through the hole that George has created. Beneath that surface is the hippocampus, coordinator of memorizing. It is also the typical pacemaker for the types of seizures from which Neil suffers. Those round-the-clock recordings several weeks ago couldn't be made from up close like this, only from the scalp. Here we have, literally, a window of opportunity through which to see whether the hippocampus is also participating in the early stages of Neil's seizures.

George tucks the little strip in through the window he has made. Close work—I can't see a thing, myself. But George finally straightens back up and plugs the little wire into the cable leading back to the EEG machine in the gallery. I look back up to the gallery and, sure enough, the platoon of EEG people has arrived, and they are already examining the voltage tracings made by Neil's hippocampus. The television monitor in the O.R. shows us exactly what they see.

This electrical activity is quite different from what we saw this morning from the surface of the temporal lobe. There is much back-and-forth talk on the intercom about the little bursts of sharp positive-going wavelets, the hallmark of an epileptic process in the time in between seizures. They're what are thought to occasionally drive the surrounding brain into seizure activity.

Someone mentions that most seem to be coming from the far end of the strip electrode. George immediately decides to move the strip electrode, to place it even further into the cavity so that it will rest against the hippocampus farther to the rear of the brain. We settle back to watch the EEG tracings once again.

No doubt about it. Now the middle sites on the strip electrode are all showing the little positive wavelets. That means that this section of hippocampus (it's a very long folded tubular structure running from front to back in the brain) ought to be removed—provided, of course, that this won't cause more trouble than it cures. Another value judgment to be made.

There is, fortunately, nearly a half century of experience with doing this kind of surgery, and many studies have been made of the patients afterward. Yes, if you run a lot of tests, there is some minor change in memory function. The more hippocampus that is removed, the more that memory is impaired. But patients don't consider it a major problem.

It's not even a close call, given how much Neil's seizures have increased in the last year. George announces that he's going to take out the front part of the hippocampus, as far back as the epileptic discharges are found, plus the uncus. Just as Portugal is the western-most part of continental Europe, so the uncus is the part of temporal lobe that comes closest to the midline. And thus the brain stem. The uncus, alas, is a common cause of trouble.

Neil still isn't really awake yet, and hasn't been heard from. But almost-awake is good enough, in this case. Many of Neil's seizures occur as he is awakening, something that wasn't realized until he was monitored around the clock. Now we've finally seen some pathophysiology that is likely close to the heart of the matter. The anesthesiologist starts the infusion pump again.

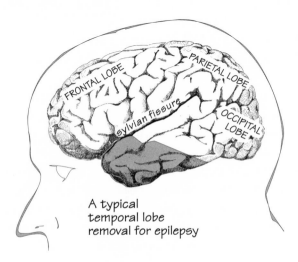

A typical
temporal lobe
removal for epilepsy

GEORGE REMOVES SOME OF THE HIPPOCAMPUS as a block for the neuroanatomists to study, and then goes to his gradual sculpturing to complete the removal.

A bit further back, he stops again to remove a little crumb-sized piece of brain tissue intact, so that the pathologists can examine it. Using some forceps with little half cups on their tips, he pinches off a peninsula of tissue that he has left behind while sculpting. Usually it comes easily. Sometimes it doesn't.

"Label that as hippocampus," he says to the scrub nurse as he hands her the forceps with the tissue still trapped inside. She drops the tissue into a little bottle that the circulating nurse holds out.

"Felt soft," he comments. In short, probably not scarred up—but the pathologist may see something more subtle.

So now we're all waiting to see what the tissue sample from the uncus will be like. George takes the cup forceps once again and begins maneuvering them down the hole. The uncus is a very short distance from the upper part of the brain stem, with only a fluid-filled gap in between. The uncus is rather like the spit of land that helps form the entrance to a harbor. And over on the other side of the gap is one of those lower-level centers of consciousness, to be carefully avoided. In between, there are a number of blood vessels. George is probably looking carefully, before closing the cup forceps around anything.

George emerges again, forceps held closed around a piece of the uncus. About the time that he passes them to the scrub nurse, Neil's head starts to shake back and forth. The anesthesiologist announces that Neil is having a seizure. But the shaking doesn't resume, lasting less time than it took to comment on it.

"It's probably the uncus that started that seizure," George says. "It felt tough when I pinched off a piece." The original source of the seizures, at last?

Cause and effect are all mixed up by now, of course. Even if there was once a single bit of anatomical pathology such as a scarred uncus, by now there are lots of well-trained followers that can cause trouble on their own. Which is why neurosurgeons remove whole regions of the cerebral cortex, the hippocampus, and the amygdala. Removing small amounts of tissue simply does not get rid of the present problem—which is seizures, not scarring. No one wants to have to subject the patient to a second or third operation, removing more tissue each time, because too little was taken the first time.

But it's still nice to know where the trouble started, decades earlier. Looks as if it was the uncus, at least in Neil. And that's a common pathological finding.

Removing all that brain tissue, of course, also leaves a scar behind. But the surgery is designed to minimize it, just as plastic surgery replaces a large, ugly scar with a fine, hard-to-see scar.

THE UNCUS IS PARTICULARLY prone to injury whenever the brain swells. Unlike the dura elsewhere, the dura in this region is pulled taut—and it has an edge. It's about the closest thing to a sharp edge inside the skull, and nearby structures may rub across it when the brain moves around inside the skull.

There are three major routes by which the uncus seems to be damaged. All occur well before the onset of seizures. It seems that damage to the uncus is only the first step in the process that leads to epilepsy.

The infant's head is somewhat compressed during birth, as it isn't as rigid as it later becomes. If the head is a very tight fit in the birth canal, the brain may be squeezed somewhat, pushing it down toward the spinal cord. When that happens, the uncus is unusually vulnerable.

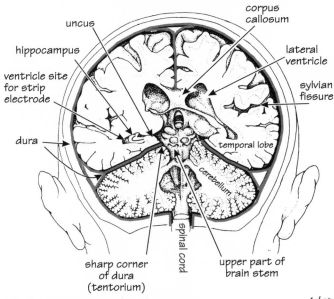

Sharp Corners and a Frequent
Cause of Temporal Lobe Epilepsy

Adapted from J. Nolte,
The Human Brain

It may be pushed into the brain stem while, at the same time, being bent around a sharp corner of dura. Such abrasion would indeed produce a scarred uncus, and sometimes a scarred hippocampus.

Febrile seizures of early childhood, while the child is running a high fever, can do the same thing if the brain swells enough. But remember that most febrile seizures, like most childbirths, do no such thing— we're talking about the extreme cases here.

Head injuries can also cause trauma in this region because of that same edge of dura. The brain sits atop a narrow stalk of brain stem, rather like the head of a mushroom sits atop its stalk. You'd think that the brain couldn't move, because of the skull. But it can be compressed. A sudden stop, as when the left side of the head encounters a car door frame, means that the right brain tries to compress the left brain. And so the brain moves atop the brain stem, potentially bruising the brain stem or the uncus.

This edge of dura near the brain stem wasn't exactly a good design. Neil's weeks of memory problems following his accident suggests that his hippocampus was damaged (but it doesn't seem to be scarred) or that its blood supply remained subnormal for a while. And that's a real possibility. The arteries supplying the hippocampus run in the space between the uncus and the brain stem, right where they too could be traumatized. When blood vessels are traumatized, they usually shrink down and restrict the blood flow.

BUT WHY SEIZURES, starting some time after the trauma to the uncus? Persisting seizures usually don't come on right after the damage, but rather months to years later, an average of eight years after birth trauma or the febrile seizures of early life.

We know which pieces of brain play a role in the genesis of the seizures because modern MRI scans show clearly the local damage, especially in the hippocampus. Yet we can only speculate on how all those pieces got involved. One presently popular theory is that there is a cascade of damage. Damaged neurons have the property of discharging in bursts of activity when they should produce only a single impulse. The neurons of the uncus have direct connections with the hippocampus. In the hippocampus are neurons with NMDA receptors—which, in response to bursts, tend to stay open a long time, letting calcium into the cell all the while.

Too much internal calcium is toxic to neurons, and so the hippocampal neurons are secondarily damaged. They, in turn—so this theory goes—start to fire in bursts. This makes the perfectly normal neurons with which they are connected—often in the front part of the temporal lobe, including the outer surface—follow in that abnormal burst-firing pattern as well.

When enough normal neurons repeatedly fire in synchronized bursts, that's a focal seizure. The hippocampal damage—in this theory—is secondary to the original damage to the uncus. And when the hippocampal damage becomes extensive enough, seizures occur. There's even some evidence that the attempts of the hippocampus to repair itself may make the whole situation worse, further increasing the chance for hippocampal neurons to fire in bursts. More subtle changes in the hippocampus following the long period of reduced blood supply might also compound the problem.

Anticonvulsant drugs may work best on the followers, reducing the chances of things temporarily spreading even further to become a bigger seizure. Anticonvulsant drugs provide adequate seizure control for up to three-quarters of those with epilepsy; it is the remaining fourth that is evaluated for surgery. It's likely that those patients whose seizures are not controlled by drugs represent a subpopulation with ongoing, progressive disease: that seizures beget seizures.

These aren't small subpopulations. Epilepsy is pretty common, about 0.5 to 1 percent of the population. That means the subpopulation with poorly controlled seizures on anticonvulsant drugs includes around 450,000 patients in the United States. New drugs for epilepsy are being continually evaluated—that's a major research interest of Neil's neurologist. And despite a cumbersome regulatory process, several new drugs for epilepsy have been approved. But these new drugs have, so far, produced only small reductions in the number of patients with poorly controlled seizures.

Drugs and operations are really only "halfway" therapies for epilepsy, not unlike the iron lung stage of polio treatment. They address the symptoms, not the causes. What's really needed is a better understanding of the causes, hopefully leading to prevention and a vast reduction in cost—as did the polio vaccine. That is what basic research is about.

One prevention step is that people with head injuries are now usually treated with anticonvulsants—just as a precaution, hoping to avoid that cascade of damage following injury to the uncus. But a real understanding of seizure spread and calcium toxicity may someday prevent the secondary damage that leads to many kinds of epilepsy.

NOW IT'S JUST A MATTER OF CLEANING UP and closing. How successful has Neil's operation been? Only time will tell for certain, but the more of the epileptic tissue removed, the better the chances of seizure control. Neil's final EEG recording, just before closing, is "clean."

In a typical group of patients coming to an operation like Neil's, around two-thirds will be free of seizures by the time the fourth and fifth postoperative years roll around. The patients with unusually localized temporal lobe disease have about an 80 percent chance of being seizure-free then. Patients with damage to both temporal lobes, but with seizures arising mostly from just one side, have only a 30 to 40 percent chance of being seizure-free—yet for the seizure-free group, it produces quite a change in their lives. They can get a driver's license. If they were employed at the time of surgery, they are likely to have a better job a few years later. If they were students, they are more likely to become employed than those epileptics who continued uncontrolled without surgery.

Evaluating patients for epilepsy surgery is complex, labor intensive, and expensive. So are the operations. That's true of many "halfway" therapies: heart transplants, kidney dialysis, artificial hips, epilepsy operations. These advances in medical technology account for much of the rapid rise in health-care costs, a rise present in all developed countries, regardless of the "system" for health-care delivery.

The health-insurance companies are already reluctant to authorize these procedures or pay their full costs. Further limits on growth in health-care costs is likely to mean restricting the resources available for these technologies: limits on O.R.s, intensive-care beds, facilities for monitoring seizures, training of specialists who know how to handle these problems that are beyond the realm of family practice. All of this is likely to diminish the availability of these technologies and lead to longer waiting lists for them.

Yet most figures indicate that the present level of epilepsy surgery takes care of only a fraction of the epileptics who need it. That number is estimated to be between 50,000 and 100,000 persons in the United

States. The number of epilepsy operations done in the United States in any one year is well under 5,000. It is such resource-intensive procedures that could well be a major casualty of health-care reform. The real losers could be the patients like Neil who would benefit from them.

SOMEHOW THE RESIDENT knows that it's time to reappear. I saw her out at the sink scrubbing again, and now she is getting gowned and gloved.

We'd heard that she was busy in the O.R. next door, helping take care of a messy head injury from a head-on collision. Eventually she clears the obstacle course and joins us at Neil's head.

"We caught the guy just as he was starting to herniate," the resident reports. I raise my eyebrows as the implications set in. She's learned the art of understatement.

You can't translate this bit of vocabulary with the usual medical dictionary. The verb *to herniate* in the present tense is not found in most of them, which instead endlessly describe various fixed hernias, things bulging out here and there, in need of fixing sometime. It's usually elective surgery. But every medical student knows what "He's herniating" means. It refers to someone's brain being seriously damaged over the course of a half hour, with fatal consequences ahead.

It's how people die from epidural hematomas, where bleeding from a leaking artery causes blood to pool outside the dura. Or from a burst aneurysm, somewhere inside the brain. The blood accumulates and pushes the brain down toward the brain stem. It's one of the major medical emergencies that needs to be treated immediately.

And it involves that same edge of dura that probably injured Neil's brain. The temporal lobe gets pushed around the edge of the dura. That's bad enough, in the long run. But it's even worse in the short run, because that portion of temporal lobe gets pushed against the brain stem. The brain stem is apt to stop working when squeezed in this way. And so the patient is apt to stop breathing. While you can always put the patient on a respirator temporarily, all sorts of irreversible neurological damage gets done—unless you catch it very quickly by opening the skull and draining off the trapped blood. That's evidently what she and the chief resident just did, the meaning of her simple words, "caught the guy."

Helping George finish up, after a few hours of that kind of action, is going to seem pretty tame to her. George has already finished with the final ultrasonic sculpturing around the biopsy sites, and has already gotten all of the bleeding under control. He takes her on a brief tour of the depths of the brain, pointing out where the scarred uncus was. She's very interested in that, as she didn't get a chance to see it in her accident victim. It was what was threatening the brain stem, causing death to rapidly approach, but the surgery consisted of stopping the bleeding near the brain's surface and relieving the pressure on the uncus.

She and George are very busy for twenty minutes, stitching up the dura, all around the three edges of the flap. George summarizes what happened during the day as they both sew away, explaining the data we obtained and his rationale for his decisions about what to remove, especially how the results from the hippocampal strip electrode changed his mind. My view of Neil's brain slowly disappears as they talk and sew. When they finish, the dura looks as taut as it normally does. If any bleeding starts outside the dura, it'll have a hard time getting through that seam.

She places some special sponges in the sites where rebleeding might occur— they are the kind that can be left behind and never removed— and then asks the scrub nurse for the drill. Time to start reattaching that big piece of Neil's skull. She drills a little hole, no bigger than a pencil lead, near the edge of the skull opening. And another diagonally opposite. And a third and fourth, each near a corner of the bony window.

George reaches across her to take the skull piece from its refuge atop the sterile tent where it has been resting for the last seven hours. He orients it to the opening, so that she can see where to drill the matching set of holes. While she does the drilling, standing off to one side, George threads four wires, very thin but very strong, through the first set of holes and bends them back into a hairpin shape. The resident holds the newly perforated skull piece up to the opening again. Everything matches. A quick look is taken around inside Neil's skull. Everything's stable.

And so they string the wires through the new little holes in the skull cap, then seat it down into the beveled edges of the skull opening. A perfect fit. Some light is presumably still coming in through the saw cuts and the access holes in the corners, but it's pretty much back to its customary darkness for Neil's brain. The window is closing.

The wires are twisted like a grocery tie, then the excess is snipped off. The next task is doing something about the five dime-sized holes that were drilled this morning to allow access for the saw. The scrub nurse has been mixing up some acrylic cement, beating it with a tongue depressor to get the desired stiffness. She scoops some up so that George can see it slowly drip back into the mixing bowl. Just the right consistency.

The resident places some of the reabsorbable sponges in the bottom of each hole, to keep the acrylic off the dura. Then she takes the tongue depressor and begins filling the holes with the acrylic, smoothing off the surface with her gloved thumb, just as a carpenter fills nail holes before finishing. The acrylic will be solid in only a few minutes. But no acrylic is placed in the saw cuts. There is something better, when the gap is so narrow. The saw cuts will be filled in over the next few months as new bone grows into the gap. Eventually the skull will be structurally sound once more, the little wires no longer playing a role.

Now it's a matter of muscle. The big fanlike temporalis muscle, which helps run the left side of Neil's jaw, is reconnected to the skull with another sewing job. Again the sutures are just to hold things in place while regrowth occurs. Then the skin flap is sewn up, though not as delicately as was the dura. The sterile tent is partially disassembled, and the rest of Neil comes into view. A sterile surgical dressing is wrapped around Neil's head. Done.

chapter 18

In Search of the Narrator

NEIL FOUND US back in our usual quiet alcove of the hospital cafeteria and carried his tray over. Other than the baseball cap he's wearing while his hair grows back—and also serving to hide the U-shaped scar—Neil looks as he did during our pre-op conversations. It's only a month since the tip of his left temporal lobe was removed.

"Well, I guess I gave you a piece of my mind!" Neil said as he unloaded his tray.

I'm afraid George and I groaned so loudly that several people turned around to look in our direction.

"But so far as I can tell, I'm not missing any marbles," he said, looking up at us with a grin.

No, only a piece of brain. Anatomy. The mind is the brain in action, its physiology. Mind is like what the computer produces, rather than the computer itself.

But Neil didn't buy my computer analogy. "Now if it were my computer," he observed, "knocking out a piece of it would cause it to crash. And it could never reboot itself."

Yes, but sometimes mental processes aren't so sensitive to crippled hardware. Just imagine computer software that can reconfigure itself to run on various combinations of hardware, after testing to see what's available.

"With consciousness as the operating system?" Neil was teasing me again. "The original user interface for the little man inside the head?"

He inspected his salad, then went on. "I think that the analogy you want is not a computer, but rather a computer network," he said. "One that can share work around among the idle processors. You ought to figure out how the brain can reorganize itself, somehow reassign space. Dynamic Reorganization, you can call it. Then patent it quickly, before a computer designer does!"

"Except for the little problem that we don't know enough about how the brain works," George replied. "Not nearly enough to be able to build a working model. One that can walk, talk, juggle cafeteria trays, worry about tomorrow, and tell bad jokes about missing marbles."

Neil grinned. "But just think what nice machines you could design with neural principles. Isn't that what the neural networks researchers are doing?"

They're trying to design machines—electronic circuits, at least— that don't have to be designed after a certain point. That instead can be tuned up or trained to perform specialized functions, such as speech recognition. The usual hyperbole, even repeated by the *New York Times* in a headline, is that the principles they use are "based on the human brain."

Which is gross overstatement. The everything-connects-to-every- thing wiring principles they utilize are found even in jellyfish nervous systems. Other principles for wiring up neural circuits have been superimposed on them, even by the time you get to the complexity of a crab nervous system—and neural-like networks haven't gotten as far as crabs yet. I wrote a letter to the *Times* suggesting that a more appropriate headline, considering the current state of the art, would have been "based on slug nerves."

"Isn't artificial intelligence trying to use them for fancier things," Neil argued, "such as pattern recognition—handwriting, fingerprints, and stuff like that?"

Yes, and maybe the simplest principles will suffice for fancy functions, without reverse-engineering the brain. I wish them well. But I'll bet they're going to have to find some fancier principles first, probably borrowing them from neurophysiology and evolutionary biology.

George had finally finished layering all possible additions atop his hamburger. Even salad dressing. He looked up at Neil. "The problem, you see, is that you're talking to a couple of biological chauvinists here. Who think that real brains are far more interesting than anything likely to be invented in silicon very soon."

"Yes, but biological brains have several drawbacks," Neil persisted. "Wouldn't you like the perfect traffic cop directing vehicles at every intersection on your way home from work, one that never got bored by the task, or demented from breathing the fumes? You'd never have to wait for the light to change, even though no traffic was coming. And it could wave you through a gap in the oncoming traffic for a quick left turn, just the way traffic cops do."

George and I allowed as how that might be nice.

"And the other problem is that human brains seem to gradually self-destruct with age. Don't you like that science-fiction idea of making a silicon working model of your brain, so that your mind can live forever?"

The disembodied mind? But the brain is intimately a part of the body, evolved to be the ultimate hand-in-glove combination. You might be able to design a thinking machine with minimal sense organs and output devices, but it's hard to imagine a human mind perking along without at least a head and a hand. Remember all those sensory isolation experiments that caused hallucinations after a little while? External reality is what keeps chaos in check—the brain has a perpetual battle between stability and flexibility, and external reality is a major arbiter.

Replicating your brain in silicon sounds like a recipe for psychosis in perpetuity. And that even assumes that they got the silicon workalike circuits tuned up right, so that the whole system didn't freeze or oscillate endlessly. No thanks.

Reverse-engineering the brain, however, is much more promising— you'd create a more stable machine, only parts of which flirted around on the edge of chaos to be creative. And then you would educate it like a child, over a period of many years. The good ones could presumably be cloned, if you'd built in readout facilities from the beginning. Different schools could have competitions to see whose star pupil got cloned, memories and all.

Neil shook his head in resignation. "Well, in any event, I've got another data point for you, in your search for the seat of the soul."

"What's that?" George responded, bemused.

"Consciousness isn't in the tip of the left temporal lobe—I can still think without it!"

"All too well," George observed. "Of course, consciousness wasn't in your brain stem either, unless you want to equate it with mere arousal. Selective-attention circuits up in the thalamus and the cortex have a lot more to do with it. Consciousness is more like a searchlight that moves around from one part of the cerebral cortex to another."

That's the problem with using the same word, *consciousness,* to describe things as different as arousal, focused attention, and talking to oneself. If you want to include selective attention within consciousness, then a three-month human fetus isn't conscious but cats are. All cells, plant and animal, have irritability—and so by some overinclusive definitions, they must be "conscious."

"Yes, I remember our first discussion of consciousness terminology," Neil said. "It was that day we first discovered this corner table where I could get my coffee fix by merely inhaling."

If you set the consciousness threshold at talking to yourself, I continued, then you've said that only humans are conscious—unless you want to believe in cartoon-strip depictions of animals that talk only to themselves and never out loud.

"Of course," George added, "if you're going to set the threshold for consciousness *that* high, you'll probably leave out some essential considerations. Such as that changing focus of selective attention, why we get bored after a while even when satisfied."

The hierarchy of mental functions builds up from the lowest level, that of deep anesthesia where very little is working, to the level of deep sleep—functionally, that's like the late part of seizures where slow electrical oscillations dominate the action.

Above that is a level of functioning like stupor and dementia, where things aren't working very well but at least aren't stuck in the limit cycle of oscillations. They're now up into the realm of chaos, at least in the mathematical sense of the word.

Expectancy is what characterizes our better mental operations, both perception and guiding movements in novel situations.

Concept formation is up there a little higher—all those new categories. And we build atop it for language and intuition, where we're always dealing with novelty and trying to apply our detailed memories to generating novel sequences of words and actions.

And then, of course, there's the issue of where in the brain these processes take place—as they could all be happening at once, but in different regions of the cortex.

"I need some examples. So let's take my train of thought during the drive to the hospital this morning," Neil proposed. "In anticipation of being at the wheel again, I've been practicing back-seat driving on all my cabbies. As I was sitting there paying attention to the red light, waiting for it to change to green, what part of my brain was working harder than usual? The visual cortex?"

"Not compared to looking around in general," George replied. "It's that right frontal area, plus that right parietal area, which is especially involved in vigilance tasks. They're what keep the driver behind you from having to honk."

"I remember drumming with my fingers, getting impatient."

That's your left supplementary motor area, plus the motor cortex, producing a nice limit-cycle oscillation.

"And, of course, I was thinking over my schedule for the day. Where's that?"

"Maintaining a mental agenda seems to be in the frontal lobes," George replied. "It's the patients with damage to the left dorsolateral frontal lobe that have trouble monitoring progress in a mental agenda."

"And then the light changes, and the landscape starts flashing past on both sides of the car. What now?"

The magnocellular pathways of the visual system, the ones that don't work as well in dyslexics. It may only be 10 percent of the visual system, but it specializes in movement and depth perception. You probably stirred up lots of activity in an area known as V5.

"A house I noticed reminded me of a rather different house, one of those Frank Lloyd Wright houses built around a little waterfall. How did I bring up that fancy set of images from memory?"

"Probably you activated some parietal-lobe areas specializing in complex forms," answered George. "And those in turn reactivated a lot of the higher-order visual areas that participated in analyzing the house when you first learned about it."

"The cab driver pointed out an Italian sports car, and so I started keeping my eyes open for another Maserati. Where's that?"

The front part of the cingulate gyrus, in the midline on both sides of the brain. At least that's what lights up when you're staying alert for particular classes of objects. I don't know where your Maserati memories are stored—maybe in the front of your temporal lobe.

"It sure isn't stored in my left temporal lobe!" grinned Neil. "That's gone now! And good riddance. Must be here," he said, pointing at his right temple.

Warming to his tour, he continued. "Then I saw this poster on the back of a bus, and tried to read it."

That ought to have stimulated more activity in the parvo parts of your visual pathways, all of those areas in the back of the temporal lobe that are involved in reading.

"But the poster had one of those tricky sentences that advertising agencies love to create," he related. "It was intentionally missing the verb, just to force you to re-read it several times to figure out what you'd missed."

"That certainly ought to have stirred up your left hemisphere," George laughed. "All of the language areas. And especially the left frontal lobe, down near your eyebrow. It gets very active when you have to supply a verb."

"And then another bout of right-hemisphere activity as we waited for a light to change," Neil continued, "followed by our grand entrance onto the freeway. But we soon slowed down to a snail's pace. So I started thinking about getting off the freeway and trying an alternate route."

Alternative courses of action are a frontal lobe function, par excellence. And surely the right parietal lobe was stirred up too, what with all those spatial tasks.

"Then I started worrying about being late, checking my watch constantly. So does the temporal lobe really have something to do with time?"

It's called the temporal lobe because it's behind the temple.

"But isn't that the same word root? For 'time'?"

The Latin word *tempus*.

"Why was the back side of the forehead named after the Latin word for 'time'?"

Because the hair there is the first to turn gray.

"Aggh! So the temporal lobe doesn't really have anything to do with time."

Well, actually it does. It just wasn't named on account of it, as the timing role was discovered much more recently. When neuro-psychologists ask you to tap a finger as fast as you can, they're checking up on how well the tips of the temporal lobes are working. Trouble there, or in the frontal lobe on the other side of the sylvian fissure, tends to slow down finger-tapping rate. It takes a lot of coordination to tap rapidly.

CATEGORIES, CONCEPTS, WORDS. They too require a lot of coordination between different regions of the cerebral cortex. You've got to be able to memorize things in versatile ways, invent new categories. Guess what another person might be thinking about. Confuse concepts, sometimes creatively. We mix and match to make metaphors.

"What about those people who seem to have categories for animal, vegetable, and mineral?" Neil asked. "Or at least, that's how I remember them. The newspaper reports say they lose all their vegetable names after a little stroke."

"Each patient shows something a little different," George said. "Some can name tools, but not animals. Others have been missing their plants, or body parts, or verbs, or the combination of food, fruits, and vegetables—as if that category was stored in the brain destroyed by the stroke. They can usually recognize the word, and write the word—what they're missing is the visual representation of that category. Sometimes they can use a word like *crack* as a verb but not as a noun. Electrical surface stimulation has shown some effects like that in the strip electrode studies. We don't know if any of these reported categories are repeatable from one patient to the next—they could just be idiosyncrasies related to how you learned words back when you were two years old."

"So do other animals have categories?" Neil asked. He was happily munching on his sandwich.

Birds can certainly learn categories. You can show pigeons pictures of sad people and happy people, and they'll learn to spot the sad ones, even in a batch of pictures they've never seen before.

But we humans can do very fancy categories, such as the various connotations of a single word. *Comb* must allow for "combing" your house in search of a lost book, as well as what a comb looks like, how it feels in your hand, the spelling c-o-m-b, the movement for combing one's hair, the sound sequence /kōm/, and so on. Combs even have a characteristic smell—if I were to ask you to close your eyes and held one up under your nose, you'd probably be able to identify it.

Rather than storing a comprehensive record of *comb* everywhere, the visual representation of a comb developed in extrastriate visual areas seems to be stored there. The auditory association areas have the stored record of what *comb* sounds like—and probably a separate record of the characteristic sound made by running your fingernail along the teeth. Other areas probably have the record of the movement sequences needed to use a comb or pronounce the word.

"But how are they tied together so one can evoke another? Seems like we're back to Pavlov's dog, associating the sound of the bell with the food."

"Good point," George said. "Associations between and among things seem to be what the cerebral cortex is particularly good at. Things like habit and skills are thought to involve subcortical structures such as your basal ganglia."

"Subroutines are made in the subcortical structures?"

"That's possible, but let's stick to categories and committees for a minute," George said. "It isn't just the cortex that does committees. For color, it starts way out in the retina. Color is a much simpler case than a comb—there's no sound associated with red, nor any feeling in the hand, nor any smell or taste."

And we know a lot about color, that it's a committee property of three types of photoreceptors peaking in short, medium, and longer

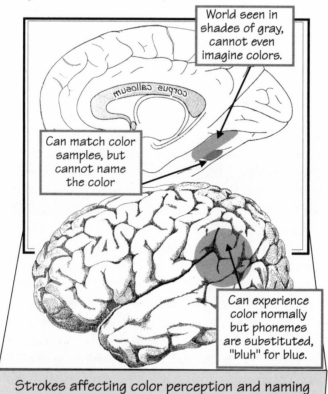

After Damasio and Damasio, 1992

World seen in shades of gray, cannot even imagine colors.

Can match color samples, but cannot name the color

Can experience color normally but phonemes are substituted, "bluh" for blue.

Strokes affecting color perception and naming

wavelengths. Equal amounts in all channels and we call it white. Long channel only, and it's red.

"I remember your Purple Principle. Short and long, but not much activity in the middle, and we say it's purple."

"There are higher-order visual areas on the underside of the temporal and parietal lobes," George resumed, "that seem essential for making use of those activity ratios. Patients with a stroke damaging those areas can't even imagine colors anymore, though they're otherwise pretty normal. They can't name the paint sample that you show them. If you ask them to match up similar paint samples, they are hopeless. Their whole concept of color is gone, replaced by the twilight world of grays. It must be like living in a world of bright moonlight."

And, of course, there are patients with strokes in the rear of the lateral language areas who can't name a color very well because they get the phonemes wrong—maybe they say "bluh" for blue, but you can get the idea that they indeed have the concept of color and can use it.

"Then there are the rare patients who have the concept of color," explained George, "but they can't give you the name. They can pronounce the name from memory just fine, if you ask them what color a banana is. They can match up paint samples correctly. But they can't name them for you. What's missing seems to be the association between the color concept and the color name. The strokes that do this are on the underside of the left temporal lobe, adjacent to the 'color concept' area."

"There are all sorts of other examples like that," George continued, "regions where certain kinds of knowledge seem to come together in a specialized way. There are patients with temporal lobe damage whose naming problems are worst when shown pictures of animals, and far less when trying to name inanimate objects such as screwdrivers."

"What about actions rather than objects?"

"Verbs give them no problems," George answered. "It's patients with frontal lobe damage that have trouble with verbs. But concepts and their nouns seem to have something to do with the lower portion of the temporal lobe—in the rear, strokes are more likely to damage a general concept. Closer to the front of temporal lobe, it's more likely to be proper names and unique episodes. That's Tony Damasio's idea of how the middle temporal lobe is organized."

"From the general to the particular," said Neil, rephrasing. "You know, that's probably the first time I've heard either of you mention some logical progression in brain organization. A principle at last."

Yes, I conceded. It's too logical, in fact—too good to be true. Brains are fundamentally irrational. They're patchworks. But we'll see— Damasio could be right.

MAKING A DECISION to say "banana" when seeing one would seem to be pretty simple, so long as it is the only object around. Neil had gone back to get dessert and returned with the banana we were discussing. He seemed in no hurry to consume it.

"So 'banana' is the activity in a collection of feature detectors," Neil speculated, "a Hebbian cell assembly. Some of which like yellow things, some of which like curved things, some of which like fruits, and so on?"

Yes, it's a spatiotemporal pattern again. A rather widespread one, extending over many millimeters or even centimeters of brain.

"And pronouncing 'banana' is another spatiotemporal pattern in the movement-control pathways up in frontal lobe," George observed, "that orchestrates the mouth and tongue and vocal cords."

But there is no need to funnel down the spatiotemporal pattern to just one command neuron for "banana." Nor to make the decision at some point in time. In fact, especially in brains less specialized than ours, there might not need to be two different spatiotemporal patterns—the sensory one might also be the movement one, because so many of the higher-order sensory neurons are also movement-associated neurons. In more complicated brains like ours, there probably are two or more distinct spatiotemporal patterns associated with "banana"—but it doesn't have to be separated in time, like some sort of 'he sings' and then 'she sings' duet. The sensory and movement spatiotemporal patterns can overlap in time—real parallel processing.

"So there's no need to have a place and a time at which the decision is made," mused Neil. "And that means no little person inside the head."

He thought a minute as he slowly peeled his banana. "So what's that 'binding problem' I've read about, that postulates some sort of synchronous activity to tie together all those feature detectors in different places? Why do they need to be tied together? Doesn't performing the action suffice to tie them together?"

It does seem regressive, doesn't it? Going backward toward what Dan Dennett mockingly calls the cartesian theater, a stage on which everything is played out, somewhere in the brain—with an implicit observer who decides.

Neil threw up his hands, smiling mischievously. "Consciousness as the graphical user interface! Didn't I tell you so?"

But the need for some limited sort of binding is real enough, once you begin to worry about *several* objects at the same time, as Hebb's colleague Peter Milner realized in 1974. Consider driving a car. There are dozens of moving objects in your field of view, each of which has a shape and color and distance away. We know from all those specialties of the higher-order visual areas that each object will set up activity in a number of the specialty areas. Some areas specialize in motion, others in shapes, others in distance away. And, of course, color.

Each object is doing that, and the positional information gets blurred in the feature detectors that are doing the motion and color tasks— they register position only crudely compared to the neurons in the parvo pathways. There is some danger of assigning the wrong color to a moving object, that of an adjacent object.

"So the traffic light appears to be moving—though it's really me, driving along—and I might think that the top light was green, if I didn't know better from memory?" Neil commented.

Synchrony could save you from that mistake, or so the theory goes. The synchrony-for-binding theory postulates a tendency for the red light's shape neurons, its color neurons, its distance neurons, and its motion neurons to all fire in near-synchrony. And for the green light's committee to all fire together, probably at a somewhat different time in a cycle.

"For example," George said, "neurons in the motor cortex tend to get synchronized when the monkey has to concentrate on a particularly difficult task, such as groping for a raisin behind its back."

"Clapping in unison, no doubt, to signal impatience."

Unlikely. But I wouldn't rule it out. There is certainly a lot of synchronized firing around, waiting to be explained—and it will probably turn out to be useful in various ways.

"So how do you create categories, if the code for an item is a Hebbian cell assembly?" Neil wondered out loud. "Or, rather, your message-board amendment that says it's a pattern, no matter where it's located in the brain?"

The Hebbian committee can be pretty sparse—maybe the neurons in a dozen active minicolumns, out of a few hundred neighboring minicolumns which otherwise keep quiet. That means that several cerebral codes, say the ones for *apple* and *orange*, can be superimposed to give you a category such as *fruit*. If you tried superimposing several letters from a dot-matrix printer, you'd get a black mess. But if the matrix is sparsely filled, you can probably recover the individual members because they each produce such distinctive spatiotemporal patterns.

WHAT SORT OF BRAIN ORGANIZATION makes for a good mechanic, or a good pianist, or a good composer? Neil and George had been comparing opinions of operas I'd never heard of.

"We don't know what the optimal brain organization for a musician is," George said, "but functional mapping techniques ought to tell us someday."

There are certainly some temporary interactions between music and intelligence that make one wonder about short-term optimal arrangements. Someone did intelligence tests after subjects had listened to a highly-structured Mozart piano sonata and got 8 to 9 percent increases—even if they didn't like Mozart! But the increase was only temporary, as if music was a good warm-up exercise for the rapid language processing and problem-solving that IQ tests require. Many researchers think that music is very similar to language—just a variation on the basic theme.

"But I still don't understand the basic theme—the long-term arrangement of the average brain," complained Neil. "Oh, I now know a lot about the departments of the brain. Reminds me a lot of modern companies, actually."

Really? A hierarchy it isn't.

"No, no. You've got a military model in mind, and most new organizations really aren't like that anymore." Now Neil was the instructor. "Taken together, the brain 'departments' remind me of an organization of knowledge specialists. Like the ones that advise communities on how to solve their garbage problems. The organizations in this building seem to practice differential diagnosis. And there are consulting firms that will tell you how to do rooftop solar power, perform all the cost calculations for you, jump the regulatory hurdles for you, and force the local electric utility to buy your surplus on the weekends. The brain's a lot more like such a knowledge-based organization—the knowledge society rather than the industrial society."

"But surely there's some management somewhere," he concluded, pointing with his fork. "Even a modern organization of equals, like an orchestra or a consulting firm, has some managers. If decisions don't get made, nothing gets done."

"Selective attention might at least qualify as middle management," George said, grinning. "But if we were to concede a vice president, you'll probably want to know where the president's office is located."

George is kidding Neil about the rotating presidency of his new company. Neil had to give up running his new company when the seizures got worse a year ago, and his partners are anxious for him to come back full time and relieve them of the burden.

"Well, let me tell you the big difference between being a vice president and a CEO," Neil said, warming to his topic. "And it isn't the size of the office or the best view. It isn't even leadership, in the sense of getting people to follow your lead. The junior people all know how to do that, by the time they get very far up the ladder."

He spread his hands wide. "But what chiefs have to do is to provide the direction. There's no one else to follow anymore. It takes real imagination to be a chief exec. All those possible different directions that the company could go—you've got to explore them in preliminary ways, and think about how the company might look in five or ten years, if you followed that path. And then decide."

"Of course, that disappoints the vice presidents who planned the other alternatives. That's why my partners and I jumped ship three years ago and started our own company. We imagined a path to some new products, saw a niche that surely was going to be filled by someone. And we had a head start on it."

A SENSE OF THE FUTURE is perhaps the most special of the higher intellectual abilities. Imagine someone—and the brighter of the autistic kids would be a good example—who has the basics of language but cannot make mental models of someone else's point of view. And so he interprets everything very literally—metaphor is beyond his abilities. He can't imagine anything very well, so even when he plays by himself, he's not creative. Because he cannot imagine another person's reaction, he gets into all sorts of trouble with social relationships. Top executives show you the other end of this spectrum.

"Oh, I agree," Neil said with mock modesty. "But you've probably got an old-fashioned idea about how top management works—it's really more like a string quartet or jazz combo, where the leadership shifts around and has little to do with rank or title in a hierarchy. That's why top management is usually called the 'President's Office' in an American company, the 'Vorstand' in a German one."

"But what it's really like is the partners in tennis doubles matches," he continued. "A player may have a preferred position, close to the net or in the back court, but they cover for one another. And not just for the situation, like getting drawn out of position, but according to their relative strengths. A good back court player will start running to cover for the weak backhand of the partner at the net, even before the ball leaves the racket on the other side of the net."

A half century ago, Kenneth Craik proposed that the brain was making a small-scale working model of external reality and of possible actions. That the brain could thus try out various alternatives, conclude which was best by utilizing stored knowledge of somewhat analogous events of the past. By having imagined alternative actions beforehand, you can react in a much fuller, safer, and more competent manner to the emergencies that come along. And you can also react to future situations before they arise, as in making a business plan that anticipates reactions by your competitors.

The brain's ability to reorganize isn't merely a matter of adapting to the loss of a piece of brain. It's also a matter of reassigning space from minute to minute, of setting up optimal arrangements in the way that listening to the Mozart sonata might have done. Of being able to marshal your resources, as you concentrate on a difficult task. Or to relax and allow those subconscious thoughts to meander—and occasionally pop some relevant old memory into your stream of consciousness. Or come up with a newfound relationship between something you saw a few minutes ago and something old, buried in the recesses of memory, as when you finally recall someone's name.

"I like it—but you're missing my point," Neil complained. "Of course you can reorganize without central coordination. Happens all the time in a decentralized economy. But there's got to be some management for other tasks, even if there isn't a hierarchy."

He gestured upward with the palm of his hand. "What shifts my attention from the traffic light to looking around for another Maserati? From emphasizing concerns of areas on the outside of right frontal and parietal lobes, then switching over—now emphasizing the stuff in the cingulate gyrus of both sides, up front of the corpus callosum?"

Maybe you're doing all those things at once, in parallel.

"It certainly seems as if I switch my attention from one thing to another. I've got a stream of consciousness, and only one thing happens at a time," he emphasized. Then he paused for a moment, looking perplexed.

"You're telling me that my stream of consciousness *seems* to be one thing after another—but that's because it is sampling, one after the other, the parallel activities of lots of areas in my brain?"

Could be something like the way that the television newscast samples the activities of its part of the world. And ignores most of the world, most of the time. Whatever it reports is only a small part of what's going on. And of course the newscast isn't causing those activities, only shining a spotlight on them, the reporters and camera crews having been drawn by other reports.

"So the one-mental-topic-after-another is *effect,* rather than cause?"

To some extent, at least. The spotlight might, of course, influence an outcome by allowing a decision to be made sooner. Orchestrating media coverage is a big part of building a consensus in politics these days. Surely there are some pathologies of such systems, just as television crews are sometimes accused of causing riots to happen by their very presence—they can act as a catalyst. Conscious attention, focused on a problem, is also a catalyst.

THE STREAM OF CONSCIOUSNESS surely works in parallel with selective attention most of the time, but they need not be identical. Selective attention may bias the activities of the subconscious as well. Schizophrenics suffer intrusive thoughts or hallucinations despite their attempts to focus on the external world. For a lot of people, the train of thought probably corresponds to what could be talked about, if you chose to speak aloud.

"You can obviously have a stream of consciousness without talking aloud," George pointed out. "And it would appear that some people can talk without much 'consciousness'—those frontal lobe patients, for example, and especially the Williams syndrome kids, that talk and talk but without much content to the sentences."

So perhaps the little person inside the head is just the stream of consciousness. A serial stream sampling parallel processes. And it, in turn, may be biased strongly toward the verbal happenings, leaving out all sorts of more mundane things like blood pressure.

"Where does this leave Julian Jaynes?" Neil asked after a moment. "His theory that talking to ourselves wasn't evolved until recent times, back between the writing of the Iliad and the Odyssey? Before then, we heard voices telling us to do things, afterward we narrated our life's story ourselves. And our mental lives became considerably more lively."

Surely language, whenever it arose during prehuman evolution, set up a big increase in mental life. But did it occur so recently? All his evidence is from literary styles—which are notoriously prone to fads. And there's an old saying in anthropology, that absence of evidence is not evidence of absence. Why assume a sudden jump if you don't have to?

"I suppose there just isn't an answer to my question, about the *management* of knowledge, about what focuses attention? About how ideas compete?"

No, but there are some testable theories. Since you insist, I suppose I'll have to tell you about Darwin Machines.

DARWINIAN PROCESSES not only evolve new species of plants and animals, but also shape up new antibodies for the immune system. It may take millennia to get a new animal species, but it only takes a week or two for a new antibody to specialize in destroying a novel invading molecule. Shifting your attention, or evolving a new thought, may involve a similar process that, because things happen much more rapidly in the electrical machinations of neurons, takes only milliseconds to minutes.

"All because of the survival of the fittest?" Neil asked skeptically.

That's a well-known aspect of darwinism, but a darwinian process has at least six essential features. First of all, you've got to have a pattern of some sort.

"Like a gene? A string of DNA bases?"

Right, and in the case of brains we're probably talking about the Hebbian cell assembly, that spatiotemporal pattern of neuron activity that represents an apple or an orange. This cerebral code is quite arbitrary—as I said, like the bar code for representing apples on a can of fruit. What's important about the pattern, so far as mental darwinism is concerned, is that copies can be made of it. For example, you can presumably send the code for *comb* over long distances in the brain, through the corpus callosum.

"Of course, you aren't literally sending the message," George clarified, "in the manner of mailing something. What you do is to make a copy of it at the other end, just as when using a fax machine."

And the original pattern isn't destroyed in the process of "sending" it. So if you feel the comb with your left hand but need to send a message from your right brain's sensory hand map over to the left-brain language areas, you'll need to make a distant copy of the comb spatiotemporal pattern. Transmission of information is one reason Hebbian cell assemblies have to be copied, but there are others too.

"So there might be many spatial patterns of neuron firing in the brain—but only some of them are capable of making copies of themselves, somehow? But why else might you want to copy the pattern?"

To produce variations on the pattern. Intentional errors, if you like. Variations over long distances can likely be minimized with the equivalent of an error-correcting code, and I've already discovered one way to do that. But sometimes you might want to turn off the error correction.

"I assume you want errors for the same reasons that mutations are sometimes useful?"

Small errors can be handy. That's certainly how the immune system produces an antibody molecule that is an even better fit to the invader. When an antibody kills an invader, reproduction is stimulated. But it isn't just a clone of the successful defender: it's a whole spread of variations around that successful defender's pattern. Some of which are even better fits to the invaders, and so reproduce more. And variations about that new, better pattern produce some variants that are better still.

"By the time all the invaders are wiped out," George explained, "the antibodies have gotten to be pretty good fits. And this type hangs around for years, ready to immediately counter a fresh invasion."

"That's the immune response. But what happens in brain circuits that's similar to that?"

Suppose that a Hebbian pattern made a copy of itself right next door. And that, just the way a crystal grows, a whole territory develops where that basic pattern repeats, over and over. As in wallpaper.

"Hundreds of copies of the Hebbian pattern. But why? The biological imperative? Because the vacant territory is there, waiting to be organized somehow?"

That's actually a good possibility. Most physical systems with a big throughput of energy tend to self-organize into patterns, so why should the electrical activity of the brain be an exception? Other patterns might be trying to organize the territory too, at the same time, so you might expect some competition.

"The way that bluegrass and crabgrass are competing in my backyard, I suppose," Neil said.

Yes, and your backyard is another essential aspect of a darwinian process: there's got to be a work space of some sort for the competition.

"But what determines who wins? Or when a standoff occurs?"

For your backyard, it's the many-faceted environment. Rainfall and watering are important. And the cropping schedule, how often you mow it. Sunshine and shade. Nutrients. Some DNA patterns in grasses reproduce better with one cluster of environmental variables than with others. The environment in the brain includes the current inputs and the memories stored in synaptic connectivity patterns, those resonances.

So pattern, copying, variations, competition for a work space, and a multifaceted environment that biases the competition are five of the six essentials of a darwinian process. The sixth is to close the loop, having many repeats on the variation-and-selection steps. Just as in the immune response, there has to be a 'next generation' where the new variants are based on the more successful of the ones in the previous generation. Most of the new variants will be worse than their parents, but some will be better—and they are mostly the ones that will reproduce with yet again more variations.

"So that's what all the neural darwinism is about, those six essentials?"

That's what I mean by it, but the word 'darwinism' is used almost as loosely in science as it is by journalists. In most cases, all someone is trying to convey is that random variations are being shaped up by selective survival into a meaningful pattern—say, the way the synapses in the infant's brain are being edited by environmental experience. It's a carving process. There's often no closing of the loop, that sixth essential. Or if there is, there's no copying of patterns involved.

Selective survival is what's usually meant when someone speaks of darwinism—and it's very important all by itself. But that's a cardboard view of darwinism—the real thing goes several steps further. It's a repeating process that produces even fancier results by using multiple generations, repeatedly copying with variation from parent patterns that were successful.

"A real engine of progress, it sounds like. That's a Darwin Machine then?"

That name refers to the whole class of computing machines, each of which uses those six essentials of a darwinian process. I named it that on the analogy to Turing Machines. It's no one particular machine or computer simulation, but the whole class. It even includes biological machinery—the immune response is a particular example of a Darwin Machine.

And if the cerebral cortex can make copies of those Hebbian spatiotemporal patterns, and have competitions between them that are biased by resonance with memories, then some of our cognitive processes could be products of a Darwin Machine in our head.

"I think I need an example," Neil said, shaking his head.

Suppose that something round went whizzing past us, I said, gesturing. And then disappeared under the tables, so you couldn't verify your first impression—that it was something like a tennis ball. Or maybe an orange or an apple. How do you come up with candidates like that, and how do you eventually decide which one it was?

"I don't know, but I trust you're going to tell me," Neil said, smiling while he rubbed an itch amid his regrowing hair.

THE SENSORY IMPRESSION creates a committee of feature-detection neurons firing away, but their spatiotemporal pattern doesn't really resonate with a stored pattern. Copies are made of the fuzzy-round-object pattern and, in the process, errors are made. Suppose an error gets the pattern close to the stored pattern for *apple*.

"I thought that stored patterns were purely spatial patterns. And that active patterns were spatiotemporal, more like a melody?"

But the active pattern resonates with the stored pattern, just as your car resonates with a washboarded road surface to enhance the teeth jarring. That does two things: it brings forth the complete details of the stored pattern, even though you provided only an approximation. Once the cortical circuits start oscillating near the chaotic attractor—that's a fancier way to describe the resonance—you start getting a more complete spatiotemporal pattern, the stored one replacing the one which prompted it.

"The way that I can supply the details of someone's face, even though I'm only looking at a cartoonist's sketch."

Right, a 'pop out' of details. Second, the resonance makes copying easier, so that the resonant pattern makes copies next door. So you start to get a territory of the active *apple* pattern even in areas that don't have the resonance from long-term synaptic patterns. Copycats.

When copying in some other direction in the cortical sheet, perhaps the fuzzy-round-object pattern made errors in the direction of the stored resonance for tennis balls. Now you have two candidates for the unknown object. And maybe a third or fourth comes along, too.

"So now that you have candidates, I suppose that you can have a competition for the work space. Just like my bluegrass and crabgrass, fighting for my backyard. And may the best resonance win?"

It's not only the stored pattern that affects copying success, but also the present situation. If you're in a cafeteria, you're more likely to guess an orange or apple than you are a tennis ball. It's a multifaceted environment that biases the competition and sets up the next generation of variants.

That *apple* does better in occupying territory doesn't mean that it wipes out the competition, any more than you ever get rid of all the crabgrass in your backyard. A little change in the environment for the competition—suppose someone says the fuzzy-round object bounced—and suddenly the boundary between *apple* and *tennis ball* starts shifting so that the latter soon becomes dominant. And therefore the best guess, the one most likely to be named as the object.

"So is that the subconscious?" Neil asked. "The alternatives lingering in the background? When I say I'm conscious of its having been a tennis ball, I'm just reporting on the currently dominant pattern?"

That's the way I'd formulate it. And the experience of consciousness could reflect the winner, as regions from all over the brain compete with each other for dominance.

"Something like the basketball championships? Where there are regional winners, and then quarter-finals, semi-finals, and finally a championship match?"

Yes, but with the competition going on constantly, so that the "spotlight" of your "conscious awareness" shifts from one part of the brain to another, as the current winner changes around. The stream of consciousness, in this formulation, is just the history of the meandering spotlight. But, of course, it really isn't a spotlight shown by someone else—it's one region of the cortex lighting up because it has become temporarily dominant over other regions.

"That's why there's no head office for consciousness," Neil mused. "Also why no stroke eliminates it?"

"A stroke might eliminate a customary concept like color from the stream of consciousness," George noted, "but seldom the switching around that produces the stream."

THERE ARE SURELY MIDDLE MANAGERS in the brain that help regulate competitions like that, just as climate change serves to stimulate evolution more generally. And I expect that they actually create fluctuations.

"Management as the equivalent of climate change, did you say?" Neil was smiling. "They didn't mention that in business school. So these managers try to sharpen the competition?"

Yes. And that creates empty niches, where a local population goes extinct. That can create a golden opportunity for a variant that, at first, might not have been able to survive a head-to-head competition. These spatiotemporal patterns are ephemeral, the work space easily wiped clean by a little inhibition that momentarily quiets things down. Most of them aren't around for long enough to change the synaptic strengths permanently and thus create a long-term memory.

That's one aspect, and fragmentation is another. In biology, the way to evolve new species quickly is in an archipelago like the Hawaiian islands. So management that segregates the cortex temporarily, to make the equivalent of lots of little islands, would be another good management strategy.

"A little inconsistency as a good management tactic? Or budgets that fluctuate unpredictably? Wait until I tell my buddies!"

In the brain, all you should have to do is to change the background level of excitation or inhibition, something that those widespread arousal and attention mechanisms ought to be good at. Just spread around some norepi or serotonin or dopamine or acetylcholine.

That way you could create cycles of climate change, and cycles of fractionation and integration—the same way that a group of islands becomes one big island during an ice age when the sea level drops. The species get a period of isolation, to go their separate ways, and then a period of competition that results in one species becoming widespread. Then when sea level or excitability rises again, that winner becomes the basis of the new fragmentation.

"Sounds like the trust-busters at work, breaking up the phone company. So what about the economic cycle? Does that fit your metaphor?"

It's a good example of how whole continents might be affected together. The economic cycle analogy might be to mood, like the manic-depressive cycling which some creative people exhibit. But suppose the neural equivalents of climate change were much more regional, like the rainfall coming off those Pacific Ocean storm systems shifting around for a few years to give California an edge over Oregon, but then it shifts back. In neural terms, that could be a management technique, both for giving the various areas a chance to show their stuff, but also to speed up evolution of new ideas—since they percolate better in the smaller copying competition work spaces.

"I'm beginning to think you're serious about this."

SEQUENCES ARE THE REAL TEST of a concept like this, however, not individual item recognition and recall. With sequences, we keep track of the order of perceived events. But most importantly, we *produce* representations that are coded by sequence, such as sentences. We generate scenarios. Because of our sequential abilities, we experience a stream of consciousness that we can recall as a sequence, that we can mull over some more, and sometimes solve problems.

The stream of consciousness that's really important is the autobiographical one, the narrative we create—telling ourselves the story of our own life. We try to explain what's happened to us, to get us where we are. We imagine scenarios of success, we worry about scenarios of failure or threat. We're always poised at a choice between alternative futures. You can hear four-year-olds narrating things out loud, but thereafter most of us narrate our mental lives silently. We are narrators of our own inner lives, thanks to our sequential abilities.

"So you want a cerebral code that's good at sequences. Isn't a sequence just a fancy form of category?"

True, and there are some strange attractors in chaos theory that seem good at doing one spatiotemporal sequence for awhile, and then shifting to another spatiotemporal sequence. That Lorenz butterfly-shaped attractor is one example.

But there are also some ways of maintaining stable sequences of cerebral codes, just by lining them up in order across the cerebral cortex in a work space. So that they could be scanned in the right sequence. The chunking limit, those seven plus or minus two items that you can hold in working memory, might correspond to the limits on such scanned mapping. And perisylvian cortex might be particularly good at maintaining such sequences. Or storing the long-term form of them in synaptic connectivity changes.

"I don't sense that an organization chart is going to describe this very well," Neil said. "Not any more than you can meaningfully map the functions of a president's office or a doubles team."

"Certainly not so far," George responded. "Just remember that the history of cerebral mapmaking has been one of discovering more and more underlying specialization, that the 'association cortex' has proved to have many maps hidden in it. Remember we've seen a lot of specialization so far, neurons active during one task but not another. Your Darwin Machine may run in the cerebral cortex as if it were just an unspecialized work space, but there may be lots of specializations, anyway."

Right. On the side of flexibility are those higher-order visual neurons that change the size of their receptive field, depending on whether the monkey's behavioral task is responding to a color or responding to shapes. In my theory, there is even more flexibility because of all the copying. The resonances for *apple* aren't everywhere, even though copying can temporarily maintain the *apple* spatiotemporal pattern without them in many other places.

"And that satisfies the other important constraint from the physiology," George went on. "There are sites that are essential for a task such as naming or reading, and then there are many other sites that are merely active during the task—but they don't seem to be essential, in the sense that the task works fine with them temporarily confused by the electrical buzz."

What my kind of dynamic reorganization theory suggests, of course, is that the region of cortex specializing in fruit—if there is one—probably spends 99 percent of its time helping out with nonfruit tasks. Something like a neurosurgeon who spends most of the time acting as a general practitioner.

"That's terrible," George groaned. "A neurosurgeon who only operates 1 percent of the time is scarcely a neurosurgeon at all!"

"So here we have," observed Neil with a tour-guide's expansiveness, "the traditional conflict in science. Between 'context is everything' on the one hand and 'specialization is essential' on the other—with, of course, its 'practice makes perfect' corollary."

The experimental neurophysiologists seek specialization, and they find it. And the theoretical neurophysiologists seek schemes for generality—dynamic reorganization and flexible assignments.

"But have to find schemes that don't conflict with all the known specialties. Right?"

We're very complementary. Any brain theory—or at least, any theory worth wading through—needs to be able to explain a lot of versatility, plus all this specificity we see. At a low level, it needs to explain those cerebral codes for apples and oranges, how Hebbian cell assemblies are created and stored—and how the full spatiotemporal pattern is recreated during recognition or recall.

At a middle level, it needs to explain how categories are formed and how metaphor might work. It needs to explain why listening to Mozart might be a good setup for problem-solving tasks.

At the high end, it needs to explain creative confusion, multiple levels of abstraction, making models of what might happen, and utilizing fancy sequential rules such as syntax and logic. Remind me to tell you about hexagons sometime.

Now there's no reason why the brain couldn't have invented some processes fancier than darwinism. But it's something of a default process in nature, simply because nature is so good at copying. At some level—and probably multiple ones—the brain is going to operate on darwinian principles.

PRODUCING NARRATIVES for one's mental autobiography and career plan is certainly one of the better candidates for "Where's the real me?" But, as Neil pointed out before leaving, a train of thought needs good nutrition.

"I'm still going fishing in my stream of consciousness," he explained. "I had a professor who used to say that you've got to feed a stream of consciousness with a variety of new facts, keep feeding it all the time—if you want to get something new and interesting to pop out, every now and then. You've got to keep reading, keep trying out ideas for size, keep rearranging them to find something better."

He resettled the baseball cap on his head. "That's about the only thing that worried me about this operation, that my memory wouldn't be good enough afterwards to keep it fed with new facts. Or to fish among the old ones."

"But so far, so good. I still have trouble with the Sunday crossword puzzle, but I'm getting faster and faster."

Postscript

A great many patients are represented in this book, usually through a question they asked or a concern they expressed. Some were the patients undergoing operations such as Neil's, who contributed much knowledge through their cooperation. We thank them all for their contributions to our understanding of the difficult issues concerning the relationship between brain and mind with which this book has been concerned.

The book is hardly comprehensive. "A personal selection" is closer to the truth, and the selection was considerably biased by the problems of constructing a story suitable for general readers. Our editor, William Patrick, was of great help in steering us to the narrative voice which we finally adopted. We must also thank our colleagues who helped straighten us out on various matters: Katherine Graubard, Linda Moretti Ojemann, Sue Savage-Rumbaugh, Derek Bickerton, Susan Goldin-Meadow, John Palka, Elizabeth Loftus, Merle Prim, and Mark Sullivan. We are grateful to our more general readers who suffered through rough drafts and flagged the bumps in the road: they include Blanche Graubard, Agnes Calvin, David and Joan Ojemann, Daryl Hochman, Steven Ojemann, Ann-Elizabeth Ojemann, Eric K. Williams, Douglas W. VanDerhoof, Diane Brown, Linda Castellani (to whom we owe the title of Chapter 3), Elaine Sweeney, Susan McCarthy, Betty Kamen, Albert Geiser, Randall Tinkerman, Patrizia DiLucchio, Richard Raucci, Lena M. Diethelm, and various fellow passengers on long airline flights.

A Note for the Professionals: You may have wondered about how one patient managed to participate in so many different tests, or happened to personify the classic teaching-case features of complex partial seizures. That is because "Neil" is not merely a pseudonym but a composite (and should not be cited in the manner of a case report) of several temporal lobe epileptics who cannot be further identified, for all the usual reasons of patient confidentiality. He is a somewhat different composite than the "Neil" of our first book, *Inside the Brain*. We often "reconstructed" patients, usually by subtracting complications from the account of an actual patient but also by adding typical features not seen in that patient. Indeed, the only unaltered case report is one contributed by Dr. C: the alexia suffered by his father, the late Fred H. Calvin.

Only the surgeons among the readership may have noticed our other literary liberty: the case of the disappearing resident. Dr. C was indeed the third pair of "sterile hands" on dozens of occasions, but he often observed that the second pair obstructed his view of the brain. The assistant surgeon was also "in the way" in a literary sense as we planned this book. Playwrights are always sending an actor offstage on some errand, leaving two actors remaining, so that dialogue is simplified; in a narrative, a three-way conversation is even more awkward than in a script. When we finally realized that Dr. C was going to have to serve as the sole narrator and report what Dr. O said, we decided to avoid the dialogue problems of including the resident in the conversations—and simultaneously promote the reader's eyes and ears to having an unobstructed view. So we dispatch the resident on an errand in the first act, only to have her return in the Shakespearean manner near the end. Otherwise, the clinical cases and the O.R. details are within the range seen in contemporary neurosurgery.

W.H.C.
G.A.O.

General References

WILLIAM H. CALVIN, *The Cerebral Symphony: Seashore Reflections on the Structure of Consciousness* (Bantam 1989).

JEAN-PIERRE CHANGEUX, *Neuronal Man* (Oxford University Press 1986; translation of *L'Homme Neuronal,* Fayard 1983).

RICHARD L. GREGORY, *The Oxford Companion to the Mind* (Oxford University Press 1987).

MICHAEL I. POSNER, MARCUS E. RAICHLE, *Images of Mind* (Freeman 1994).

Scientific American special issues on the brain, September 1979 and September 1992.

Texts and Collections

JOHN E. DOWLING, *Neurons and Networks: An Introduction to Neuroscience* (Harvard University Press 1992).

DANIEL GARDNER (ed.), *The Neurobiology of Neural Networks* (MIT Press 1993).

ERIC R. KANDEL, JAMES H. SCHWARTZ, THOMAS M. JESSELL, *Principles of Neural Science*, 3d edition (Elsevier 1991).

STEPHEN M. KOSSLYN, RICHARD A. ANDERSEN (eds.), *Frontiers in Cognitive Neuroscience* (MIT Press 1992). Collected articles on vision, audition, somatosensory system, attention, memory, language, and reasoning.

JOHN G. NICHOLLS, A. ROBERT MARTIN, BRUCE G. WALLACE, *From Neuron to Brain: A Cellular and Molecular Approach to the Function of the Nervous System*, 3rd edition (Sinauer, Sunderland MA, 1992).

LLOYD D. PARTRIDGE, L. DONALD PARTRIDGE, *The Nervous System* (MIT Press 1993).

ROBERT F. SCHMIDT, GERHARD THEWS, *Human Physiology*, 2nd edition (Springer Verlag 1989, translation of *Physiologie des Menschen*, 1987).

GORDON M. SHEPHERD, *The Synaptic Organization of the Brain*, 3rd edition (Oxford University Press 1990).

End Notes

Rather than citing the earliest observations in the research literature, we have attempted to cite recent articles in books and journals that are widely found in college and public libraries; most of our citations, unfortunately, will be found only in medical libraries.

Chapter 1. *A Window into the Brain*

Some of the history of attempts to localize functions in the human brain can be found in ANNE HARRINGTON, "Beyond phrenology: localization theory in the modern era," in *The Enchanted Loom: Chapters in the History of Neuroscience,* edited by PIETRO CORSI, pp. 207–239 (Oxford University Press 1991).

See also STANLEY FINGER, *Origins of Neuroscience: A History of Explorations into Brain Function* (Oxford University Press 1994).

A. R. LURIA, "The functional organization of the brain," *Scientific American* (March 1970).

10   The sensory strip figure is modified from the version found in WILDER PENFIELD, THEODORE RASMUSSEN, *The Cerebral Cortex of Man* (Macmillan 1950).

13   WILDER PENFIELD, HERBERT JASPER, *Epilepsy and the Functional Anatomy of the Human Brain* (Little, Brown 1954). Although most cortical movements and sensation relate to the opposite side of the body, there are connections between primary motor and sensory cortices and ipsilateral body, especially for the face and to a lesser extent the leg. Only fine finger movement seems to be totally dependent on contralateral motor cortex. These ipsilateral connections are probably important in recovery from damage to primary motor and sensory areas. Only very rarely will electrical stimulation of the primary motor or sensory cortex evoke ipsilateral responses. However, stimulation of some of the secondary motor or sensory maps will more often yield ipsilateral effects.

15   The comparative neuroanatomist Irving Diamond argues that the "motor cortex" isn't restricted to the motor strip but is the fifth layer of the entire cerebral cortex. This is true because the fifth layer, no matter where it is, contains neurons that send their mass mailings down to the spinal cord, with copies to the brain stem, basal ganglia, and hypothalamus. Diamond likewise argues that the fourth layer everywhere is the "sensory cortex" and that second and third layers everywhere are the "association cortex." See "The subdivisions of neocortex: A proposal to revise the traditional view of sensory, motor, and association areas," in J. M. SPRAGUE, A. N. EPSTEIN (eds.), *Progress in Psychobiology and Physiological Psychology*, 8:1–43 (Academic Press 1979).

15   D. J. FELLEMAN, DAVID C. VAN ESSEN, "Distributed hierarchical processing in the primate cerebral cortex," *Cerebral Cortex* 1:1–47 (1991).

Chapter 2. ***Losing Consciousness***
For some general background on the EEG and its relation to chaos theory, see WALTER J. FREEMAN, "The physiology of perception," *Scientific American* 264(2):78–85 (February 1991).

RODOLFO R. LLINÁS, D. PARÉ, "Of dreaming and wakefulness," *Neuroscience* 44:521–535 (1991).

J. ALLAN HOBSON, *Sleep* (Freeman 1989).

19   J. ALLAN HOBSON, *The Dreaming Brain* (Basic Books 1988), p. 133.

20   MARVIN MINSKY, quoted by CLIVE DAVIDSON, "I process therefore I am," *New Scientist* 1866:22–26 (27 March 1993).

24   Neurons are only one of the cell types in the brain. There are even more astrocytes, the glial cells that line every surface of the brain and surround the nonmyelinated parts of most neurons. They surround the blood vessels and contribute to the so-called blood-brain barrier that keeps many substances (such as antibiotics) from reaching further into the brain. The myelin wrapping on the axons inside the central nervous system is due to the oligodendrocytes (that in the peripheral nervous system is due to Schwann cells).

24   Serotonin neurons are concentrated in the *raphe nuclei*, which get their name from the Greek word *rhaphe*, which means "seam" and refers to the midline crease that can be seen along the top surface of the brain stem. Besides norepi and serotonin, there are also diffuse projecting systems for dopamine and acetylcholine. These four diffuse systems can be thought of as like a set of four underground sprinkler systems that spray out various mixes of short-acting fertilizer over broad areas of the brain.

25   The illustration of stages of sleep is modified from NANCY C. ANDREASEN, *The Broken Brain* (Harper & Row 1984).

25   ADAM N. MAMELAK, J. ALLAN HOBSON, "Dream bizarreness as the cognitive correlate of altered neuronal behavior in REM sleep," *Journal of Cognitive Neuroscience* 1:201–222 (Summer 1989).

25   JONATHAN WINSON, "The meaning of dreams," *Scientific American* 263(5):86–96 (November 1990).

27   RENÉ DESCARTES, *Meditations on First Philosophy* (1641, various editions).

35   SUZANNE STENSAAS, D. EDDINGTON, AND W. DOBELLE, "The topography and variability of the primary visual cortex in man," *Journal of Neurosurgery* 40:747 (1973).

36   Cortical surface area in various species, calculated from the figures in JEAN-PIERRE CHANGEUX, *Neuronal Man* (1983, Random House translation from the French in 1985).

36   NANCY C. ANDREASEN et al., "Intelligence and brain structure in normal individuals," *American Journal of Psychiatry* 150:130–134 (January 1993).

36   ARTHUR R. JENSEN, "Understanding *g* in terms of information processing," *Educational Psychology Review* 4:271–308 (1992).

Chapter 3. ***Seeing the Brain Speak***

The blood flow studies of seeing words, hearing words, speaking and generating words are from the work of MARCUS RAICHLE and his collaborators; the original color illustration can be readily found in GERALD D. FISCHBACH, "Mind and brain," *Scientific American* 267(3):48–57 (September 1992). For more on both reading and PET methods, see JULIE A. FIEZ, STEVEN E. PETERSEN, "PET as part of an interdisciplinary approach to understanding processes involved in reading," *Psychological Science* 4:287–293 (September 1993).

WILDER PENFIELD, LAMAR ROBERTS, *Speech and Brain Mechanisms* (Princeton University Press 1959).

ALBERT M. GALABURDA, "Asymmetries of cerebral neuroanatomy," *Ciba Foundation Symposia* 162:219–226 (1991). Two-thirds of human brains have a larger planum temporale on the left.

ANTONIO R. DAMASIO, HANNA DAMASIO, "Brain and language," *Scientific American* 267(3):63–71 (September 1992).

ANTONIO R. DAMASIO, "Aphasia," *New England Journal of Medicine* 326:531–539 (20 February 1992).

GEORGE OJEMANN, "Cortical organization of language," *Journal of Neuroscience* 11:2281–2287 (1991). See also *Scientific American* (to appear).

ALAN S. GEVINS, JUDY ILLES, "Neurocognitive networks of the human brain," *Annals of the New York Academy of Sciences* 620:22–44 (1991). Scalp-recorded EEG and evoked potentials.

40   There is a fascinating story concerning personality differences in rats whose left brain is larger than the right: see VICTOR H. DENNENBERG, "Hemispheric laterality in animals and the effects of early experience," *Behavioral and Brain Sciences* 4(1):1–50 (March 1981).

40   NORMAN GESCHWIND, "Specializations of the human brain," *Scientific American* (September 1979). *Caution: the planum temporale is mislabeled in the next-to-last illustration of this article.* The planum temporale asymmetry has recently been challenged on the grounds that infolding (within the sylvian infolding itself) is greater on the right, compensating for the differences in gross appearance: see WILLIAM C. LOFTUS, MARK JUDE TRAMO, CATHERINE E. THOMAS, RONALD L. GREEN, ROBERT A. NORDGREN, MICHAEL S. GAZZANIGA, "Three-dimensional quantitative analysis of hemispheric asymmetry in the human superior temporal region," *Cerebral Cortex* 3:348–355 (July/August 1993).

42   The appearance of asymmetry in the planum temporale during human fetal development is described in J. WADA, R. CLARKE, A. HAMM, "Cerebral hemispheric asymmetry in humans," *Archives of Neurology* 32:239–246 (1975). And see ALBERT M. GALABURDA, "Anatomical asymmetries," in *Cerebral Dominance,* edited by NORMAN GESCHWIND, ALBERT M. GALABURDA, pp. 11–25 (Harvard University Press 1984).

44   Harry Whitaker recently pointed out that Wernicke was not the first person to describe the pattern of aphasia with temporal lobe damage. There is an earlier case report by Theodore Meynert, an Austrian neurologist, of a patient with a left temporal lobe stroke, and the pattern of language changes we would now call "Wernicke's" aphasia, a case cited by Wernicke in his book.

48   E. SUE SAVAGE-RUMBAUGH, JEANNINE MURPHY, ROSE A. SEVCIK, KAREN E. BRAKKE, SHELLEY L. WILLIAMS, AND DUANE RUMBAUGH, *Language Comprehension in Ape and Child* (University of Chicago Press 1993). Monographs of the Society for Research on Child Development 58(3).

48   DEREK BICKERTON, *Language and Species* (University of Chicago Press 1990).

51   The illustration of mental rehearsal of finger movements is adapted from P. E. ROLAND, E. SKINHØJ, N. A. LASSEN, B. LARSEN, "Different cortical areas in man in organization of voluntary movements in extrapersonal space," *Journal of Neurophysiology* 43:137–150 (1980).

51   RODOLFO LLINÁS, U. RIBARY, "Coherent 40-Hz oscillation characterizes dream state in humans," *Proceedings of the National Academy of Sciences (U.S.A.)* 90:2078–2081 (1 March 1993).

52   J. W. BELLIVEAU, D. N. KENNEDY, JR., R. C. MCKINSTRY, B. R. BUCHBINDER, R. M. WEISSKOFF, M. S. COHEN, J. M. VEVEA, T. J. BRADY, B. R. ROSEN, "Functional mapping of the human visual cortex by magnetic resonance imaging," *Science* 254:716–719 (1 November 1991).

54   Mapping by neural activity altering the reflectance of light from the brain's surface: while this may be, in part, a matter of blood flow changing the average color of the surface, it has been known since the 1940s that even isolated peripheral nerves change their reflectance when kept busy conducting impulses. Reflectance changes also occur in brain slices kept alive by an oxygenated bath without any blood supply, making it likely that reflectance changes are at least in part also a result of swelling of neurons and glia with activity. The first full report of reflectance changes in human cortex during movements and language is MICHAEL M. HAGLUND, GEORGE A. OJEMANN, DARYL HOCHMAN, "Optical imaging of epileptiform and functional activity in human cerebral cortex," *Nature* 358:668–671 (20 August 1992).

54   A detailed analysis of the size and location of sites where stimulation altered naming in 117 patients is found in GEORGE OJEMANN, JEFF OJEMANN, ETTORE LETTICH, MITCHELL BERGER, "Cortical language localization in left, dominant hemisphere," *Journal of Neurosurgery* 71:316–326 (September 1989). This report also includes correlations between the location of sites related to naming by stimulation, and patient sex and verbal IQ. Further evidence that a removal of brain that encroaches on sites where stimulation alters naming is likely to result in a postoperative language deficit is presented in GEORGE A. OJEMANN, "Electrical stimulation and the neurobiology of language," *Behavioral and Brain Science* 6:221–226 (1983).

56   The illustration of how male and female brains are organized for language and hand movements is adapted (with the percentages recalculated) from DOREEN KIMURA, "Sex differences in the brain," *Scientific American* 267(3):118–125 (September 1992). Further evidence of differences in language organization in males and females, derived from stimulation mapping, is reported in CATHERINE MATEER, SAMUEL POLEN, GEORGE OJEMANN, "Sexual variation in cortical localization of naming as determined by stimulation mapping," *Behavioral and Brain Science* 5:310–311 (1982), and in the 117 patient series above.

Chapter 4. *If Language Is Left, What's Right?*
Any of the textbooks on human neuropsychology is a good starting place to read more, e.g., BRYAN KOLB, IAN Q. WHISHAW, *Fundamentals of Human Neuropsychology*, 3d edition (Freeman 1990). For a somewhat skeptical view of the left-right overemphasis, see ROBERT EFRON, *The Decline and Fall of Hemispheric Specialization* (Erlbaum 1990) and WILLIAM H. CALVIN, *The Throwing Madonna*, Chapter 10 (Bantam 1991).

E. D. ROSS, "The aprosodias: Functional-anatomical organization of the affective components of language in the right hemisphere," *Archives of Neurology* 38:561–569 (1981).

RICHARD B. IVRY, PAUL C. LEBBY, "Hemispheric differences in auditory perception are similar to those found in visual perception," *Psychological Science* 4(1):41–45 (January 1993).

ROBERT J. ZATORRE, ALAN C. EVANS, ERNST MEYER, ALBERT GJEDDE, "Lateralization of phonemic and pitch discrimination in speech processing," *Science* 256:846–849 (8 May 1992).

59 Juhn Wada actually invented the intracarotid amobarbital test in 1949 to test for language dominance. It was about a decade later when its primary use became one of pre-operative testing for memory function in the two hemispheres, following the report on H.M. by W. B. SCOVILLE, BRENDA MILNER, "Loss of recent memory after bilateral hippocampal lesions," *Journal of Neurology, Neurosurgery, and Psychiatry* 20:11–21 (1957).

60 EDWIN A. WEINSTEIN, *Woodrow Wilson: A Medical and Psychological Biography* (Princeton University Press 1981).

61 The Justice Douglas story is in HOWARD GARDNER, HIRAM H. BROWNELL, WENDY WAPNER, DIANE MICHELOW, "Missing the point: the role of the right hemisphere in the processing of complex linguistic materials," in *Cognitive Processing in the Right Hemisphere*, pp. 169–191 (Academic Press 1983). For the press release, see p. 361 of BOB WOODWARD, SCOTT ARMSTRONG, *The Brethren* (Simon and Schuster 1979).

62 Some of the implications for presidential disability under the 25th Amendment to the U.S. Constitution are discussed, along with Woodrow Wilson's stroke, by WILLIAM H. CALVIN, *The Throwing Madonna: Essays on the Brain* (McGraw-Hill 1983).

63 The series of self-portraits by Anton Räderscheidt, covering the period from before his right-hemisphere stroke through his partial recovery, is illustrated in HOWARD GARDNER, *The Shattered Mind: The Person After Brain Damage* (Knopf 1975), pp. 330–331.

66 The data on proportions of left- or right-brain lesions producing aphasias, constructional apraxias, or dressing apraxias was derived from R. J. JOYNT, M. N. GOLDSTEIN, "Minor cerebral hemisphere," *Advances in Neurology* 7:147–183 (1975).

66 PETER F. MACNEILAGE, MICHAEL G. STUDDERT-KENNEDY, BJORN LINDBLOM, "Hand signals: Right side, left brain and the origin of language," *The Sciences* 33(1):32–37 (January–February 1993). This contains a good summary of the animal lateralization literature. See also the letter by WILLIAM H. CALVIN in the November–December 1993 issue.

67 When visual-spatial functions and language are crammed into one hemisphere (as in a child who has had one side of the brain removed in infancy for Sturge-Weber disease), language may be nearly normal, but visual-spatial functions are poorly developed. That suggests that one hemisphere isn't adequate to house both major groups of cortical functions.

It has long been known that left-handedness is much more common in those who stutter than in the overall population. Evidence of an unusually high incidence of bilateral language representation in stutterers, using the dichotic technique, has been reported by J. P. BRADY, J. BERSON, "Stuttering, dichotic listening, and cerebral dominance," *Archives of General Psychiatry* 32:1449–1452 (1975). Cases in which damage to one side of the brain, in what would ordinarily be language areas on the left side, have cured lifelong stuttering are collected in R. K. JONES, "Observations on stammering after localized cerebral injury," *Journal of Neurology, Neurosurgery, and Psychiatry* 29:192–195 (1966).

J. MONDLOCK, L. CAPLAN, "Behavioral abnormalities after right hemisphere stroke," *Neurology* 33:337–344 (1983).

68   ROBERT DESIMONE, "Face-selective cells in the temporal cortex of monkeys," *Journal of Cognitive Neuroscience* 3 (Winter 1991).

68   OLIVER SACKS, *The Man Who Mistook His Wife for a Hat* (Simon and Schuster 1985).

68   Changes in the labeling of facial emotional expressions with right posterior temporal stimulation are reported in ITZHAK FRIED, CATHERINE MATEER, GEORGE OJEMANN, RICHARD WOHNS, PAUL FEDIO, "Organization of visuospatial functions in human cortex: evidence from electrical stimulation," *Brain* 105:349–371 (1982). Evidence for right-brain lateralization of mechanisms for identifying facial emotional expressions, derived with a variety of techniques, is also reviewed there.

69   Changes in human temporal lobe neuronal activity with faces is reported in JEFF OJEMANN, GEORGE OJEMANN, ETTORE LETTICH, "Neuronal activity related to faces and matching in human right nondominant temporal cortex," *Brain* 115:1–13 (1992).

71   JUSTINE SERGENT, S. OHTA, BRENNAN MACDONALD, "Functional neuroanatomy of face and object processing. A positron emission tomography study," *Brain* 115:15–36 (February 1992). A face-gender categorization resulted in activation changes in the right extrastriate cortex, and a face-identity condition produced additional activation of the fusiform gyrus and anterior temporal cortex of both hemispheres, and of the right parahippocampal gyrus and adjacent areas. Cerebral activation during an object-recognition task occurred essentially in the left occipito-temporal cortex and did not involve the right-hemisphere regions specifically activated during the face-identity task.

JUSTINE SERGENT, JEAN-LOUIS SIGNORET, "Functional and anatomical decomposition of face processing: evidence from prosopagnosia and PET study of normal subjects," *Philosophical Transactions of the Royal Society of London (Biology)* 335:55–61 (29 January 1992). See the news story in *American Scientist* 80(6):537–539 (November–December 1992).

71   Localization of memories, see MARTHA J. FARAH, "Neuropsychological inference with an interactive brain: a critique of the locality assumption," *Behavioral and Brain Sciences* (to appear, 1994).

72   The effects of cortical stimulation on simple arithmetic calculations are from an unpublished study of A. FORBES, G. OJEMANN. A more general review of the brain basis for mathematical calculation is found in F. GREWEL, volume 4 of *Handbook of Neurology* (VINKEN and BRUYN, eds., Amsterdam, North Holland) pp. 181–194 (1969).

72   T. G. BEVER, R. J. CHIARELLO, "Cerebral dominance in musicians and non-musicians," *Science* 185:137–139 (1974).

73   Changes in human temporal lobe neuronal activity while listening to various types of music are reported in OTTO CREUTZFELDT, GEORGE OJEMANN, "Neuronal activity in the human lateral temporal lobe. III. Activity changes during music," *Experimental Brain Research* 77:490–498 (1989). A particularly good discussion of the effects of brain damage on artistic abilities of all types, including professional musicians, is found in chapter 8 of HOWARD GARDNER, *The Shattered Mind* (Knopf 1975).

73   GARDNER et al. (1983).

Chapter 5.   **The Problems with Paying Attention**

A good discussion of Penfield's "evoked memories" is in LARRY R. SQUIRE, *Memory and Brain* (Oxford University Press 1987), pp. 76–84.

76   ELIZABETH F. LOFTUS, GEOFFREY R. LOFTUS, "On the permanence of stored information in the human brain," *American Psychologist* 35:409–420 (May 1980).

77   Penfield's own summary of his experience with evoking memories is in WILDER PENFIELD, PHANOR PEROT, "The brain's record of auditory and visual experience—a final summary and discussion," *Brain* 86:595–696 (1963). That report indicates some of the association between the presence of experiential responses with stimulation, and as part of the same patient's seizures. Further evidence that these responses occur only when stimulation evokes a small seizure is provided by PIERRE GLOOR, ANDRE OLIVIER, L. QUESNEY, FRED ANDERMANN, S. HOROWITZ, "The role of the limbic system in experiential phenomena of temporal lobe epilepsy," *Annals of Neurology* 12:129–144 (1982). The patient who heard Led Zeppelin is reported in more detail in GEORGE OJEMANN, "Brain mechanisms for consciousness and conscious experience," in McMaster-Bauer Symposium on Consciousness, *Canadian Psychology* 27:158–168 (1986).

81   JOSÉ V. PARDO, PETER T. FOX, MARCUS E. RAICHLE, "Localization of a human system for sustained attention by positron emission tomography," *Nature* 349:61–64 (3 January 1991).

81   MICHAEL I. POSNER, STEVEN E. PETERSEN, PETER T. FOX, MARCUS E. RAICHLE, "Localization of cognitive operations in the human brain," *Science* 240:1627–1631 (1988). MICHAEL I. POSNER, "Attention as a cognitive and neural system," *Current Directions in Psychological Science* 1:11–14 (February 1992).

84   The effects of thalamic stimulation on language and recent verbal memory performance are summarized in GEORGE OJEMANN, "Language and the thalamus: object naming and recall during and after thalamic stimulation," *Brain and Language* 2:101–120 (1975).

86   Thalamic stimulation effects on recent memory for complex shapes, and the contrast with effects on recent verbal memory, is reported in GEORGE OJEMANN,

"Altering memory with human ventrolateral thalamic stimulation," in *Modern Concepts in Psychiatric Surgery*, edited by E. HITCHCOCK, T. BALLANTINE, B. MEYERSON (Elsevier/North Holland Biomedical Press 1979), pp. 103–109.

87   UTA FRITH, "Autism," *Scientific American* 268(6):108–114 (June 1993). UTA FRITH, JOHN MORTON, ALAN M. LESLIE, "The cognitive basis of a biological disorder: Autism," *Trends in the Neurosciences* 14:433–438 (October 1991). OLIVER SACKS, "A neurologist's notebook: an anthropologist on Mars," *The New Yorker*, pp. 106–125 (27 December 1993).

Chapter 6. *The Personality of the Lowly Neuron*

A good introduction to the physiology is by CHARLES F. STEVENS, "The neuron," *Scientific American* 241(3):55–65 (September 1979). For the local circuits of the cerebral cortex, see the special issue of the journal *Cerebral Cortex* 3 (September/October 1993) edited by KATHLEEN S. ROCKLAND.

89   SANTIAGO RAMÓN Y CAJAL, *Histologie du système nerveux de l'homme et des vertébrés* (Paris: Malone, 1909–1911).

89   Six layers of neocortex: The original classification has been subject to some lumping and splitting. Layers II and III can usually be lumped together; one will see "layer 2/3" or "the superficial layers" as a way of lumping them (layer I doesn't have many cell bodies in it, so the "cells of the superficial layers" usually means those of 2/3). But layer IV has had to be repeatedly subdivided, especially in the visual cortex where we talk about layers IVa, IVb, and IVc (and sometimes subdivide it into IVcα and IVcβ).

91   The best pictures of the horizontal connections are in BARBARA A. MCGUIRE, CHARLES D. GILBERT, PATRICIA K. RIVLIN, TORSTEN N. WIESEL, "Targets of horizontal connections in macaque primary visual cortex," *Journal of Comparative Neurology* 305:370–392 (1991) and in CHARLES D. GILBERT, "Circuitry, architecture, and functional dynamics of visual cortex," *Cerebral Cortex* 3:373–386 (1993). Some axons continue for another gap to produce a second patch of terminals, and so forth. The dimensions are from JENNIFER S. LUND, TAKASHI YOSHIOKA, JONATHAN B. LEVITT, "Comparison of intrinsic connectivity in different areas of macaque monkey cerebral cortex," *Cerebral Cortex* 3:148–162 (March/April 1993). The "0.5 mm" distance to the center of the terminal patch is about 0.43 mm in the primary visual cortex, 0.65 mm in the secondary visual areas, 0.73 mm in the sensory strip, and 0.85 mm in the motor cortex of monkeys. The diameter of the patch of terminals (and that of the basal dendritic spread) is about half the center-to-center distance (our "block length"); thus, the "mass mailing" does not go only to the "third house on each block," but to a spread of addresses near it. In humans, the center-to-center dimensions (at least in the primary visual cortex) are in the range of 0.6–1.0 mm, about twice that of monkeys: ANDREAS BRUKHALTER, KERRY L. BERNARDO, "Organization of corticocortical connections in human visual cortex," *Proceedings of the National Academy of Sciences (U.S.A.)* 86:1071–1075 (1989).

91   Horizontal connections are also found among the pyramidal neurons of the deep layers (V and VI), but the regular spacing has been noted only for the pyramids of the superficial layers. The latter also may send myelinated axons (the horizontal collaterals are unmyelinated) out of the cortical layers into the white matter; their eventual targets are other cortical areas, sometimes via the corpus callosum. Roughly 70 percent of the excitatory synapses on any superficial pyramid, but less than 1 percent of those on layer V pyramids, are derived from pyramidal neurons less than 0.3 mm away: ANDREW NICOLL, COLIN BLAKEMORE, "Patterns of local connectivity in the neocortex," *Neural Computation* 5:665–680 (September 1993).

91   CHARLES F. STEVENS, "How cortical interconnectedness varies with network size," *Neural Computation* 1:473–479 (1989).

91   The corpus callosum illustration is adapted from one in JONAS SZENTÁGOTHAI, "The neuron network of the cerebral cortex, a functional interpretation," *Proceedings of the Royal Society, London* B201:219–248 (1978).

92   A. J. ROCKEL, R. W. HIORNS, T. P. S. POWELL, "The basic uniformity in structure of the neocortex," *Brain* 103:221–244 (1980).

92   At least in the sensory cortices, there are "minicolumns" whose dimensions are about 30 μm, such as the orientation columns of the visual cortex; these may be due to vertical bundles of apical dendrites, as proposed by ALAN PETERS, C. SETHARES, "Organization of pyramidal neurons in area 17 of monkey visual cortex," *Journal of Comparative Neurology* 306:1–23 (1991), and ALAN PETERS, ENGIN YILMAZ, "Neuronal organization in area 17 of cat visual cortex," *Cerebral Cortex* 3:49–68 (January/February 1993). Then there are "macrocolumns" of closer to 0.4–0.7 mm (e.g., eye preference columns, Mountcastle's original columns in the sensory strip). There are about 300 minicolumns in a macrocolumn, and about 100 neurons in a minicolumn (142 for monkey visual cortex). See VERNON B. MOUNTCASTLE, in *The Neurosciences Fourth Study Program*, edited by F. O. SCHMITT and F. G. WORDEN, pp. 21–42 (MIT Press 1979). See the discussion of columns in association cortex in *Trends in the Neurosciences* 15:362–368 (1992) and 16:178–181 (1993).

95   LUIGI F. AGNATI, BÖRJE BJELKE, KJELL FUXE, "Volume transmission in the brain," *American Scientist* 80:362–373 (July–August 1992).

98   Impulses are not the only way to trigger release of the neurotransmitter packets; indeed, there are neurons that rarely use impulses. The photoreceptors in the eye, and the next layer or so of interneurons, normally operate without impulses. Any cell lacking a long axon is a candidate for such "graded release synapses," where the release rate is proportional to the net excitatory synaptic current. See Chapter 8 in W. H. CALVIN, *The Throwing Madonna: Essays on the Brain* (Bantam 1991).

98   A synonym for *impulse* is *action potential*. Another common synonym is *spike,* but we have avoided it here because of the EEG terminology's use of "spike" for the characteristic resting activity of an epileptic focus, in between seizures. This EEG spike is not an impulse from a single neuron, but the summed activity of many synchronized excitatory postsynaptic potentials (EPSPs).

98 Myelinated conduction of the impulse is sometimes called *saltatory*, after the Latin *saltare*, "to leap." The gaps in the myelin insulation, about 1 mm apart, are where the sodium channels through the axon membrane cluster.

99 If the presynaptic neuron fires a few impulses in rapid succession, the successive EPSPs will add together to reach a higher peak voltage ("temporal summation"). EPSPs from other sources ("spatial summation") also sum together; a cortical neuron has between 3,000 and 60,000 input synapses, with about 40 percent of them being inhibitory.

We talk of the neuron "firing" as if the voltage trigger had finally been pulled hard enough to set it off. Sometimes the EPSPs are so brief that only one impulse occurs. But a neuron can fire an impulse every few milliseconds (usually to send a rather imperative signal). In many neurons of the brain and spinal cord, the firing rate is almost a linear function of the summed synaptic currents (to use the more precise word instead of *flow*), at least once past a minimum requirement. It is rather like court fines for speeding: no output when beneath the threshold (speed limit), court costs of $25 and $2 for each mph in excess of the threshold. So, too, a neuron may produce no impulses for below-threshold synaptic currents, then jump up to a minimum rhythmic firing rate (say, 25 each second), and add two more impulses per second for nanoampere current increments in excess of the minimum requirement. A few neurons, most notably the motor neurons of spinal cord that run the muscles, change their properties at a second threshold, rather like the sliding scale for speeding fines that goes up to $4 for each mph over 70 mph.

The neuron can appear to be remarkably "analog" (adding and subtracting linearly, for example) when the postsynaptic potentials are individually small and there are enough of them to keep the neuron above the repetitive firing minimum. The spinal cord "motor neurons" that run the muscles are a good example of this computational style. And a neuron's style can be more "digital" when postsynaptic strengths are larger, and a few EPSPs can stand on one another's shoulders to reach impulse threshold. Cortical neurons appear to be capable of both styles. That cortical neurons can grade their rhythmic firing rate over a wide range, analogous to motor neurons and many sensory neurons, is reviewed by WILLIAM H. CALVIN, "Normal repetitive firing and its pathophysiology," in *Epilepsy: A Window to Brain Mechanisms* (JOAN S. LOCKARD, ARTHUR A. WARD, JR., editors, Raven Press, New York 1980), pp. 97–121. That many cortical neurons in awake monkeys demonstrate intervals between impulses that are more consistent with a nonrhythmic, and possibly digital, process is demonstrated by WILLIAM R. SOFTKY, CHRISTOF KOCH, "Cortical cells should fire regularly, but do not," *Neural Computation* 4:643–646 (September 1992); "The highly irregular firing of cortical cells is inconsistent with temporal integration of random EPSPs," *Journal of Neuroscience* 13:334–350 (January 1993).

99 In neurons, the ten-fold higher concentration of sodium ions outside the cell constitutes a battery across the cell membrane of about 60 millivolts. The potassium inside the neuron is about thirty times more concentrated than it is just outside the neuron, and that acts as if a battery of –90 millivolts were straddling the cell membrane. Chloride ions are also pumped out the cell, and that produces a battery equivalent of nearly –90 millivolts.

The actual voltage inside the neuron depends on these (and other) opposing influences. It can be momentarily varied anywhere between +60 and –90 millivolts, much like a mixing faucet can give you any temperature between that of the hot water heater and that of the cold water source. Ordinarily most of the membrane pores that can pass sodium ions are kept closed, and the voltage inside the neuron stays down near –70 millivolts. But occasionally some sodium pores are opened, and the positive-charged sodium ions rush in, raising the internal voltage—sometimes a little, sometimes a lot. Sometimes the potassium or chloride pores are opened to move the voltage down nearer –90 millivolts.

The impulse is simply a result of enough sodium channels being opened so that the internal voltage shoots up from –70 to perhaps +30 millivolts, a 0.1 volt excursion. One consequence is that the potassium pores then open up— and that hauls the voltage back down again. If potassium didn't "reset" the internal voltage in this manner, the impulse would last much longer. And that would release even more neurotransmitter from the presynaptic terminal.

99 The flows are also equal at the resting potential, but this is a stable equilibrium; if the voltage is slightly displaced, it drifts back toward the resting potential in tens of milliseconds. Actually, sodium ion (Na^+) and potassium ion (K^+) are not the only players in this game; chloride ion, Cl^-, also moves, but its membrane pores aren't as likely to open and close as those of the two positive ions. In some regions of the cell (though not usually the axon), calcium ion (Ca^{++}) is also a major player.

100 "Sodium pores tend to slowly shut themselves off at higher voltages" is known as sodium inactivation, and it is largely responsible for the inability to initiate another impulse for a while (the refractory period).

101 Wrong-way impulses spreading down side branches along the way: this is known as the *axon reflex*. Sometimes the backward impulses will fail when reaching a branch point because of geometric considerations, a problem discussed by WILLIAM H. CALVIN, "Some design features of axons and how neuralgias may defeat them," in *Advances in Pain Research and Therapy* (JOHN J. BONICA, ed.), 3:297–309 (1979).

103   Properly speaking, only the postsynaptic pores of a synapse can be excitatory or inhibitory. But the upstream neuron is often so labeled because its "mass mailings" usually all have the same type of postsynaptic effect at the thousands of synapses made by its axon terminals.

104   EDWARD L. WHITE with ASAF KELLER, *Cortical Circuits: Synaptic Organization of the Cerebral Cortex* (Birkhäuser 1989).

105   The nonpyramidal neuron axon almost never enters the white matter, while pyramidal neurons usually (but not always) have a more distant projection in addition to all their local axon branches. There is one type of nonpyramidal neuron in primate cerebral cortex that may be a modified pyramidal neuron and excitatory: JENNIFER S. LUND, "Spiny stellate cells," in *Cerebral Cortex*, vol. 1, A. PETERS, E. G. JONES, editors, (Plenum 1984), pp. 255–308.

106   The illustration of three types of motor cortex neurons is from WILLIAM H. CALVIN, GEORGE W. SYPERT, "Fast and slow pyramidal tract neurons: An intracellular analysis of their contrasting repetitive firing properties in the cat," *Journal of Neurophysiology* 39:420–434 (1976). The calibration bars represent 20 millivolts, 20 nanoamperes of injected current, and 20 milliseconds.

107   For each neurotransmitter such as glutamate, there are usually a number of somewhat different postsynaptic receptors, each controlling a channel through the membrane and/or an intracellular process of some sort. That acetylcholine had "nicotinic" and "muscarinic" receptors was known a half-century ago; now we are faced with dozens of serotonin receptors in postsynaptic cells. So synaptic actions are not merely a matter of how much membrane current is generated in the first millisecond, but also a matter of how the released neurotransmitter affects regulatory processes in the cell on a slower timescale.

107   Blood flow is some unknown function of the number of neurons active and their firing rates—but it doesn't distinguish between excitatory and inhibitory neurons. Were inhibitory neurons to increase their activity to the point of canceling out the excitatory activity, the blood-flow–based techniques would simply report that the cortex was twice as busy—when it was only stalemated.

107   Actually, synaptic strength isn't the only thing that can be adjusted for learning and memory. Some neurotransmitters and their second messengers inside the postsynaptic neuron can change the mode of impulse initiation from beating to bursty. But this affects the whole cell, and adjusting synaptic strengths at or near the synapse is capable of fine-tuning.

108   LTP has both pre- and postsynaptic aspects, NMDA being an example of how the same amount of neurotransmitter can cause more postsynaptic current to flow. But LTP also has presynaptic aspects, where more transmitter seems to be released. It is thought that there are certain "retrograde neurotransmitters" that allow the postsynaptic cell to stimulate more transmitter release presynaptically by later impulses. Both NO and CO gases are candidates, e.g., CHARLES F. STEVENS, YANYAN WANG, "Reversal of long-term potentiation by inhibitors of haem oxygenase," *Nature* 364:147–149 (8 July 1993)—and the news article in the same issue at pp. 104–105.

108 ATSUSHI IRIKI, CONSTANTINE PAVLIDES, ASAF KELLER, HIROSHI ASANUMA, "Long-term potentiation of thalamic input to the motor cortex induced by coactivation of thalamocortical and corticocortical afferents," *Journal of Neurophysiology* 65:1435–1441 (1991).

Chapter 7. **The What and Where of Memory**

A prime reference is LARRY R. SQUIRE, *Memory and Brain* (Oxford University Press 1987). In addition, some background reading might include:

DANIEL C. ALKON, *Memory's Voice: Deciphering the Mind-Brain Code* (HarperCollins 1992).

NEAL J. COHEN, HOWARD EICHENBAUM, *Memory, Amnesia, and the Hippocampal System* (MIT Press 1993).

LARRY R. SQUIRE, STUART ZOLA-MORGAN, "The medial temporal lobe memory system," *Science* 253:1380–1386 (1991).

GEOFFREY E. HINTON, "How neural networks learn from experience," *Scientific American* 267(3):105–109 (September 1992).

PATRICIA S. GOLDMAN-RAKIC, "Working memory and the mind," *Scientific American* 267(3):73–79 (September 1992).

ENDEL TULVING, *Elements of Episodic Memory* (Oxford University Press 1983). And his "Remembering and knowing the past," *American Scientist* 77:361–367 (1989), or "What is episodic memory?" *Current Directions in Psychological Science* 2(3):67–70 (June 1993).

SUZANNE CORKIN, "Lasting consequences of bilateral medial temporal lobectomy: Clinical course and experimental findings in H.M.," *Seminars in Neurology* 4:249–259 (1984).

110 WILLIAM SCOVILLE, BRENDA MILNER, "Loss of recent memory after bilateral hippocampal lesions," *Journal of Neurology, Neurosurgery and Psychiatry* 20:11–21 (1957).

110 The autopsy findings in the patient with recent memory loss after a left temporal removal, showing focal damage in the remaining hippocampus, are in WILDER PENFIELD, G. MATHIESON, "An autopsy and a discussion of the role of the hippocampus in experiential recall," *Archives of Neurology* 31:145–154 (1974).

111 A detailed summary of H.M.'s memory deficits is in ARTHUR SHIMAMURA, "Disorders of memory: the cognitive science perspective," in *Handbook of*

Neuropsychology, edited by FRANÇOIS BOLLER, JORDAN GRAFMAN, v. 3, pp. 37–42 (Elsevier 1988).

113   G. STILLHARD, T. LANDIS, R. SCHIESS, M. REGARD, G. SIALER, "Bitemporal hypoperfusion in transient global amnesia: 99m-Tc-HM-PAO SPECT and neuropsychological findings during and after an attack," *Journal of Neurology, Neurosurgery, and Psychiatry* 53:339–342 (1990).

114   A good review of Milner's findings is "Hemispheric specialization: scope and limits," in *The Neurosciences: Third Study Program,* edited by F. O. SCHMITT, F. G. WORDEN (MIT Press 1974), pp. 75–89.

115   HERMANN EBBINGHAUS, *Memory: A Contribution to Experimental Psychology* (Dover 1964).

116   ULRIC NEISSER, NICOLE HARSCH, "Phantom flashbulbs: False recollections of hearing the news about Challenger," in E. WINOGRAD, U. NEISSER (Eds.), *Affect and accuracy in recall: Studies of "flashbulb" memories* (Cambridge University Press 1992).

117   ELIZABETH F. LOFTUS, "When a lie becomes memory's truth," *Current Directions in Psychological Science* 1:121–123 (1992). ELIZABETH F. LOFTUS, GEOFFREY R. LOFTUS, "On the permanence of stored information in the human brain," *American Psychologist* 35:409–420 (May 1980). Actually, a videotape was not used but rather a series of 30 slides, and the yield sign misinformation was subtly incorporated into a different question, and then later tested by asking subjects to choose between a picture of the intersection and a nearly identical one in which the stop sign had been replaced by a yield sign.

117   D. STEPHEN LINDSAY, "Eyewitness suggestibility," *Current Directions in Psychological Science* 2:86–89 (June 1993).

118   TULVING (1989) and DAVID H. INGVAR, "Ideography: Mapping ideas in the brain," in *Brain Work and Mental Activity,* edited by N. A. LASSEN, D. H. INGVAR, M. E. RAICHLE, L. FRIBERG (Munksgaard, Copenhagen 1991), pp. 346–359.

118   Cortical stimulation mapping effects on recent verbal memory are reported in GEORGE OJEMANN, "Organization of short term verbal memory in language areas of human cortex: evidence from electrical stimulation," *Brain and Language* 5:331–340 (1978) and "Brain organization for language from the perspective of electrical stimulation mapping," *Behavioral and Brain Sciences* 6:189–206 (1983). Evidence that these cortical memory sites contribute to memory deficits after left temporal removals is found in GEORGE OJEMANN, CARL DODRILL, "Verbal memory deficits after left temporal lobectomy for epilepsy: Mechanism and intraoperative prediction," *Journal of Neurosurgery* 62:101–107 (1985). The effects of stimulation elsewhere in the brain, including the hippocampus, are reviewed in GEORGE OJEMANN, OTTO CREUTZFELDT, "Language in humans and animals: contribution of brain stimulation and recording," in *Handbook of Physiology, the Nervous System,* volume 5, *Higher Functions of the Brain,* edited by VERNON MOUNTCASTLE, FRED PLUM, STEVEN GEIGER, (American Physiological Society 1987), pp. 675–699.

Chapter 8. *How Are Memories Made?*

123   GEORGE A. MILLER, "The magical number seven: plus or minus two. Some limits on our capacity for processing information," *Psychological Review* 9:81–97 (1956).

124   E. PAULESU, C. D. FRITH, R. S. J. FRACKOWIAK, "The neural correlates of the verbal component of working memory," *Nature* 362:343–346 (25 March 1993).

125   PHILIP LIEBERMAN, *Uniquely Human: The Evolution of Speech, Thought, and Selfless Behavior* (Harvard University Press 1991).

125   P. M. GRASBY, C. D. FRITH, K. J. FRISTON, C. BENCH, R. S. J. FRACKOWIAK, R. J. DOLAN, "Functional mapping of brain areas implicated in auditory-verbal memory function," *Brain* 116:1–20 (1993).

126   JOAQUIN FUSTER, "Neuronal discrimination and short-term memory in association cortex," in *Neurobiology of Higher Cognitive Function,* ARNOLD SCHEIBEL, ADAM WECHSLER, editors, (Guilford Press 1990), pp. 85–102.

126   WILLIAM H. CALVIN, GEORGE A. OJEMANN, ARTHUR A. WARD, JR., "Human cortical neurons in epileptogenic foci: Comparison of inter-ictal firing patterns to those of 'epileptic' neurons in animals," *Electroencephalography and Clinical Neurophysiology* 34:337–351 (1973).

127   GEORGE OJEMANN, OTTO CREUTZFELDT, ETTORE LETTICH, MICHAEL HAGLUND, "Neuronal activity in human lateral temporal cortex related to short-term verbal memory, naming and reading," *Brain* 111:1383–1403 (1988).

127   MICHAEL HAGLUND, GEORGE OJEMANN, TED SCHWARTZ, ETTORE LETTICH, "Neuronal activity in human lateral temporal cortex during serial retrieval from short-term memory," *Journal of Neuroscience* (in press 1993).

127   The learning-associated changes in cerebral blood flow patterns are especially pronounced in the supplementary motor area, e.g., R. J. SEITZ, P. E. ROLAND, C. BOHM, T. GREITZ, S. STONE-ELANDER, "Motor learning in man: a positron emission tomography study," *NeuroReport* 1:17–20 (1990). For language learning, PET blood flow changes have been better seen in the region of the cingulate gyrus and in the traditional language areas. MARCUS RAICHLE, "Exploring the mind with dynamic imaging," *Seminars in the Neurosciences* 2:307–315 (1990).

129   WILLIAM H. CALVIN, "Binding forms a cerebral code which error corrects: Scattered feature detectors generate a hexagonal code via synchronizing excitation among pyramidal neurons," *Society for Neuroscience Abstracts* 19:398.22 (1993).

129   MALCOLM P. YOUNG, S. YAMANE, "Sparse population coding of faces in the inferotemporal cortex," *Science* 256:1327–1331 (1992).

130   Simpler mechanisms for *Post hoc ergo propter hoc* are discussed in chapter 9 of WILLIAM H. CALVIN, *The Throwing Madonna: Essays on the Brain* (Bantam 1991).

131   The washboarded road illustration is from WILLIAM H. CALVIN, lectures for *Dutch National Science* Week (October 1992).

131   FRANKLIN B. KRASNE, "Extrinsic control of intrinsic neuronal plasticity: a hypothesis from work on simple systems," *Brain Research* 140:197–206 (1978).

132   ERIC R. KANDEL, ROBERT D. HAWKINS, "The biological basis of learning and individuality," *Scientific American* 267(3):52–60 (September 1992).

132   ANITA M. TURNER, WILLIAM T. GREENOUGH, "Differential rearing effects on rat visual cortex synapses. I. Synaptic and neuronal density and synapses per neuron," *Brain Research*, 329:195–203 (1985).

FRED R. VOLKMAR, WILLIAM T. GREENOUGH, "Rearing complexity affects branching of dendrites in the visual cortex of the rat," *Science* 176:1445–1447 (1972).

WILLIAM T. GREENOUGH, "Experiential modification of the developing brain," *American Scientist* 63:37–46 (1975).

132   Evidence that drugs that block protein synthesis interfere with formation of long term memories in experimental animals has been available for several decades. S. BARONDES, H. COHEN, "Memory impairment after subcutaneous injection of acetoxycycloheximide," *Science* 160:556–557 (1968). However, interpretation of these findings is complicated by the possibility that these drugs also have other effects besides blocking protein synthesis.

132   DONALD O. HEBB, *The Organization of Behavior* (Wiley 1949). Includes what we now call the "Hebbian synapse" which, like the modern NMDA synapse, strengthens when there are near-simultaneous arrivals on the same dendrite. Hebb also proposed the cell assembly, the "Hebbian ensemble," as the active form of the memory. And Hebb noted that memory really required a "dual trace" system with an underlying pattern of connectivities that allowed the cell assembly to recreate its characteristic activity. All of this Hebb recognized on a theoretical basis from the psychological and brain lesion experiments, a few years before the first microelectrode recordings were made from mammalian central nervous systems. See PETER M. MILNER, "The mind and Donald O. Hebb," *Scientific American* 268(1):124–129 (January 1993).

133   The NMDA channel at glutamate synapses was named after *N*-methyl-D-aspartate because it, rather than glutamate, is what opens the channel in the lowest concentrations. But glutamate opens it just fine, and that's what is usually released as a neurotransmitter.

134   JOHN G. TAYLOR, *When the Clock Strikes Zero* (Pan Macmillan 1992) discusses the role of hippocampus rehearsing cerebral cortex during REM sleep.

Chapter 9.   ***What's Up Front***

For general background on the psychiatric disorders, see NANCY C. ANDREASEN, *The Broken Brain* (Harper and Row 1984) and PETER D. KRAMER, *Listening to Prozac* (Viking 1993).

U. HALSBAND, N. ITO, J. TANJI, H.-J. FREUND, "The role of premotor cortex and the supplementary motor area in the temporal control of movement in man," *Brain* 116:243–266 (February 1993).

138   The darwinian notion of consciousness is developed by W. H. CALVIN, *The Cerebral Symphony: Seashore Reflections on the Structure of Consciousness* (Bantam 1989), and in "Islands in the mind," *Seminars in the Neurosciences* 3:423–433 (1991). It is an old idea, dating back to WILLIAM JAMES in 1880.

141   JUSTINE SERGENT, "Music, the brain, and Ravel," *Trends in the Neurosciences* 16:168–172 (May 1993). The illustration shows right-handed piano playing, sight-reading, and listening, subtracting the activity map obtained when merely playing scales; there is little activation of midline cortex such as supplementary motor area, and the only right-sided activation is in the rear of the superior parietal lobule.

JUSTINE SERGENT, ERIC ZUCK, SEAN TERRIAH, BRENNAN MACDONALD, "Distributed neural network underlying musical sight-reading and keyboard performance," *Science* 257:106–109 (3 July 1992).

142   TIM SHALLICE, PAUL W. BURGESS, "Deficits in strategy application following frontal lobe damage in man," *Brain* 114:727–741 (April 1991). A description of three patients with head injuries, more typical of frontal lobe patients than those discussed in our chapter, who had more localized lesions.

142   WILDER PENFIELD, J. EVANS, "The frontal lobe in man: a clinical study of maximum removals," *Brain* 58:115–133 (1935). The meal preparation story is usually told as by WILLIAM H. CALVIN, in *The River That Flows Uphill: A Journey from the Big Bang to the Big Brain* (Macmillan 1986) at p. 460, with the meal-preparation distress as part of the diagnosis of the tumor, but the 1935 paper reveals that it actually occurred 15 months *after* the surgery which removed all of the right frontal lobe to within 1 cm of the motor strip.

143   A. J. WILKINS, TIM SHALLICE, R. MCCARTHY, "Frontal lesions and sustained attention," *Neuropsychologia* 25:359–365 (1987).

143   JOSÉ V. PARDO, PETER T. FOX, MARCUS E. RAICHLE, "Localization of a human system for sustained attention by positron emission tomography," *Nature* 349:61–64 (3 January 1991).

143   PAUL J. ESLINGER, ANTONIO R. DAMASIO, "Severe disturbances of higher cognition after bilateral frontal lobe ablation: patient E.V.R.," *Neurology* 35:1731–1741 (1985).

143   NANCY C. ANDREASEN, "Brain imaging: Applications in psychiatry," *Science* 239:1381–1388 (1988).

JUDITH L. RAPOPORT, "The biology of obsessions and compulsions," *Scientific American* 260(3):82–89 (March 1989). And her book *The Boy Who Couldn't Stop Washing: The Experience and Treatment of Obsessive-Compulsive Disorder* (E. P. Dutton 1989).

146   Evidence for reduced glucose metabolism in the left frontal lobe in several different types of depression is presented by L. BAXTER, JR., J. SCHWARTZ, M. PHELPS, J. MAZZIOTTA, B. GUZE, C. SELIN, R. GERNER, R. SUMIDA, "Reduction of prefrontal glucose metabolism common to three types of depression," *Archives of General Psychiatry* 46:243–250 (1989).

146   ANTONIO R. DAMASIO, DANIEL TRANEL, HANNA DAMASIO, "Individuals with sociopathic behavior caused by frontal damage fail to respond autonomically to social stimuli," *Behavioral Brain Research* 41:81–94 (1990).

147   The dorsolateral prefrontal cortex projects directly to the superior colliculus, a midbrain structure that has a prominent role in the control of eye and head movements. The orbitofrontal cortex, in contrast, projects directly to the brain stem and the spinal visceral motor structures related to the autonomic nervous system and is also an important olfactory and visceral sensory area. See the review by EDWARD J. NEAFSEY, "Prefrontal autonomic control in the rat: anatomical and electrophysiological observations," *Progress in Brain Research* 85:147–166 (1990).

148   SIMON LEVAY, *The Sexual Brain* (MIT Press 1993). And see the news article on genetic linkages in *Science* 261:291–292 (16 July 1993).

Chapter 10.   ***When Things Go Wrong with Thought and Mood***
ELLIOT S. GERSHON, RONALD O. RIEDER, "Major disorders of mind and brain," *Scientific American* 267(3):89–95 (September 1992). For a text (from which most of the statistics in this chapter have been taken): NANCY C. ANDREASEN, DONALD W. BLACK, *Introductory Textbook of Psychiatry* (American Psychiatric Press 1991).

SAMUEL H. BARONDES, *Molecules and Mental Illness* (Freeman 1992).

IRVING I. GOTTESMAN, *Schizophrenia Genesis* (Freeman 1991).

151   PETER D. KRAMER, *Listening to Prozac* (Viking 1993), p. 165.

151   KAY REDFIELD JAMISON, *Touched with Fire: Manic-depressive illness and the artistic temperament* (Free Press 1993), p. 125.

153   M. M. MESULAM, "Slowly progressive aphasia without generalized dementia," *Annals of Neurology* 11:592–598 (June 1982).

153 SERGENT (1993).

154 J. WILLIAM LANGSTON, "The case of the tainted heroin: a trail of tragedies leads to a new theory of Parkinson's disease," *The Sciences* 25(1):34–40 (January 1985). See also *Science* (25 February 1983).

154 MATTI VIRKKUNEN, JUDITH DEJONG, JOHN BARTKO, FREDERICK K. GOODWIN, MARKKU LINNOILA, "Relationship of psychobiological variables to recidivism in violent offenders and impulsive fire setters. A follow-up study," *Archives of General Psychiatry* 46:600–603 (July 1989). Follow-up articles in the January and February 1994 issues of that journal explore the personality profiles and state-related aggressiveness in Finnish alcoholic, violent offenders, fire setters, and healthy volunteers, along with suicide attempts. Of particular importance are the CSF biochemistries, glucose metabolism, and diurnal activity rhythms.

155 JAMISON (1993), p. 29. See also ARNOLD M. LUDWIG, *The Price of Greatness* (Guilford, in press), who found that manic-depressives are 17 percent of actors, 13 percent of poets, but less than 1 percent of physical scientists (a rate like that of the general population).

156 NANCY C. ANDREASEN, "Creativity and mental illness: prevalence rates in writers and their first-degree relatives," *American Journal of Psychiatry* 144:1288–1292 (1987).

156 JAMISON (1993), pp. 60–89. And see the *New York Times* feature (12 October 1993).

159 ERIC R. KANDEL, ROBERT D. HAWKINS, "The biological basis of learning and individuality," *Scientific American* 267(3):79–86 (September 1992).

159 Evidence that many effective antidepressants (and electroconvulsive therapy) decrease the release of cyclic adenosine monophosphate that occurs within a neuron when norepinephrine or related compounds bind to their receptors is reviewed in ELLIOT S. GERSHON, RONALD O. RIEDER, "Major disorders of mind and brain," *Scientific American* 267(3):89–95 (September 1992).

159 MURRAY A. FALCONER, "Reversibility by temporal-lobe resection of the behavioral abnormalities of temporal-lobe epilepsy," *New England Journal of Medicine*, 289:451–455 (1973).

159 R. L. SUDDATH, M. F. CASANOVA, T. E. GOLDBERG, D. G. DANIEL, J. R. KELSOE, JR., D. R. WEINBERGER, "Temporal lobe pathology in schizophrenia: a quantitative magnetic resonance imaging study," *American Journal of Psychiatry* 146:464–472 (April 1989). The volume of temporal lobe gray matter was 20 percent smaller in the patients than in the control subjects (but this need not mean that there are fewer neurons: see GREENOUGH 1975).

RUE L. CROMWELL, "Searching for the origins of schizophrenia," *Psychological Science* 4:276–279 (September 1993).

I. I. GOTTESMAN, *Schizophrenia Genesis: The Origins of Madness* (Freeman 1991).

DANIEL R. WEINBERGER, K. F. BERMAN, R. SUDDATH, E. F. TORREY, "Evidence of dysfunction of a prefrontal-limbic network in schizophrenia: a magnetic resonance imaging and regional cerebral blood flow study of discordant monozygotic twins," *American Journal of Psychiatry* 149:890–897 (July 1992). The more an affected twin differed from the unaffected twin in left hippocampal volume, the more they differed in prefrontal blood flow activation during the Wisconsin Card Sorting Test. In the affected twins as a group, prefrontal activation was strongly related to both left and right hippocampal volume, suggesting dysfunction within a widely distributed neocortical-limbic neural network that has been implicated in working memory.

160   ERIC M. REIMAN, MAUREEN J. FUSSELMAN, PETER T. FOX, AND MARCUS E. RAICHLE, "Neuroanatomical correlates of anticipatory anxiety," *Science* 243:1071–1074 (1989). A PET study showing that the tip of the temporal lobe activates in both normal volunteers and panic disorder patients.

160   There is also evidence for a role of one of the structures on the inner side of the temporal lobe, the amygdala, in uncontrolled anger. There are rare patients with episodic uncontrolled rage. Few people have ever witnessed such rage behavior. It is not the anger of most domestic violence, barroom brawls or riots. Rather, these rare patients may be triggered into trying to kill a stranger by a stimulus as innocuous as a touch on the coat sleeve. Such patients may be too dangerous to be allowed near other people even in an institutional environment. This pattern of behavior has followed damage to the front and inner sides of the temporal lobe including the amygdala, and removal of those damaged structures has reversed the episodic rage behavior, though not preventing normal anger. Local destruction of the amygdala has also ameliorated episodic rage. An evaluation of this type of surgery for this problem is in EDWARD HITCHCOCK, V. CAIRNS, "Amygdalotomy," *Postgraduate Medicine* 49:894–904 (1973) and VERNON MARK, FRANK ERWIN, WILLIAM SWEET in *Neural Basis of Violence and Aggression,* edited by WILLIAM SWEET and WILLIAM FIELDS (St. Louis, Warren Green, 1975), pp. 379–391.

163   See the news article "Psychosurgery: National Commission issues surprisingly favorable report," *Science* 194:299 (15 October 1976). And the *Federal Register* 43(221):53242 (1978).

164   E. TAN, I. M. MARKS, P. MARSET, "Bimedial leucotomy in obsessive-compulsive neurosis: a controlled serial inquiry," *British Journal of Psychiatry* 118:155–164 (1971). I. M. MARKS, J. L. BIRLEY, M. G. GELDER, "Modified leucotomy in severe agoraphobia: a controlled serial inquiry," *British Journal of*

Psychiatry 112:757–769 (1966). R. STROM-OLSEN, S. CARLISLE, "Bi-frontal stereotactic tractotomy. A follow-up study of its effects on 210 patients," *British Journal of Psychiatry* 118:141–54 (1971). For the studies where behavioral and intelligence tests were done before and after, see N. MITCHELL-HEGGS, D. KELLY, A. RICHARDSON, and MCLEISH, pp. 327–336 in *Modern Concepts in Psychiatric Surgery*, edited by EDWARD HITCHCOCK, et al. (Elsevier 1979); CORKIN, TWITCHELL, SULLIVAN at pp. 253–272; N. MITCHELL-HEGGS, D. KELLY, A. RICHARDSON, "Stereotactic limbic leucotomy—a followup at 16 months," *British Journal of Psychiatry* 128:226–40 (1976).

168   ROBERT M. SAPOLSKY, "Stress in the wild," *Scientific American* 262(1):116–123 (1990). And his book *Stress, the Aging Brain, and the Mechanisms of Neuron Death* (MIT Press 1992).

168   The behavioral tics of Tourette's are described by OLIVER SACKS, "A surgeon's life," *The New Yorker*, pp. 85–94 (16 March 1992).

169   JEROME KAGAN, J. STEPHEN REZNICK, NANCY SNIDMAN, "Biological basis of childhood shyness," *Science* 240:167–171 (1988). And see the discussion in KRAMER (1993).

Chapter 11. ***Tuning Up the Brain by Pruning***

DAVID H. HUBEL, *Eye, Brain, and Vision* (Freeman 1988).

176   A theoretical analysis of the left vs. right eye zones in visual cortex, which includes many of the relevant citations to the literature, is by KENNETH D. MILLER, JOSEPH B. KELLER, MICHAEL P. STRYKER, "Ocular dominance column development: analysis and simulation," *Science* 245:605–615 (11 August 1989).

176   The retinal sketch is adapted from one in JOHN E. DOWLING, BRIAN B. BOYCOTT, "Organization of primate retina: electron microscopy," *Proceedings of the Royal Society, London* B166:80–111 (1966).

181   P. R. HUTTENLOCHER, "Synapse elimination and plasticity in developing human cerebral cortex," *American Journal of Mental Deficiency* 88:488–496 (1984).

181   J. TIGGES, J. G. HERNDON, A. PETERS, "Neuronal population of area 4 during the life span of the rhesus monkey," *Neurobiology of Aging* 11:201–208 (May–June 1990). A significant loss of approximately one-third was observed in the total number of motor strip neurons in maturing monkeys (less than 5.5 years). In contrast, in adult monkeys no age-associated loss of neurons was observed.

182   PETER F. DRUCKER, *Post-capitalist Society* (HarperCollins 1993), p. 57.

184   DAVID H. HUBEL, "Effects of distortion of sensory input on the visual system of kittens," *The Physiologist* 10:43 (1967).

Chapter 12. *Acquiring and Reacquiring Language*

PATRICIA S. KUHL, "Auditory perception and the evolution of speech," *Human Evolution* 3:21–45 (1988).

JOHN L. LOCKE, *The Child's Path to Spoken Language* (Harvard University Press 1993).

OLIVER SACKS, *Seeing Voices: A Journey into the World of the Deaf* (University of California Press 1989).

185   NOAM CHOMSKY, "Language and the mind," *Psychology Today* (February 1969).

186   See, for example, the news story at p. 535 accompanying the article by PATRICIA K. KUHL, KAREN A. WILLIAMS, FRANCISCO LACERDA, KENNETH N. STEVENS, BJÖRN LINDBLOM, "Linguistic experience alters phonemic perception in infants by 6 months of age," *Science* 255:606–608 (31 January 1992). For more, see M. J. S. WEISS, P. R. ZELAZO, editors, *Newborn Attention* (Ablex 1991).

186   STEVEN HARNAD, editor, *Categorical Perception* (Cambridge University Press 1987).

188   JON H. KAAS, "Plasticity of sensory and motor maps in adult mammals," *Annual Reviews of Neuroscience* 14:137–167 (1991).

WILLIAM M. JENKINS, MICHAEL M. MERZENICH, GREG H. RECANZONE, "Neocortical representational dynamics in adult primates: implications for neuropsychology," *Neuropsychologia* 28:573–584 (1990).

MICHAEL M. MERZENICH, GREG H. RECANZONE, WILLIAM M. JENKINS, K. A. GRAJSKI, "Adaptive mechanisms in cortical networks underlying cortical contributions to learning and nondeclarative memory," *Cold Spring Harbor Symposia for Quantitative Biology* 55:873–887 (1990).

188   ALVARO PASCUAL-LEONE, FERNANDO TORRES, "Plasticity of the sensorimotor cortex representation of the reading finger in Braille readers," *Brain* 116:39–52 (February 1993).

188   TIM C. PONS, PRESTON E. GARRAGHTY, ALEXANDER K. OMMAYA, JON H. KAAS, EDWARD TAUB, MORTIMER MISHKIN, "Massive cortical reorganization after sensory deafferentation in adult macaques," *Science* 252:1857–1860 (28 June 1991). See also PRESTON E. GARRAGHTY, JON H. KAAS, "Large-scale functional reorganization in adult monkey cortex after peripheral nerve injury," *Proceedings of the National Academy of Sciences (U.S.A.)* 88(16):6976–6980 (15 August 1991). Incidentally, these are the very "Silver Springs" monkeys that the animal rights people tried to gain custody of, claiming in lawsuits and publicity that it was worthless science. Many motorcycle riders who are thrown over the handlebars in an accident, while still hanging on tightly to the handgrips, tend to suffer injuries analogous to those created in these monkeys, severing the sensory axons that come from the hand and arm as they enter the spinal cord. After reading these scientific reports, it is instructive to read back over the journalistic accounts and see the role that arrogant ignorance played in the controversy. A popular treatment is CAROLYN FRASER, "The raid at Silver Springs," *The New Yorker* (19 April 1993), pp. 66ff.

190   MAUREEN DENNIS, HARRY WHITAKER, "Language acquisition following hemidecortication: Linguistic superiority of the left over the right hemisphere," *Brain and Language* 3:404–433 (1976).

191   An example of language localization in a four-year-old derived from stimulation mapping during naming of common objects can be found in GEORGE OJEMANN, JEFF OJEMANN, ETTORE LETTICH, MITCHELL BERGER, "Cortical language localization in left, dominant hemisphere," *Journal of Neurosurgery* 71:316–326 (1989).

192   The graph showing the acquisition of language is adapted from one in ERIC H. LENNEBERG, *Biological Foundations of Language* (Wiley 1966), p. 133.

195   RICHARD P. MEIER, "Language acquisition by deaf children," *American Scientist* 79:60–70 (January–February 1991).

195   National Institutes of Health, Office of the Director, "Early identification of hearing impairment in infants and young children," *NIH Consensus Statement* 11 (1 March 1993). Their recommendation is that all hearing-impaired infants be identified, and treatment initiated, before six months of age.

195   OLIVER SACKS, *Seeing Voices* (University of California Press 1989).

197   SUSAN CURTISS, *Genie: A Psycholinguistic Study of a Modern-Day "Wild Child"* (Academic Press 1977).

198   Lack of success with late-start relatives of the two successful bonobos: personal communication, E. SUE SAVAGE-RUMBAUGH, 1993.

199   Factors influencing spontaneous recovery from aphasia are reviewed in AUDREY HOLLAND, "Recovery in aphasia," in *Handbook of Neuropsychology,* edited by FRANÇOIS BOLLER, JORDAN GRAPHMAN (Elsevier 1989) vol. 2, pp. 83–90. Studies evaluating the effects of therapy on this are reviewed in MARTHA SARNO, "Recovery and rehabilitation in aphasia," in *Acquired Aphasia,* edited by MARTHA SARNO (Academic Press 1981) pp. 485–529.

199   MICHAEL GAZZANIGA, "Right hemisphere language following brain bisection: a 20-year perspective," *American Psychologist* 38:525–537 (1983).

199   Lack of naming sites in unusual places in stroke patients: G. A. OJEMANN, unpublished data.

201   J. WILLIAM LANGSTON, "The case of the tainted heroin: a trail of tragedies leads to a new theory of Parkinson's disease," *The Sciences* 25(1):34–40 (January 1985). P. L. MCGEER, E. G. MCGEER, J. S. SUZUKI, "Aging and extrapyramidal function," *Archives of Neurology* 34:33–35 (1977). And also P. L. MCGEER, E. G. MCGEER, "Aging and neurotransmitter systems," in *Parkinson's Disease—II. Aging and Neuroendocrine Relationships,* edited by C. E. FINCH et al., pp. 41–57 (Plenum 1978). For a more recent discussion, see JAMES A. MORTIMER, "Human motor behavior and aging," *Annals of the New York Academy of Sciences* 515:54–65 (1988).

Chapter 13. *Taking Apart the Visual Image*

DAVID H. HUBEL, *Eye, Brain, and Vision* (Scientific American Books 1988).

SEMIR ZEKI, *A Vision of the Brain* (Blackwell Scientific Publications 1993).

MARGARET LIVINGSTONE, DAVID H. HUBEL, "Segregation of form, color, movement, and depth: Anatomy, physiology, and perception," *Science* 240:740–749 (1988).

DALE PURVES, D. R. RIDDLE, A.-S. LAMANTIA, "Iterated patterns of brain circuitry (or how the brain gets its spots)," *Trends in the Neurosciences* 15:362–368 (1992).

JENNIFER S. LUND, "Anatomical organization of macaque monkey striate visual cortex," *Annual Reviews of Neuroscience* 11:253–288 (1988).

203   E. M. GOMBRICH, *Art and Illusion: A Study in the Psychology of Pictorial Representation* (Phaidon Press 1959).

205   FLOYD RATLIFF, *Mach Bands: Quantitative Studies on Neural Networks in the Retina* (Holden-Day 1965).

206   The maps showing responses from two retinal ganglion cells is adapted from ROBERT W. RODIECK, *The Vertebrate Retina: Principles of Structure and Function* (Freeman 1973).

206   ROY M. PRITCHARD, "Stabilized images on the retina," *Scientific American* pp. 72–91 (June 1961).

209   MARGARET S. LIVINGSTONE, "Art, illusion and the visual system," *Scientific American* 258(1):78–85 (January 1988).

209   MARGARET S. LIVINGSTONE, GLENN D. ROSEN, FRANK W. DRISLANE, ALBERT M. GALABURDA, "Physiological and anatomical evidence for a magnocellular defect in developmental dyslexia," *Proceedings of the National Academy of Sciences (U.S.A.)* 88:7943–7947 (15 September 1991). The visual evoked potentials for low-contrast stimuli are delayed in dyslexics. While the lateral geniculate nucleus looks normal in the parvocellular layers, there is a 27 percent reduction in cell bodies in the magnocellular layers of dyslexics.

209   DAVID H. HUBEL, TORSTEN N. WIESEL, "Brain mechanisms of vision," *Scientific American* 241(3) (September 1979).

212   DAVID H. HUBEL, TORSTEN N. WIESEL, "Functional architecture of macaque monkey visual cortex," *Proceedings of the Royal Society, London* 198B:1–59

(1977). For a text, see JOHN G. NICHOLLS, A. ROBERT MARTIN, BRUCE G. WALLACE, *From Neuron to Brain,* 3d ed. (Sinauer 1992).

213   GIAN E. CHATRIAN, ETTORE LETTICH, L. H. MILLER, JOHN R. GREEN, "Pattern-sensitive epilepsy. I. An electrographic study of its mechanisms," *Epilepsia* 11:125–149 (1970).

213   MARGARET S. LIVINGSTONE, DAVID H. HUBEL, "Psychophysical evidence for separate channels for the perception of form, color, movement, and depth," *Journal of Neuroscience* 7:3416–3468 (1987).

213   SEMIR ZEKI, "The visual image in mind and brain," *Scientific American* 267(3):42–50 (September 1992).

213   D. C. VAN ESSEN, C. H. ANDERSON, D. J. FELLMAN, "Information processing in the primate visual system: an integrated systems perspective," *Science* 255:419 (1992).

214   Triangle detectors are actually possible: see GYULA SÁRY, RUFIN VOGELS, GUY A. ORBAN, "Cue-invariant shape selectivity of macaque inferior temporal neurons," *Science* 260:995–997 (14 May 1993).

214   For color vision, see the entries "Colour vision" and "Thomas Young" in *The Oxford Companion to the Mind,* edited by RICHARD L. GREGORY (Oxford University Press 1987). The cone types are discussed by EDWARD F. MACNICHOL, JR., "Three-pigment color vision," *Scientific American,* p. 64 (December 1964).

216   The combination theory for taste is covered by ROBERT P. ERICKSON, "On the neural bases of behavior," *American Scientist* 72:233–241 (May-June 1984). An endnote in *The Cerebral Symphony,* at p. 359, discusses its application to orientation-sensitive neurons of visual cortex with eighteen types of elementary templates.

216   DONALD O. HEBB, *The Organization of Behavior* (Wiley 1949). And see PETER M. MILNER, "The mind and Donald O. Hebb," *Scientific American* 268(1):124–129 (January 1993).

216   ANTONIO DAMASIO, "Prosopagnosia," *Trends in the Neurosciences* 8:132–145 (1985). ANTONIO DAMASIO, DANIEL TRANEL, HANNA DAMASIO, "Facial agnosia and the neural substrates of memory," *Annual Review of Neuroscience* 13:9–109 (1990). JUSTINE SERGENT, JEAN-LOUIS SIGNORET, "Varieties of functional deficits in prosopagnosia," *Cerebral Cortex* 2:375–388 (1992).

Chapter 14. ***How the Brain Subdivides Language***

GEORGE A. OJEMANN, OTTO D. CREUTZFELDT, "Language in humans and animals: contribution of brain stimulation and recording," in *Handbook of Physiology. Section 1: The Nervous System, Volume 5 part 2, The Higher Functions of the Brain,* edited by VERNON B. MOUNTCASTLE, FRED PLUM, and STEVEN R. GEIGER (American Physiological Society 1987).

STEVEN E. PETERSEN, P. T. FOX, A. Z. SNYDER, "Activation of extrastriate and frontal cortical areas by visual words and word-like stimuli," *Science* 249:1041–1044 (1990).

M. PARADIS, "Bilingualism and aphasia," *Studies in Neurolinguistics* 3:65–122 (1977).

220   GEORGE OJEMANN, HARRY WHITAKER, "The bilingual brain," *Archives of Neurology* 35:409–412 (1978). Separate sites have even been identified as essential for naming in different Chinese dialects in one patient. Whether there are specific patterns for first or second languages, or for languages that one speaks more or less fluently, is not clear.

221   URSULA BELLUGI, HOWARD POIZNER, EDWARD S. KLIMA, "Language, modality, and the brain," *Trends in Neurosciences* 12(10):380–388 (1989). See also MICHAEL M. HAGLUND, GEORGE A. OJEMANN, ETTORE LETTICH, URSULA BELLUGI, DAVID CORINA, "Dissociation of cortical and single unit activity in spoken and signed languages," *Brain and Language* 44:19–27 (January 1993).

222   A patient with preservation of naming for tools, but not animals, is described in ANTONIO DAMASIO, "Synchronous activation in multiple cortical regions; a mechanism for recall," *Seminars in the Neurosciences* 2:287–296 (1990). Another patient with preservation of one semantic category, but not another, after a stroke is presented in J. HART, R. BERNDT, A. CARAMAZZA, "Category-specific naming deficit following cerebral infarction," *Nature* 316:439–440 (1985). Stimulation mapping evidence for separation of sites essential for naming, from those utilized to generate verbs from nouns, is presented in JEFF OJEMANN, GEORGE OJEMANN, ETTORE LETTICH, "Cortical stimulation during a language task with known blood flow changes," *Society for Neuroscience Abstracts* 19:1808 (1993). PET scan localization of the brain areas active during generation of verbs from nouns is described in MARCUS RAICHLE, "Exploring the mind with dynamic imaging," *Seminars in the Neurosciences* 4:307–315 (1990). That group has recently presented evidence that the PET localization for this language function is different, depending on whether the subject has previous experience with the particular list of nouns from which the verbs are to be generated. Stimulation mapping effects on speech sound identification and orofacial speech gestures (movements) is in GEORGE A. OJEMANN, CATHERINE MATEER, "Human language cortex: localization of memory, syntax, and sequential motor-phoneme identification systems," *Science* 205:1401–1403 (1979).

222   Syntax examples, see GEORGE A. OJEMANN, "Brain organization for language from the perspective of electrical stimulation mapping," *Behavioral and Brain Sciences* 6(2):189–230 (1983).

226   The rate of change of sounds may be particularly important: J. SCHWARTZ, PAULA TALLAL, "Rate of acoustic change may underlie hemispheric specialization," *Science* 207:1380–1381 (1980).

227   ITZHAK FRIED, GEORGE OJEMANN, EBERHARD FETZ, "Language-related potentials specific to human language cortex," *Science* 212:353–356 (1981). And GEORGE OJEMANN, ITZHAK FRIED, ETTORE LETTICH, "Electrocorticographic (ECoG) correlates of language: I. Desynchronization in temporal language cortex during object naming," *Electroencephalography and Clinical Neurophysiology* 73:453–463 (1989).

228   The usually transient but dramatic language deficits after removal of the supplementary motor area are described in detail in ROBERT ROSTOMILY, MITCHELL BERGER, GEORGE OJEMANN, ETTORE LETTICH, "Postoperative deficits and functional recovery following removal of tumors involving the dominant hemisphere supplementary motor area," *Journal of Neurosurgery* 75:62–68 (1991).

Investigations into monkey vocalization, using both stimulation mapping and neuronal recording, are reviewed in GEORGE OJEMANN, OTTO CREUTZFELDT, "Language in humans and animals: contribution of brain stimulation and recording," in *Handbook of Physiology, the Nervous System,* volume 5, *Higher Functions of the Brain,* edited by VERNON MOUNTCASTLE, FRED PLUM, STEVEN GEIGER, pp. 675–699 (American Physiological Society 1987).

Chapter 15. ***Why Can We Read So Well?***
For general background on language per se, see David Crystal, *The Cambridge Encyclopedia of Language* (Cambridge University Press 1987).

ANTONIO DAMASIO, HANNA DAMASIO, "The anatomic basis of pure alexia," *Neurology* 33:1573–1583 (1983).

ALBERT M. GALABURDA (ed.), *Dyslexia and Development* (Harvard University Press 1993).

MARGARET LIVINGSTONE, "Parallel processing in the visual system and the brain: Is one subsystem selectively affected in dyslexia?", in *Dyslexia and Development,* edited by ALBERT M. GALABURDA (Harvard University Press 1993).

PAULA TALLAL, ROSLYN HOLLY FITCH, "Hormones and cerebral organization: implications for the development and transmission of language and learning disabilities," in *Dyslexia and Development,* edited by ALBERT M. GALABURDA (Harvard University Press 1993).

233   Alexia and attentional disorders are reviewed by MICHAEL I. POSNER, "Attention as a cognitive and neural system," *Current Directions in Psychological Science 1:11–14 (February 1992).*

234   MARGARET S. LIVINGSTONE, GLENN D. ROSEN, FRANK W. DRISLANE, ALBERT M. GALABURDA, "Physiological and anatomical evidence for a magnocellular defect in developmental dyslexia," *Proceedings of the National Academy of Sciences (U.S.A.)* 88:7943–7947 (15 September 1991).

234   Dyslexia is more common in males, though with a somewhat smaller predominance than previously thought. See W. JAMES, "The sex ratios of dyslexic children and their sibs," *Developmental Medicine and Child Neurology* 34:530–533 (1992). Evidence linking abnormalities in chromosome 15 to some cases of familial dyslexia is presented in S. SMITH, W. KIMBERLING, B. PENNINGTON, H. LUBS, "Specific reading disability: identification of an inherited form through linkage analysis," *Science* 219:1345–1347 (1983). A recent evaluation of Geschwind's hypothesis on the origin of dyslexia, allergies, left-handedness and unusually good mathematical abilities is to be found in ALBERT GALABURDA, "The testosterone hypothesis: reassessment since Geschwind and Behan," *Annals of Dyslexia* 40:18–38. More on mice with autoimmune and learning disorders can be found in V. DENNENBERG, G. SHERMAN, L. SCHROTT, G. ROSEN, A. GALABURDA, "Spatial learning, discrimination learning, paw preference, and neocortical ectopias in two autoimmune strains of mice," *Brain Research* 562:98–104 (1991).

236   GEORGE A. OJEMANN, "Some brain mechanisms for reading," in *Brain and Reading*, edited by CURT VON EULER (Macmillan 1989), pp. 47–59.

237   The costs and patient numbers for the neurological disorders are those assembled by the Society for Neuroscience in 1993 from various federal sources. The 1990 estimate of 3.3 percent R&D expenditures is from DONALD C. HARRISON, "Science for the 21st Century: the coming biomedical revolution," in *Preparing for Science in the 21st Century,* edited by DONALD C. HARRISON, MARIAN OSTERWEIS, ELAINE R. RUBIN (Association of Academic Health Centers, Washington DC, 1991), p.5.

239   Paperwork costs, see article and editorial in *New England Journal of Medicine* (5 August 1993).

240   CHRISTINA ENROTH-CUGELL, JOHN G. ROBSON, "The contrast sensitivity of retinal ganglion cells of the cat," *Journal of Physiology* 187:517–552 (1966).

240   Ignorance abounds concerning how useful discoveries actually come about, and so legislatures tend to earmark research funds for specific diseases rather than allowing researchers to simply follow their well-honed instincts about "interesting problems."

241   The quotations from LEWIS THOMAS are reprinted with his permission and that of the *New England Journal of Medicine,* where they originally appeared. They may be found reprinted in LEWIS THOMAS, *The Lives of a Cell* (Viking 1974), pp. 36–42.

Chapter 16.   *Stringing Things Together*

Recent overviews of human language cortical organization include the following:

DOREEN KIMURA, *Neuromotor Mechanisms in Human Communication* (Oxford University Press 1993).

GEORGE A. OJEMANN, "Cortical organization of language," *Journal of Neuroscience* 11:2281–2287 (August 1991); "Cortical organization of language and verbal memory based on intraoperative investigations," *Progress in Sensory Physiology* 12:193–230 (1991).

DAVID CORINA, JYOTSNA VALD, URSULA BELLUGI, "The linguistic basis of left hemisphere specialization," *Science* 255:1258–1260 (6 March 1992).

244   GEORGE A. OJEMANN, CATHERINE MATEER, "Human language cortex: localization of memory, syntax, and sequential motor-phoneme identification systems," *Science* 205:1401–1403 (1979).

245   J. P. MOHR, "Broca's area and Broca's aphasia," in *Studies in Neurolinguistics*, edited by HARRY WHITAKER, HANNA A. WHITAKER (Academic Press 1976).

246   Many primatologists would expand JANE GOODALL'S list of 36 vocalizations in *The Chimpanzees of Gombe* (Harvard University Press 1986). But the point remains: the human list of meaningless phonemes is about as long as the chimpanzee list of meaningful vocalizations.

247   For hominid brain changes, see DEAN FALK, *Braindance* (Henry Holt 1992). For a more general discussion of infolding, see JOHN W. PROTHERO, JOHN W. SUNDSTEN, "Folding of the cerebral cortex in mammals," *Brain, Behavior, and Evolution* 24:152–167 (1984).

248   JOHN HUGHLINGS JACKSON, "Remarks on evolution and dissolution of the nervous system," *The Journal of Medical Science* 33:25–48 (1887–88).

248   WILLIAM H. CALVIN, "A stone's throw and its launch window: timing precision and its implications for language and hominid brains," *Journal of Theoretical Biology* 104:121–135 (1983).

249   OTTO CREUTZFELDT, GEORGE OJEMANN, ETTORE LETTICH, "Neuronal activity in the human lateral temporal lobe. I. Responses to speech," *Experimental Brain Research* 77:451–475 (1989).

OTTO CREUTZFELDT, GEORGE OJEMANN, ETTORE LETTICH, "Neuronal activity in the human lateral temporal lobe. II. Responses to the subject's own voice," *Experimental Brain Research* 77:476–489 (1989).

OTTO CREUTZFELDT, GEORGE OJEMANN, "Neuronal activity in the human lateral temporal lobe. III. Activity changes during music," *Experimental Brain Research* 77:490–498 (1989).

250   DOREEN KIMURA, "Sex differences in the brain," *Scientific American* 267(3):81–87 (September 1992).

251   Sequencing abilities as the key element in hominid brain evolution: see W. H. CALVIN, *The Ascent of Mind: Ice Age Climates and the Evolution of Intelligence* (Bantam 1990).

251   A modern discussion of the confusions generated by talking of cortical specializations can be found in ROBERT EFRON, *The Decline and Fall of Hemispheric Specialization* (Erlbaum 1990), pp. 3–16.

Chapter 17.   **Deep in the Temporal Lobe, Across from the Brain Stem**

The proper name of the usual epilepsy operation is *anterior temporal lobectomy*. Some background may be found in WILDER PENFIELD, THEODORE RASMUSSEN, *The Cerebral Cortex of Man* (Macmillan 1950). The Latin appellation for the scarring of the uncus is *mesial sclerosis*. Our illustration of uncal herniation is adopted from that in JOHN NOLTE, *The Human Brain: An Introduction to its Functional Anatomy*, 3rd edition (Mosby 1993); note that the level of section is different on the left and right sides, and that the uncus is actually located two-thirds of the way forward along the undersurface of the temporal lobe.

257   R. IVNIK, F. SCHARBOUGH, E. LAWS, "Effects of anterior temporal lobectomy on cognitive functions," *Journal of Clinical Psychology* 43:128–137 (1987); ROBERT EFRON, PAUL CRANDALL, "Central auditory processing. II. Effects of anterior temporal lobectomy," *Brain and Language* 19:237–253 (1983); ROBERT EFRON, PAUL CRANDALL, B. KOSS, P. DIVENYI, E. YUND, "Central auditory processing. III. The 'cocktail party' effect and anterior temporal lobectomy," *Brain and Language* 19:254–263 (1983).

261   Evidence that the reinnervation that is part of the repair process of human hippocampus in epilepsy may lead to further hyperexcitability can be found in THOMAS BABB and others, "Aberrant synaptic reorganization in human epileptic hippocampus: evidence for feedforward excitation," *Dendron* 1:7–25 (1992) and TOM SUTULA and others, "Mossy fiber synaptic reorganization in epileptic human temporal lobe," *Annals of Neurology* 26:321–330 (1989).

262   Five years after epilepsy surgery, those patients who are seizure-free view their quality of life as having significantly improved, using several standardized measures. Those who were employed are likely to have a better job, and those who were in school at the time of operation and have joined the work force in the five years since the operation are much more likely to be employed than are similar patients who were managed medically during those five years. LARRY BATZEL, ROBERT FRASER, "Resection surgery for epilepsy: outcome and quality of life," in *Epilepsy Surgery,* edited by DAN SILBERGELD, GEORGE OJEMANN, *Neurosurgical Clinics of North America,* 4:345–351 (April 1993). That study found, as have others, that in contrast to these two groups of patients, those who were out of school but unemployed seldom became employed even when their seizures were controlled by surgery. This is a major argument for considering surgery in adolescence for those patients with seizures not responding to antiepileptic drugs.

262   MICHAEL M. HAGLUND, LINDA MORETTI OJEMANN, "Seizure outcome in patients undergoing temporal lobe resections for epilepsy," *Neurosurgical Clinics of North America* 4:337–344 (April 1993).

262   "National Institutes of Health Consensus Conference: Surgery for Epilepsy," *Journal of the American Medical Association* 264:729–733 (1990). The conference concluded that resective surgery for epilepsy had been proven effective for control of seizures in appropriate patients.

262   One state, Oregon, initially tried to eliminate state funding for epilepsy surgery in their rationing effort to increase the availability of other medical care.

Chapter 18.   ***In Search of the Narrator***
The general background for this chapter may be found in W. H. CALVIN, *The Cerebral Symphony: Seashore Reflections on the Structure of Consciousness* (Bantam 1989).

MARVIN MINSKY, *The Society of Mind* (Simon & Schuster 1985).

ANTONIO R. DAMASIO, "Synchronous activation in multiple cortical regions: a mechanism for recall," *Seminars in the Neurosciences* 2:287–296 (August 1990).

FRANCIS CRICK, CHRISTOF KOCH, "The problem of consciousness," *Scientific American* 267(3):111–117 (September 1992). And their "Towards a neurobiological theory of consciousness," *Seminars in the Neurosciences* 2:262–276 (August 1990).

HOWARD EICHENBAUM, "Thinking about brain cell assemblies," *Science* 261:993–994 (20 August 1993).

CHRISTOF KOCH, JOEL E. DAVIS, editors, *Large-Scale Neuronal Theories of the Brain* (MIT Press 1994).

MICHAEL S. GAZZANIGA, editor, *The Cognitive Neurosciences* (MIT Press 1994).

271   B. L. J. KACZMAREK, "Neurolinguistic disturbances of verbal utterances in patients with focal lesions of frontal lobes," *Brain and Language* 21:52–58 (1984).

271   The extrastriate visual area known as Middle Temporal (MT) in monkeys is sometimes called V5 because, in humans, it appears to be located on the border of the occipital and temporal lobes, somewhat on the undersurface but mostly peeking around the lateral edge. The visual areas may have scaled up only about twofold between monkey and human, while the overall cortical area increase is more like tenfold. Consequently many of the visual cortical areas that in monkeys are located in the middle temporal lobe may, in humans, be much closer to the occipital lobe.

272 ANTONIO R. DAMASIO, DANIEL TRANEL, "Nouns and verbs are retrieved with differently distributed neural systems," *Proceedings of the National Academy of Sciences (U.S.A.)* 90:4957–4760 (1 June 1993).

GREGORY MCCARTHY, ANDREW M. BLAMIRE, DOUGLAS L. ROTHMAN, ROLF GRUETTER, ROBERT G. SHULMAN, "Echo-planar magnetic resonance imaging studies of frontal cortex activation during word generation in humans," *Proceedings of the National Academy of Sciences (U.S.A.)* 90:4952–4956 (1 June 1993).

273 JOHN HART, BARRY GORDON, "Neural subsystems for object knowledge," *Nature* 359:60–64 (1992). Offers evidence for a major division between visually based and language-based higher-level representations. Some background is in *The New York Times* article, p. C3 (15 September 1992).

275 The areas of the lingual gyrus associated with color concepts are thought to be the homologues of the extrastriate visual areas known in the monkey literature as V2 and V4. See HANNA DAMASIO, ANTONIO R. DAMASIO, *Lesion Analysis in Neuropsychology* (Oxford University Press 1989).

ANTONIO R. DAMASIO, HANNA DAMASIO, DANIEL TRANEL, JOHN P. BRANDT, "Neural regionalization of knowledge access: preliminary evidence," *Cold Spring Harbor Symposia on Quantitative Biology,* 55:1039–1047 (1990).

ANTONIO R. DAMASIO, "Time-locked multiregional retroactivation: a systems-level proposal for the neural substrates of recall and recognition," *Cognition* 33:25–62 (1989).

277 DANIEL C. DENNETT, *Consciousness Explained* (Little, Brown 1991).

277 PETER M. MILNER, "A model for visual shape recognition," *Psychological Reviews* 81:521–535 (1974).

277 ANDREAS K. ENGEL, PETER KÖNIG, ANDREAS K. KREITER, THOMAS B. SCHILLEN, WOLF SINGER, "Temporal coding in the visual system: new vistas on integration in the nervous system," *Trends in Neuroscience* 15:218–226 (June 1992). And WOLF SINGER, "Synchronization of cortical activity and its putative role in information processing and learning," *Annual Review of Physiology* 55:349–374 (1993). See also STEVEN H. STROGATZ, IAN STEWART, "Coupled oscillators and biological synchronization," *Scientific American* 269(6): 102–109 (December 1993).

277 VENKATESH N. MURTHY, EBERHARD E. FETZ, "Coherent 25- to 35-Hz oscillations in the sensorimotor cortex of awake behaving monkeys," *Proceedings of the National Academy of Sciences (U.S.A.)* 89:5670–5674 (June 1992).

278 Temporal patterns of thalamic neuronal activity in humans that seem to be specific for particular semantic categories have been reported by NATALIA BECHTEREVA and her associates at the Institute for Experimental Medicine in St. Petersburg. See N. P. BECHTEREVA, P. V. BUNDZEN, Y. L. GOGOLITSIN, V. N. MALYSHEV, P. D. PEREPELKIN, "Neurophysiological codes of words in subcortical

330 — Conversations with Neil's Brain

structures of the human brain," *Brain and Language* 7:145–163 (1979). Temporal lobe neurons apparently with specific patterns of activity for specific words are illustrated in OTTO CREUTZFELDT, GEORGE OJEMANN, ETTORE LETTICH, "Neuronal activity in human lateral temporal lobe. I. Responses to speech," *Experimental Brain Research* 77: 451–475 (1989).

278   FRANCES H. RAUSCHER, GORDON L. SHAW, KATHERINE N. KY, "Music and spatial task performance," *Nature* 365:611 (14 October 1993). Listening to Mozart improves subsequent performance on spatial IQ tests by about nine points for perhaps fifteen minutes.

278   PETER F. DRUCKER, *Post-capitalist Society* (HarperCollins 1993).

280   KENNETH J. W. CRAIK, *The Nature of Explanation* (Cambridge University Press 1943), p. 61.

282   URSULA BELLUGI, A. BIHRLE, T. JERNIGAN, D. TRAUNER, S. DOHERTY, "Neuropsychological, neurological, and neuroanatomical profile of Williams syndrome," *American Journal of Medical Genetics, Supplement* 6:115–125 (1990). Language and cognitive functions in Williams syndrome adolescents, in contrast to age- and IQ-matched Down's syndrome adolescents. The Williams syndrome individuals exhibit an unusual fractionation of higher cortical functioning, with marked cognitive deficits, but selective sparing of syntax.

285   WILLIAM H. CALVIN, "The brain as a Darwin Machine," *Nature* 330:33–34 (5 November 1987).

285   Another example is the computational technique called the "genetic" algorithm, e.g., JOHN H. HOLLAND, "Genetic algorithms," *Scientific American* 267(1):66–72 (July 1992). By tapping evolution's creative power, genetic algorithms have become a widely used search technique, used in nonlinear symbolic regression, automatic programming, plant scheduling, etc.

288   WILLIAM H. CALVIN, "Islands in the mind: dynamic subdivisions of association cortex and the emergence of a Darwin Machine," *Seminars in the Neurosciences* 3(5):423–433 (1991).

289   FREDERICK DAVID ABRAHAM with RALPH H. ABRAHAM, CHRISTOPHER D. SHAW, *A Visual Introduction to Dynamical Systems Theory for Psychology* (Aerial Press, Santa Cruz, 1990). JAMES GLEICK, *Chaos* (Viking 1987), p. 140.

289   JOHN H. R. MAUNSELL, WILLIAM T. NEWSOME, "Visual processing in monkey extrastriate cortex," *Annual Review of Neuroscience* 10:363–401 (1987).

290   WILLIAM H. CALVIN, "Error-correcting codes: Coherent hexagonal copying from fuzzy neuroanatomy," *World Congress on Neural Networks* 1:101–104 (1993). And WILLIAM H. CALVIN, "The emergence of intelligence," *Scientific American* (September 1994).

Index

Authors' Note

Our first book, *Inside the Brain* (NAL 1980), has been out of print for years; while it also followed a patient named Neil through a day of neurosurgery, the present book is not a revision of that book. Except for several pages on psychosurgery and a few illustrations, this is an entirely new book using a similar literary device. *Inside the Brain* covers a number of topics, such as pain and regeneration, which we have not been able to include in this book because of our focus on the cerebral cortex. In the fourteen years between books, our understanding of cortical mechanisms has increased enormously.

153   Calvin, William H.,
CALV   1939-

           Conversations with
           Neil's brain.

DATE			
APR 1 6 000			